SHAKESPEARE'S TRAGIC PERSPECTIVE

Shakespeare's
Tragic Perspective

LARRY S. CHAMPION

THE UNIVERSITY OF GEORGIA PRESS
ATHENS

Library of Congress Catalog Card Number: 74–75943
International Standard Book Number: 0–8203–0363–1

The University of Georgia Press, Athens 30602

© 1976 by the University of Georgia Press
All rights reserved

Set in 11 on 13 pt. Intertype Garamond
Printed in the United States of America

for Nancy
and for Katherine, Becky, and Stephen

ACKNOWLEDGMENTS

Portions of this study in somewhat different form have appeared previously in *Shakespeare Quarterly, English Studies,* and *Ball State University Forum.* Permission to reprint this material is gratefully acknowledged. I also wish to thank the Department of English at North Carolina State University for supporting this study through its research program.

CONTENTS

ABBREVIATIONS

CE	*College English*
CLAJ	*College Language Association Journal*
CQ	*Critical Quarterly*
EJ	*English Journal*
ELN	*English Language Notes*
HLQ	*Huntington Library Quarterly*
JEGP	*Journal of English and Germanic Philology*
JGE	*Journal of General Education*
MLQ	*Modern Language Quarterly*
MLR	*Modern Language Review*
MP	*Modern Philology*
PLL	*Papers on Language and Literature*
PQ	*Philological Quarterly*
REL	*Review of English Literature*
RES	*Review of English Studies*
SAB	*South Atlantic Bulletin*
SAQ	*South Atlantic Quarterly*
SEL	*Studies in English Literature*
SJ	*Shakespeare-Jahrbuch*
SP	*Studies in Philology*
SQ	*Shakespeare Quarterly*
TSLL	*Texas Studies in Literature and Language*
UR	*University Review*

I

INTRODUCTION

A definition of tragedy is possible only within the context of one's philosophy of life. This perspective establishes the value structure against which the individual is measured and thus determines whether emphasis is upon the consequences of sin in a Christian universe, the struggle for self-will in a world controlled by whimsical Olympian gods, the inability to live up to an inner standard or code in the face of external disaster, the consequences of error or misjudgment in a world in which man at least partially is master of his own fate, or even the logical absurdity of life in a nihilistic universe.

The essence of tragedy, in any case, involves human failure, weakness, and suffering. Elizabethan England, caught like the present age in the spiritual agony of philosophic transition, could no longer sanction without question the Judaeo-Christian assumptions about man and his universe inherited from the Middle Ages; nor could it place full credence in the secular impulses of self-assertion that seemed to lie at the very heart of man's astronomical, geographical, economic, and political discoveries. From this profound ambivalence emerges in the dramatic literature of the period—primarily in the work of Marlowe, Shakespeare, and Webster—a concept that failure of a particular nature is mysteriously a kind of progress, success, or enlightenment. Such a view in no way minimizes the sense of suffering, destruction, or loss; nor does it in any way disguise the vicious and animalistic cruelty that man is capable of inflicting upon those around him, frequently those whose love is most sincere. It does not deny the existence of a teleological universe and a power who exercises supreme control, although by focusing upon man's human destiny as reflected in his relationships with his fellow man it suggests the inscrutability of such a metaphysical force.

One of the purposes of the present study is to trace this development of Shakespeare's tragic vision. While his interpretation of the experience varies, the framework of his tragic perspective has become reasonably firm by the turn of the seventeenth century. Action has come to focus on a single figure of noble stature whose experiences during a limited part of his life provide a fundamental unity. Facing some critical decision or provoked to some critical act, this individual is imbued with a sensitive conscience and with at least a latent conviction that he is the cause of his own undoing and that he is responsible for the consequences of his actions both for himself and for others. At the same time, in a world of opposing values, each ambivalent and each possessing the potential of both salvation and destruction, his dilemma is not to be resolved through simplistic moral or ethical choices. The resulting paradox lends dignity to the hero's inevitable error and subsequent misery; it projects him, in the eye of the beholder, at least, beyond what N. J. Calarco has recently described as "naked, unmediated suffering, and beyond the despair" that results from such "suffering [which] can neither be ignored nor made intelligible in some context larger than the individual experience of pain."[1] In the full pattern this central figure will experience some form of an anagnorisis, either wisdom spawned by suffering followed by reconciliation and spiritual peace or tragic insight resulting from the power to endure and the power to apprehend (even if he himself is incapable of regeneration), followed by a restitution of harmony in the order of man and the order of nature.[2]

Shakespeare was instrumental, of course, in the establishment of a form that subsequent generations and countless critics have viewed as the supreme literary contribution of the age. Certainly in large measure this success is the result of his careful concern, even in the late

1. *Tragic Being: Apollo and Dionysus in Western Drama* (Minneapolis: Univ. of Minnesota Press, 1968), p. 9. Excellent general discussions of tragedy include J. M. R. Margeson, *The Origins of English Tragedy* (Oxford: Clarendon Press, 1967); A. P. Rossiter, *Angel with Horns*, ed. Graham Storey (New York: Theatre Arts Books, 1961); Norman Rabkin, *Shakespeare and the Common Understanding* (New York: Free Press, 1967); and Geoffrey Brereton, *Principles of Tragedy* (London: Routledge and Kegan Paul, 1968).

2. As Howard Baker writes, suffering must "become articulate. Articulation goes hand in hand with ultimate understanding and adjustment; and understanding and adjustment, though they do not prevent the fates, though they see only death before them, are nevertheless the soul of tragedy" (*Induction to Tragedy* [Baton Rouge: Louisiana State Univ. Press, 1939], p. 105). On the same point, see Northrop Frye, *Fools of Time* (Toronto: Toronto Univ. Press, 1967).

1580s and early 1590s, for a coherent plot to accommodate his protagonist's adventures as its consuming interest—"to excite expectation and keep it up throughout," as the nineteenth-century actor-playwright James Sheridan Knowles describes it.[3] To be sure, his tragedy at its best does not escape Sidney's neoclassical criticism (leveled against earlier English tragedy) that the play is "faulty both in place and time," portraying "Asia of the one side, and Afric of the other" with "two armies fly[ing] in, represented with swords and bucklers." Above all his contemporaries, however, Shakespeare comes to know "the difference betwixt reporting and representing," which demands that either "history" or "new matter" be framed "to the most tragical conveniency" in order that the plot will be capable of "stirring the effects of admiration and commiseration" whereby to teach "the uncertainty of this world."[4]

A second purpose of this study, then, is to examine the developing sophistication of Shakespeare's dramatic technique, the nature of his control of the action and his manipulation of the spectators' view of it. Specifically the attention will be directed to the various structural devices by which Shakespeare creates and sustains in the spectators the necessary pattern of anticipation and the double vision provoking them simultaneously to participation in the protagonist's spiritual anguish and to judgment on the decisions and actions that destroy him as well as those he loves. Secondary characters, for example, who comment significantly on the protagonist's actions or personality; character parallels and foils, whose presence serves primarily to heighten certain aspects of his nature; a subplot or diversionary episodes, scenes that function either comically or seriously to reiterate the issues of major importance; cosmic ramifications: ghosts, omens, portents, oracles, magic, witchcraft (which in the best plays are far more than contrivances for exhilaration)—all such apparatus direct the spectators' attention to the protagonist and control their attitude toward him. Analytic asides and soliloquies from the protagonist or from those

3. *Lectures on Dramatic Literature Delivered . . . During the Years 1820–1850*, ed. Francis Harvey (London, 1873), p. 125.

4. Sir Philip Sidney, *An Apology for Poetry*, ed. Geoffrey Shepherd (London: Nelson, 1965), pp. 114, 118, 135.

centrally involved in his struggle result in a new and complex form of drama that sets in motion an inner pattern of events simultaneous with the action that proceeds on the external level.[5] The dramatist in this manner is able to penetrate and explore the spiritual depths of the personality, to reveal both the full motivation and the inner anguish.

While Shakespeare's initial tragedies are significant achievements in their own right when compared with earlier sixteenth-century drama, their most remarkable quality—for our present purposes—lies in what they anticipate. Inconsistent and rudimentary in many ways, the individual play nonetheless reflects Shakespeare's concern for controlling the spectators' dramatic experience and demonstrates particular structural techniques by which he will achieve the firm tragic perspective of his major work. These experiments range from the potentially effective pattern of Titus' characterization as established through the extensive use of comments from the surrounding characters, and the misdirected soliloquies of the melodramatic villain Aaron who is never successfully integrated into the plot, to the numerous soliloquies in *Richard III* which, coupled with the elaborate curses of Queen Margaret and Lady Anne, both foreshadow the action and provide for it a philosophical frame of reference. The middle tragedies focus on the experience of a central figure whose guilt, suffering, and tragic insight are registered essentially on the private level. Through the devices of internalization, utilized first by Iago and then by Othello, for example, the spectators' attention is progressively restricted; in the climactic moments it is confined to the privacy of a bedroom and to an isolated character whom pride and circumstance have blinded. By contrast the late plays—structurally the most complex works, if not the most successful dramatically—chart Shakespeare's final tragic dimensions in his apparent determination to reflect both the individual and collective nature of tragedy. While the spectators continue to catch significant—if only sporadic—glimpses of the protagonist's internal struggle, major emphasis, through the comments of secondary characters and multiple foils, is also on the selfish-

5. An excellent discussion of the significance of the soliloquy is provided by Wolfgang Clemen, *Shakespeare's Soliloquies* (Cambridge: Cambridge Univ. Press, 1964).

ness of those who use and misuse him for their own material or emotional ends.

In this respect Shakespeare's final tragedies are obviously closely related in theme and tone to the work of such playwrights as Tourneur, Webster, Middleton, and Ford, who also depict a darkened and decadent world in which the individual is as much a victim of the evil in those around him as he is an agent of his own destruction. In Coriolanus' and Antony's compassionate moments, however—and above all in the development of a secondary character who can profit directly from the insights gained from the tragic experience—Shakespeare continues to suggest that it is the action of the individual and the manner in which he touches the lives of those around him, not the action of society, by which the value of human existence must ultimately be measured.

The Renaissance was an age intensely engaged in a search for literary form, a fact well documented by both Madeleine Doran in *Endeavors of Art* and Austin Warren in *Rage for Order*.[6] The specific development of the Elizabethan tragic pattern has best been described as the result of a synthesis of the native with the classical tradition. Critical terms for these traditions abound, to be sure; the native tradition, for example, has been characterized as *de casibus* (from the narrative pattern of Boccaccio's *De Casibus Virorum Illustrium* and John Lydgate's translation as *The Fall of Princes*) or Gothic tragedy, while the classical tradition has been referred to variously as Senecan, Italianate intrigue, or *Novelle* tragedy. And the evolution of this synthesized form is undeniably multifaceted even in Shakespeare's age, as demonstrated by V. K. Whitaker's need for twelve categories to classify the fewer than one hundred extant tragedies in England from 1560 to 1613.[7] Certainly, though, that is the kind of exercise to which the age itself would have been sympathetic: one needs only to recall the second player's Polonius-like observation to Aminadab in Thomas

6. Madeleine Doran, *Endeavors of Art* (Madison: Univ. of Wisconsin Press, 1954); Austin Warren, *Rage for Order* (Chicago: Univ. of Chicago Press, 1948).

7. *The Mirror Up To Nature* (San Marino, Calif.: Huntington Library, 1965), pp. 7–8.

Middleton's *The Mayor of Queensborough* that he and his colleagues
are "comedians, tragedians, tragi-comedians, comi-tragedians, pas-
toralists, humourists, clownists, satirists" moving deftly "from the hug
to the smile, from the smile to the laugh, from the laugh to the handkerchief."[8] In any event Miss Doran (p. 105) has aptly noted that the
"great service of ancient drama was to give English drama a point of
view in handling story other than mere successiveness of event."
Tragedy was possible when the nature of the human experience became more significant to the plot than the state of the central figure's
soul or the theological doctrine by which he could achieve salvation.

Despite the age's demonstrable concern for form, Shakespeare—
except for an occasional comment within a play (such as Hamlet's
famous assertion that the purpose of playing is to hold the mirror up
to nature and his quips to the players, like Peter Quince's earlier, concerning the proper fashion for acting—nowhere provides a statement
of dramatic theory. Consequently any such theory must be constructed
from inference; and, whatever the method, the critic must consider
the individual play in relationship to Shakespeare's total production.
He must be alert also to recurring patterns that might reveal something of the playwright's attitude toward character, the nature of the
tragic dilemma, and the consequences of suffering. Perhaps above all
he must be alert to the recurring techniques by which Shakespeare
establishes and develops these patterns of character and action and by
which he controls the spectators' reaction to his dramatic material. Such
inferential construction, moreover, is admittedly cumulative. Many
aspects of this book are indebted to the efforts and to the insights of
previous critics, and several studies which bear upon my thesis in at
least a general way have appeared only quite recently.[9] In a significant

8. *Thomas Middleton*, ed. Havelock Ellis (London: Vizetelly, 1890), II,
373 (V, i).
9. Emrys Jones, *Scenic Form in Shakespeare* (Oxford: Clarendon Press,
1971); Kenneth Muir, *Shakespeare's Tragic Sequence* (London: Hutchinson
Univ. Press, 1972); Mark Rose, *Shakespearean Design* (Cambridge, Mass.:
Harvard Univ. Press, 1972); J. L. Simmons, *Shakespeare's Pagan World: The
Roman Tragedies* (Charlottesville: Univ. of Virginia Press, 1973); J. Leeds
Barroll, *Artificial Persons: The Formation of Character in the Tragedies of
Shakespeare* (Columbia: Univ. of South Carolina Press, 1973); Ruth Nevo,
Tragic Form in Shakespeare (Princeton: Princeton Univ. Press, 1972); Philip

manner also the study builds upon my earlier effort to trace in Shakespeare's comedies the manner in which he utilized structural devices to maintain a comic perspective even while his dramatic vision of character and of situation became increasingly more profound and problematic.[10] Specifically my principal concern in the chapters which follow will be to examine through each of the twelve tragedies the developing complexity of Shakespeare's tragic form and to explore the increasingly more functional manner in which he transmits this vision to the audience.

Edwards, *Shakespeare and the Confines of Art* (London: Methuen, 1968); Bernard McElroy, *Shakespeare's Mature Tragedies* (Princeton: Princeton Univ. Press, 1973).

10. *The Evolution of Shakespeare's Comedy: A Study in Dramatic Perspective* (Cambridge, Mass.: Harvard Univ. Press, 1970).

II

THE SEARCH FOR A PERSPECTIVE:
TITUS ANDRONICUS, RICHARD III,
RICHARD II, ROMEO AND JULIET

Analysis of *Titus Andronicus* would be largely an exercise in futility did it not provide a base from which to measure and evaluate the nature of Shakespeare's growth as a tragic playwright. Despite what we now denounce as its crudeness and barbarity[1] and despite the ease with which we can now point out flaws in structure, character, and language, the play was evidently one of the dramatic highlights of the early 1590s, and almost twenty-five years later it was still sufficiently popular to provoke Jonson's sneering observation in the Induction to *Bartholomew Fair* that any playgoer who still insists it is the best play "shall passe vnexcepted at, heere, as a man whose Judgement shewes it is constant, and hath stood still, these five and twentie, or thirtie yeeres." Moreover it is not very dissimilar to Kyd's horrific *Spanish Tragedy*, which presumably set the popular tradition in this mode a few years earlier. Post hoc critical carping about this individ-

1. Edward Ravenscroft, in the *Address* to his adaptation of the play in 1687, refers to *Titus* as "the most incorrect and indigested piece in all his Works" (quoted in E. K. Chambers, *William Shakespeare* [Oxford: Oxford Univ. Press, 1930], II, 255). Recent opinion is substantially the same. "Barbaric, lusty, bloodthirsty" (Margaret Webster, *Shakespeare Without Tears* [New York: McGraw-Hill, 1942], p. 101), a "concentrated brew of blood and horror" (H. C. Goddard, *The Meaning of Shakespeare* [Chicago: Univ. of Chicago Press, 1951], I, 3), the tragedy—"like some broken-down cart, laden with bleeding corpses from an Elizabethan scaffold, and driven by an executioner from Bedlam" (J. D. Wilson, ed., *Titus Andronicus* [Cambridge: Cambridge Univ. Press, 1948], p. xii)—is "one of the stupidest and most uninspired plays ever written" (T. S. Eliot, quoted in E. M. W. Tillyard, *Shakespeare's History Plays* [London: Chatto and Windus, 1944], p. 160), its author a virtuoso of horror (W. Hastings, "The Hard Boiled Shakespeare," *SAB*, XVII [1942], 122). Wilson (p. liv), Goddard (p. 34), and Mark Van Doren (*Shakespeare* [New York: Holt, 1939], p. 32) suggest that Shakespeare may have been consciously parodying the revenge tragedy.

ual play, then, in a sense tends to be reduced to an academic condemnation of late sixteenth-century English dramatic taste.[2]

The play anticipates much about the extensive developments that are to occur in the art of English stagecraft (most strikingly Shakespeare's) during the next two decades. For whether Shakespeare is responsible for all or only a part of the play,[3] the tragic perspective is a touchstone to the artistry of his later work. Most significant is the establishment in the initial scene of a powerful tragic protagonist. Specifically the juxtaposition in Act I of Titus' magnitude and heroism (as visualized in the words of others and in his posture as conquering hero) with his precipitous actions and bestial fury logically establishes the thematic anticipation of a great man, flawed to the core, whose

2. In "a period of crude and careless drama" (Arthur M. Sampley, "Plot Structure in Peele's Plays as a Test of Authorship," *PMLA,* LI [1936], 689), *Titus*—"clearly the work of a young dramatist whose main interest is the principal one of conforming to accepted popular taste" (D. A. Traversi, *An Approach to Shakespeare* [New York: Doubleday, 1956], pp. 13–14)—was written for an audience "to which no exhibition of horror or cruelty could give anything but a pleasurable shock" (Arthur Symons, *Studies in the Elizabethan Drama* [New York: Dutton, 1919], p. 64). Robert Y. Turner has recently examined the principles of rhetoric and characterization in this play and Shakespeare's other earliest pieces (*Shakespeare's Apprenticeship* [Chicago: Univ. of Chicago Press, 1974]).

3. A few earlier critics have denied Shakespeare any portion (see, for example, Samuel Johnson, ed., *Shakespeare* [London, 1765], VI, 364; and John Bailey, *Shakespeare* [London: Longmans, Green, 1929], p. 86). While this view is no longer posited, critics have continued to disagree concerning the extent of Shakespeare's contribution since Ravenscroft's comment in the late seventeenth century that Shakespeare "only gave some master-touches" to the play (Chambers, II, 246). One group (for example, Edmond Malone [quoted in Chambers, II, 258]; A. W. Verity, ed., *Shakespeare* [London, 1890], VII, 259; T. W. Baldwin, *On the Literary Genetics of Shakespeare's Plays* [Urbana: Univ. of Illinois Press, 1959], pp. 402–20; J. C. Maxwell, "Peele and Shakespeare: A Stylometric Test," *JEGP,* XLIX [1950], 558; and J. D. Wilson [p. lvii]) have described Shakespeare's role as that of a collaborator or a reviser. Another group (for example, Walter Raleigh, ed., *Shakespeare* [London: Macmillan, 1907], pp. 84, 108, 125; Harold Fuller, "The Sources of *Titus Andronicus,*" *PMLA,* IX [1901], 65; Robert Adger Law, "The Roman Background of *Titus Andronicus,*" *SP,* XL [1943], 153; and H. T. Price, "The Authorship of *Titus Andronicus,*" *JEGP,* XLII [1943], 55–81) argue Shakespeare's hand in every line.

implacable pride has provoked distastrous error and who in the subsequent scenes must be expected to endure a spiritual wheel of fire.[4]
This concept of character, along with the structural devices that control the spectators' attitude, need not be explained away as unworthy
of a fledgling Shakespeare. To be sure, the design is executed only in
part, the full potential of the protagonist never realized. But as D. A.
Stauffer has remarked, the play is a "storehouse of themes and episodes and attitudes and images and situations which Shakespeare later
was to develop."[5] Titus himself recent critics have described as "ex-
quisitely conceived, in the mould of later Shakespearian tragic heroes,"[6] a "real prophecy" of the characters to come.[7]

Certainly Shakespeare consciously underscores Titus' merits at the
outset. Marcus, the Captain, Lavinia, the Tribunes—all through their
comments guide and control the spectators' initial response. A brave
warrior, renowned, favored by honor and fortune, a patron of virtue
and a champion of Rome, he is a "noble lord and father" "whose
fortunes Rome's best citizens applaud" (I, i, 161, 167).[8] That Marcus

4. John P. Cutts ("Shadow and Substance: Structural Unity in *Titus Andronicus*," *Comparative Drama*, II [1968], 163–64) claims that both Titus'
sacrifice of Alarbus and his support of Saturninus stem directly from the
"groaning shadow of his own ambition," while Price ("The Authorship," p.
75) and Fredson T. Bowers (*Elizabethan Revenge Tragedy* [Princeton: Princeton Univ. Press, 1940], p. 112) use Tamora's charge of "cruel, irreligious impiety" to describe Titus' flaw. Viewing the pattern of events from a greater
distance, Tillyard (p. 162) finds the unity of the play in the issues of "title and
succession [which] were crucial in Elizabethan thought"; see also J. Leeds
Barroll ("Shakespeare and Roman History," *MLR*, LIII [1958], 328). Northrop Frye observes that "perhaps we could make more dramatic sense out of
Titus Andronicus if we could see it as an unharrowed hell, a satyr-play of obscene gibbering demons" (*Anatomy of Criticism* [Princeton: Princeton Univ.
Press, 1957], p. 292); Jan Kott (*Shakespeare Our Contemporary*, trans. Boleslaw Taborski [New York: Doubleday, 1964], pp. 5–6), on the other hand,
quite predictably proclaims that Titus' horrors, atrocities, and political dilemmas place him in close contact with the readers and spectators of the present
age and its tragedy of the absurd.
5. *Shakespeare's World of Images* (New York: Norton, 1949), p. 13.
6. Virgil K. Whitaker, *The Mirror Up To Nature* (San Marino, Calif.:
Huntington Library, 1965), p. 97.
7. Alan Sommers, " 'Wilderness of Tigers': Structure and Symbolism in
Titus Andronicus," *Essays in Criticism*, X (1960), 288.
8. All line references to Shakespeare's plays throughout this study are to

and the people of Rome have selected Titus to stand as a candidate for emperor attests to their regard. When he modestly refuses the honor and factionalism bursts forth again between Saturninus and Bassianus, that the citizens would readily accept Titus' word for selecting the next ruler suggests virtual idolatry.

Yet, directly in the face of what others have said about him, Titus' actions in the first act reflect a man who is furiously proud and stubborn beyond measure. The spectator can only be disturbed by the hero's implacable determination to sacrifice Alarbus before the monument of the Andronici. Indeed Shakespeare takes some pains to focus the worst light of this situation on Titus. The human sacrifice is never justified; the occasional comments that these are rites enacted to appease the dead simply fail to provide the rationale so distinctly needed when the action has been openly challenged; no god's name is invoked, no spiritual efficacy described. Titus agrees to the sacrifice in the face of a description that exhibits its most gruesome and inhuman aspects. Lucius requests his father to give him "the proudest prisoner" so that he may "hew his limbs" and "sacrifice his flesh" (99–101); moments later he reports that Alarbus' limbs are "lopp'd," his entrails feeding the fire. Even more emphatically, Titus' determination to proceed with the ritual death assumes cruelty when juxtaposed with Tamora's impassioned pleas that her son be spared:

> Rue the tears I shed,
> A mother's tears in passion for her son:
>
> . . . .
>
> Wilt thou draw near the nature of the gods?
> Draw near them then in being merciful.
> (108–9, 120–21)

In effect it is she who, invoking the names both of mother and gods, momentarily captures the spectator's emotional fancy.

If Titus' pride is implicit in his treatment of Alarbus, certainly it is explicit in his brutal slaying of his son. When Mutius attempts to

---

the Pelican Shakespeare, *William Shakespeare: The Complete Works*, general editor Alfred Harbage: Penguin Books, 1969).

prevent his father's pursuing Bassianus and Lavinia, Titus strikes him down with a monstrous arrogance. And to Lucius' charge that Titus is unjust and has slain his son wrongfully, the father retorts that anyone who dishonors him is no real son. So, too, in his wrath, he for a time denies Mutius burial in the family tomb, spurning the charge of impiety and branding sons and brother traitor. Obsessed with a sense of his own importance, he claims that Marcus has wounded his honor and that Bassianus, who later attempts to defend him before Saturninus, has also dishonored him. Unbalanced thus by passion, he is easily duped by Tamora into believing that she, who a few moments earlier was coldly repudiated in pleading for the life of her son, is now a merciful intercessor on behalf of the murderer. Just as earlier he could use his own injured ego as justification for atrocities, so now he is unable to see beyond the glitter of his reconciliation and the apparent restitution of his wonted dignity and adulation.

The structure of Act I establishes a fundamental thrust for the plot: the juxtaposition of numerous choric characters parroting Titus' heroics with a flurry of actions precipitated by the sudden and uncontrolled fury of his pride creates for the spectator a pattern of anticipation in which the focus is on the central character and the consequences he must suffer as a result of his tragic foolishness and, if the cycle is to be complete, the insights he may ultimately achieve. Indeed for a time the experiences of Titus in moving from wrath to self-pity to madness—and the interpretation of them as the spectator is directed by the choric character—support this assumption. Through Act II and the first scene of Act III destruction strikes at him from all directions: his three remaining sons are apparently doomed—Quintus and Martius charged with the murder of Bassianus and Lucius banished for attempting to defend them, his only daughter ravished and horribly mutilated, his willing sacrifice of his own hand to save his sons cruelly mocked with the subsequent presentation of his hand and their heads. While these disasters are not—as in *King Lear*—directly prompted by the protagonist's passion, the spectators inevitably relate them to his earlier posture.

Quite pointedly, his wrath is converted to self-pity in Act III. Lying on the ground before the judges, senators, and tribunes, he pleads for his sons, calling for pity because of his age, his blood, and his tears; his entreaties spurned, he moans that he will tell his "sorrows to the stones" because at least they receive his tears and "seem to weep" with him (III, i, 37, 42). In his grief he avers that Lucius, banished, should be a happy man; no longer will the son be attacked by Rome, the "wilderness of tigers" (54) for which he fought in vain and for which now he and his family afford prey. Confronted with the horrible sight of the mutilated Lavinia, he can only proclaim:

> It was my dear, and he that wounded her
> Hath hurt me more than had he killed me dead;
>
> · · · · · · · · · · · · · ·
>
> O, what a sympathy of woe is this:
> As far from help as Limbo is from bliss!
>
> (91–92, 148–49)

He insists on sacrificing his hand because "such with'red herbs as these / Are meet for plucking" (177–78), and, as Aaron departs with the hand, he implores aid from any power that pities tears of wretchedness. His sorrow he descibes as bottomless, as a deluge beyond control; and his remaining hand is an instrument to "tyrannize" upon his breast (III, ii, 8).

Throughout the act the comments of the surrounding characters maintain the focus on Titus and his reactions to his sufferings. Lucius, for example, informs Titus, pleading before the judges, that he laments in vain because he recounts his sorrows to a stone; the choric function is similar later in the scene when, the ravished Lavinia standing before her father, Lucius implores Titus to cease weeping because of the effect it is having upon her. Marcus provides such comments most extensively. He observes that Lavinia's sight will make her father blind, and he warns Titus to "prepare [his] aged eyes to weep" and his "noble heart to break" because he brings "consuming sorrow" to his age (III, i, 59, 60, 61). At other points he implores Titus to dry his eyes and to "let reason govern [his] lament" (218). Even his grandson on one occasion begs Titus to "leave [his] bitter deep laments" (III, ii, 46).

In Act IV his sanity is the victim of his extreme pride stretched on the rack of ignominy and suffering. Certainly his actions suggest a mounting degree of insanity—his macabre laughter when the mutilated Lavinia kisses her grieving father (III, i, 264),[9] his assertion that he is "mad with misery" (III, ii, 9) and that "no man should be mad but I" (24), his berating Marcus for killing a fly (54 ff.), his suggestion of inscribing words on a leaf of brass to be blown by the angry northern wind (IV, i, 102 ff.), his presents to the empress' sons, his assertion that justice has abandoned the earth:

> This wicked emperor may have shipped her hence;
> And, kinsmen, then we may go pipe for justice.
>
> . . . .
>
> And, sith there's no justice in earth nor hell,
> We will solicit heaven, and move the gods
> To send down Justice for to wreak our wrongs.
>
> (IV, iii, 23–24, 49–51)

His subsequent act in his cruelest and, in a sense, his maddest, as he mistakes a clownish rustic for a messenger from heaven, bringing response to his pleas to the gods for justice.[10] Without the least qualm of sanity Titus gives him a messsage to Saturninus, assures him justice at the emperor's hands and that Andronicus himself will "be at hand" (110) to look to his reward, and sends him to a sure death.

9. M. C. Bradbrook (*Shakespeare and Elizabethan Poetry* [New York: Oxford Univ. Press, 1952], pp. 105–6) calls his laughter the turning point in the play, the signal for his assuming the role of the revenger. Perhaps so, but the spectator does not catch the signal; there is no reason whatever—except that of hindsight—for the spectator to believe Titus anything but insane from this point until the fifth act.

10. The brutality of this incident and the manner in which it confirms our assumptions of Titus' insanity have not been considered by previous critics. E. W. Talbert (*Elizabethan Drama and Shakespeare's Early Plays* [Chapel Hill: Univ. of North Carolina Press, 1963], p. 54) sees it as a comic element akin to the death of the dizzard in folk merriment. Howard Baker (*Induction to Tragedy* [Baton Rouge: Louisiana State Univ. Press, 1939], p. 128) describes the clown as a role consciously created as a parallel to Hieronimo's mistaking the old man for a supernatural emissary in *The Spanish Tragedy*. He is, write W. A. Neilson and C. H. Hill (eds. *The Complete Plays and Poems of William Shakespeare* [Boston: Houghton Mifflin, 1942], p. 943), "prophetic of things to come," anticipating "a long line of witless and genial bumpkins."

As the surrounding characters reinforce Titus' statements of sufferings and self-pity in Act III, so their remarks—coupled with his
actions and the absence of any comment from him to suggest that such
action is but an antic posture—convince the spectators that he is indeed mad. Even at the height of Titus' passion in Act I, Martius anticipates the action that follows with the observation that Andronicus
"is not with himself" (I, i, 371). In similar fashion young Lucius
later glosses Lavinia's actions: "I have heard my grandsire say full
oft, / Extremity of griefs would make men mad" (IV, i, 18–19).
Marcus, again, is the most significant tragic pointer. Of his brother's
actions in the fly scene, he notes that grief has so distracted him that
he "takes false shadows for true substances" (III, ii, 80). So, later,
after Lavinia has revealed the identity of her attackers, Marcus' attempt to initiate some form of revenge indicates his assumption that
Titus—plagued by his mutinous thoughts—is unable to mount such
an effort:

> O heavens, can you hear a good man groan
> And not relent, or not compassion him?
> Marcus, attend him in his ecstasy,
> That hath more scars of sorrow in his heart
> Than foemen's marks upon his batt'red shield.
> (IV, i, 123–27)

As Titus in a subsequent scene directs his arrows with their requests
for justice to the various gods, Marcus laments, "O Publius, is not this
a heavy case / To see thy noble uncle thus distract? . . . Kinsmen, his
sorrows are past remedy" (IV, iii, 25–26, 31). Aaron speaks to Chiron and Demetrius of the "mad message" from young Lucius' "mad
grandfather" (IV, ii, 3); the emperor, of the "sorrows" that "have so
overwhelmed his wits" (IV, iv, 10); and the empress, of his lunacy
and his brainsick humors—as she and her sons dress as Revenge,
Rape, and Murder to "fit" his condition (V, ii).

Demonstrably, Shakespeare has focused the first four and one-half
acts on the character of Titus. Largely through the consistent pattern
of comments from the surrounding characters, the spectators' attention has been directed to a powerful Roman soldier who, once past the

awesomely furious and active moments of his pride in Act I, is by degrees broken through pain and madness. He has, in effect, become
relatively passive and impotent, on occasions speaking of vengeance
but apparently incapable of a concerted effort. Certainly, then, the
thrust of the play is toward some final and climactic development in
the character of Titus—whether some form of stoic resignation by
which spiritually to rise above the conditions that destroy him, or some
recognition of the destructive nature of uncontrolled passion, or some
form of poetic redress by which a chastened Titus could regain something of his former status without his former abilities, or some scheme
of vengeance directed by Marcus through which Titus either in life or
death could enact some measure of retributive justice. At least the
structure of the play could accommodate such a conclusion.

What Shakespeare provides is the very conclusion the structure will
not support—the sudden and (from the perspective of the audience)
absolutely unanticipated emergence of Titus as a sophisticated revenger outwitting his adversaries at their own game. One is shocked to
hear Titus, in an aside well into Act V (indeed 264 lines from the
end), suddenly affirm his sanity:

> I knew them all, though they supposed me mad,
> And will o'erreach them in their own devices,
> A pair of cursèd hellhounds and their dame.
>
> (V, ii, 142–44)

Even here, of course, the spectators have no assurance of a degree of
sanity sufficient for his devising a scheme; nor for that matter is the
audience made aware of what Titus' macabre designs are until he explains them to Chiron and Demetrius even at the point of cutting their
throats. In no way arising from the pattern of the plot and in no
way consistent with the character of Titus, the events of the final moments occur so rapidly and so amazingly as to command interest as an
end in themselves, and—the perspective for the spectator destroyed—
the emphasis is on narrative rather than drama. Within moments Lavinia has entered carrying between her stumps a basin in which to receive the blood of her ravishers, and moments after that Titus, dressed
as a cook, is—Virginius-like—sacrificing his own daughter, serving

16

his macabre dish, itemizing its contents to the horrified Tamora and Saturninus, and fatally stabbing the former queen of the Goths.

The central problem of the play, then, is the protagonist—the direction in which he is developed in the first twelve scenes and the anomalous point at which he has suddenly arrived in the last two scenes. Clearly it is patently inaccurate to assert that Titus is totally flat, a character without development. The development from wrath to self-pity to madness, which Shakespeare is to reiterate in Lear, is profoundly human and, even amidst the bombastic rhetoric and the diversionary horrors of Aaron the Moor, not totally ineffective. But to develop a character and to provide him with philosophic depth are two different matters. In this play the playwright, to indicate the progressive degeneration in Titus, depends almost exclusively upon the external structural device of the pointer characters—Marcus primarily but, on occasion, other figures such as the sons, young Lucius, Publius, the Captain, Aaron, Tamora, and Saturninus. Absent are significant soliloquies and asides, devices that permit the spectator to see within the character where the struggle that gives universal meaning to external actions occurs.

Titus speaks an incredible total of only six such lines in the entire play. His one soliloquy (I, i 341–43), in which he reacts with dismay to public repudiation by Saturninus, does serve to underscore his egocentricity in the early moments of the play; but at the same time the absence of even the slightest concern for the son he has brutally murdered earlier demonstrates his total lack of introspection. In Act V (ii, 142–44) he suddenly asserts his sanity and privately reveals to the spectators his intention to overreach Tamora. Even this aside is not a truly significant statement; its importance is narrative rather than dramatic in that it merely announces a course of action instead of revealing any aspect of the struggle by which the decision was reached. There is, in short, absolutely no indication (as in Kyd's Hieronimo) of inner conflict concerning the nature of public vengeance, no indication (as in Hamlet) of inner struggle concerning the morality of revenge or the relationship of the avenger to the gods, no assertion (implicit as in Chapman's Bussy, explicit as later in Ford's Orgilus) of the validity of private values in a corrupt society. Nor—beyond the possible implications (*if* we could believe him sane) of Titus' exclamation, "Ah, Rome! Well, well, I made thee miserable" (IV, iii, 18)—is there ever a hint of remorse arising from a recognition of his withering and destructive wrath, or, for that matter, a suggestion of inner peace resulting from a debt of justice successfully paid in full. Titus, in fact, never goes so far as to assert the justice of revenge and his ready willingness to sacrifice his own life, if need be, to achieve it.

Shakespeare himself may well have realized something of the weakness arising from the lack of philosophic dimension. References to the gods and the heavens are quite frequent in the last half of the play (seventeen to the gods, fifteen to the heavens). The effect, however, is entirely peripheral; no relationship is developed at any time between Titus and the heavens or his concept of the will of the gods. In the "fly scene" (III, ii), first printed in the folio version of the text,[11] apparently Shakespeare attempted, albeit clumsily, to supply a part of that deficiency. This scene, in which Titus berates Marcus for killing a fly, in part underscores Andronicus' madness; yet the conversation turns directly on the morality of killing the innocent. Titus calls his brother a murderer; his eyes are "cloyed with view of tyranny. / A deed of death done on the innocent" (55–56). He is concerned for the father and mother of the harmless fly. When informed that the fly was black like the empress' Moor, however, his attitude suddenly alters, and he calls the deed a "charitable" one. The forced analogy, then, seems to compel Titus to consider the moral ramifications of retaliation in kind. Although murder is itself an abominable violence, Aaron's villainy is so detestable that his destruction might well be an act of kindness. The incident, however, is grotesque, and the idea of such mental conflict is never functionally developed. Moreover the Moor is one of the few principals who survive Titus; vengeance falls

11. The scene was probably in the play from the outset, omitted from the quarto publications because the players would not release the leaf which bore the license (see W. W. Greg, *The Shakespeare First Folio* [Oxford: Clarendon Press, 1955], pp. 203–9); H. T. Price claims that Aaron's reference to a fly in V, i, 141–42 is a "clear echo in Q_1 of the incident with the fly [and] makes it certain that III, ii, is not a later addition" ("Mirror Scenes in Shakespeare," in *Joseph Q. Adams Memorial Studies* [Washington: Folger Library, 1948], p. 109). Whether in the original play or added later, the significance of the scene is obviously not altered.

instead upon Tamora and her children, who play no significant role
in the parallel.

Whatever the nature of Titus' development, the spectators' emotions are never engaged. A successful revenger who, in the process,
shocks us further by sacrificing his daughter without warning, Titus in
the final act experiences no form of regeneration that in itself would
strengthen such a rapport. Again the playwright depends upon the
comments of the surrounding characters to create an impression of
sympathy and nobility. Marcus, for instance, standing amidst the carnage of Titus' final banquet, stresses the cause that provoked Titus,
the unspeakable wrongs that pushed him beyond what any mortal man
could bear. While his performance does succeed in calming the people
and in establishing Lucius as emperor, actually his subsequent request
(that the people show him what he has done wrong) skirts the morality of the issue, just as the entire play has done. Both Lucius, with a
kiss upon his lips as the last duty of a noble son, and Marcus, with
tear for tear and kiss for kiss, pay their final respects to Titus, after
which the young grandson cries:

> O grandsire, grandsire! ev'n with all my heart
> Would I were dead, so you did live again!
> O Lord, I cannot speak to him for weeping;
> My tears will choke me if I ope my mouth.
>
> (172–75)

At the same time these kinsmen of Titus denigrate the character of
Aaron, the only villain still alive. Defiant, blasphemous, and cruelly
unrepentant to the end, he asserts that if he could have his will he
would perform deeds ten thousand times worse than those of record.
Obviously he provides a convenient foil for Titus against which the
Roman will shine the brighter and appear the more human.

By pointers and character contrast, then, the playwright attempts to
elevate Titus to a final tragic stature even though he experiences no
true regeneration. Aside from his single three-line soliloquy and his
single three-line aside, the play contains six soliloquies and eight
asides. On eight occasions these passages are used to establish dramatic irony and thus, for a brief moment at least, to create a pattern

of anticipation which the narrative will shortly satisfy. The remaining passages are soliloquies and asides in name only; that is, the character, who merely happens to be alone on stage, reveals nothing significant about his own or Titus' personality and might well have been speaking with, or overheard by, any number of characters.

Only one soliloquy approximates the device that Shakespeare is to use with such powerful effect in his more profound tragedies. Here the passage, spoken by Aaron (II, i, 1–25), is used not to delineate a spiritual struggle between opposing values, but to provide significant self-analysis. The Moor—philosophically an incipient Iago, Edmund, Flamineo, or Bosola—asserts his determination to use his opportunities for advancement.[12] Doffing both "slavish weeds and servile thoughts," he will "be bright and shine in pearl and gold" (18, 19) and will "arm [his] heart and fit [his] thoughts / To mount aloft with [the] imperial mistress" (12–13) whom he long has held prisoner in "amorous chains" (15). Unfortunately, however, Aaron is never functionally made a part of the plot; he moves against Titus without Tamora's knowledge and, insofar as the spectators can perceive, without apparent reason. On the one hand there is no visible development of Tamora's and Aaron's relationship as lovers to the point that the two share in some kind of joint effort to destroy her enemy, with Aaron acting as both designer and executor. On the other hand neither is there a development of Aaron as the Machiavellian opportunist who performs blindly and dispassionately the deeds he knows will make his rise the more meteoric. Certainly the Moor is no DeFlores acting blindly and passionately in *The Changeling* for the sake of dotage; if anything Tamora is the passionate one and Aaron

---

12. "A leaf from Marlowe's book" (Hardin Craig, ed., *The Complete Works of Shakespeare* [Chicago: Scott, Foresman, 1951], p. 367), a legacy of the vice who delights with his wit (Ann Righter, *Shakespeare and the Idea of the Play* [London: Chatto and Windus, 1962], p. 87; Bernard Spivack, *Shakespeare and the Allegory of Evil* [New York: Columbia Univ. Press, 1958], 380), the conventional Machiavellian (C. Coe, *Shakespeare's Villains* [New York: Bookman Associates, 1957], p. 11), a parody of the humor of melancholy (Eldred D. Jones, "Aaron and Melancholy in *Titus Andronicus*," *SQ*, XIV [1963], 179), Aaron has been labeled by more than one critic the best indication in the play of Shakespeare's potential (J. S. G. Bolton, "*Titus Andronicus*: Shakespeare at Thirty," *SP*, XXX [1933], 221; Talbert, p. 44).

the cold-blooded egotist who would find it difficult to love or to be fascinated by anyone other than himself. In short, for the play as it stands, Aaron is another of the unexplained ingredients. Whether he is the dramatist's concession to a popular stage type only peripherally attached to the plot or whether he is intended to be the confidant and henchman of Tamora to assist her against Titus—and whether he is intended to be lethally serious or grotesquely comic, he does not (as the soliloquy suggests) function coherently at the center of the plot. To furnish him with the single significant soliloquy, which by its very nature makes the spectators feel more intimately familiar with him than with any other character, is to blur even more seriously the focus and the design of the play.

Tamora, of course, would have credible motivation for seeking vengeance against Titus. Indeed, her entreaties spurned and her son brutally sacrificed in the first act, she avows a passionate hatred for Titus and, when her fortunes rise as empress, assures Saturninus that in due time she will "find a day to massacre them all" (I, i, 453). Yet she never devises a plan, and her opportunities to destroy Titus arise almost by accident. For instance, the rape of Lavinia, the murder of Bassianus, and the framed charges against Quintus and Martius are virtually faits accomplis before she is aware of them. Without her knowledge Aaron has dug the pit, buried the gold, and carefully directed the lust of Chiron and Demetrius for Lavinia; she is suddenly told to deliver a "fatal-plotted scroll" with evidence against Titus' son Saturninus. Her opportunity to refuse mercy callously to Lavinia again is in no way of her own making. Nor is the ruse by which Titus is brought willingly to permit his hand to be amputated. Indeed her one attempt to move directly against Titus (in disguise along with her sons) is ironically the fatal step by which she is caught in Andronicus' trap.

One could also easily enumerate general flaws in the language and the action. The imagery, for example, on occasion fragments the effect of the play.[13] There are moments when the language is incon-

---

13. The language of the characters is inconsistent (H. T. Price, "The Language of *Titus Andronicus*," *Papers of the Michigan Academy*, XXI [1935], 501-7), the images of cruelty and brutality opposed by others of a remarkably

sistent with the characterization, as in Tamora's pastoral set-piece description of the secret spot at which she and Aaron meet ("everything doth make a gleeful boast," "birds chaunt melody," "cheerful sun," "cooling wind," "checkered shadow," "sweet shade," "babbling echo," "golden slumber," "melodious birds," "nurse's song / Of lullaby" [II, iii, 10–29 passim]). Moments later in equally lavish terms she describes the same place as a spot to which Bassianus and Lavinia have enticed her ("pale," "barren detested vale," "forlorn and lean," "moss and baleful mistletoe," "never shines the sun," "nightly owl or fatal raven," "abhorrèd pit," "thousand fiends," "hissing snakes," "swelling toads," "urchins," "fearful and confusèd cries," "dismal yew" [II, iii, 91–115 passim]). At other moments the imagery is so excessive or so grotesque that it virtually blocks the spectator's sympathetic reaction to the scene he beholds. Marcus, for example, laments over the mutilated and ravished Lavinia: her body has been made bare of "branches, those sweet ornaments"; her tongueless mouth is "a crimson river of warm blood," a "bubbling fountain stirred with wind"; she is "a conduit with three issuing spouts" (II, iv, 17–18, 22, 23, 30). So, later, in bringing her to her father, Marcus describes the "delightful engine of her thoughts" as "torn from forth that pretty hollow cage" (III, i, 82, 84). During moments of Titus' apparent sanity, the baroque imagery of self-pity tends to block our response. He declares that his "two ancient urns" "will befriend" the earth with more rain than "youthful April"; "with warm tears" he will "in winter . . . melt the snow" and "keep eternal spring-time on [the earth's] face" (III, i, 16–21). A few lines later he compares himself to

a rock,
Environed with a wilderness of sea,

---

pastoral and peaceful nature (A. Yoder, *Animal Analogy in Shakespeare's Character Portrayal* [New York: King's Crown Press, 1947]). Both E. M. Waith ("The Metamorphosis of Violence in *Titus Andronicus*," *Shakespeare Survey*, X [1957], 39–49) and A. C. Hamilton ("*Titus Andronicus*: The Form of Shakespearian Tragedy," *SQ*, XIV [1963], 208, 210) believe the juxtaposition to be deliberate; through "control over language, Shakespeare controls the horror which the play arouses."

Who marks the waxing tide grow wave by wave,
Expecting ever when some envious surge
Will in his brinish bowels swallow him.

(III, i, 93–97)

Even more disconcerting than these lapses in language, which smell more of the study than the playhouse, are the sudden unmotivated actions that prevent the material from functioning as a frame within which the spectator can intelligently observe and share in Titus' tragic development. For instance, Bassianus' seizing Lavinia as his betrothed in the opening action provokes Titus to his woeful attack upon Mutius. Like Titus the spectator has had no premonition of this betrothal which, oddly enough, the rest of her family (Marcus, Lucius, Mutius, Quintus, and Martius) apparently know about or at least choose to support without question or explanation, even though it involves defiance of the emperor. Obviously the spectator finds himself so busy attempting to understand the baffling action that his full attention is far from Titus' reaction. Similarly the love-lust rivalry for Lavinia between Chiron and Demetrius suddenly set forth in Act II is convenient for Aaron to overhear and to mold to his own plan, but, without preparation, it seems hardly plausible. So, also, the blackamoor child which the nurse proffers Aaron in Act IV as the fruit of his relationship with Tamora strikes one as a deus ex machina maneuver to separate the two and thus prepare the empress for what we later learn will be her fate. And, as noted earlier, the events of the final act are the most shocking of all—Lavinia's (so far as we know in no way privy to Titus' full designs) trailing on stage after her father with a knife and basin with which to participate in the grisly execution of her assailants and (without the slightest indication that he has weighed the consequences and formulated his plan in advance) Titus' striking down his daughter with the feebly self-righteous remark that he is as woeful as Virginius was.

Even with these structural inconsistencies, it would be quite easy to extol the virtues of *Titus Andronicus* by pointing to the formlessness and the total lack of dramatic focus in Preston's *Cambises* (c. 1569), the scenes of mounting tyranny and atrocities leading nowhere—ex-

23

cept to the Persian ruler's sudden and accidental death provoked by his stabbing himself with his sword while mounting his horse. Or one might point to the confused melange of scenes in the anonymous *Warres of Cyrus* (1594), a romantic narrative which offers two precipitous deaths in the final act, or to the chaotic structure of Peele's *The Battle of Alcazar* (1594); indeed the character of Aaron, however peripheral, is an improvement on that of the villain Muly Mahamet. Or, even later, one could point to the formlessness of *The Death of Robert, Earl of Huntington* by Munday and Chettle, or *A Christian Turn'd Turk* by Daborne.

The dramatic heritage of the Elizabethan age results, of course, not from such work, but from those playwrights who, in the last fifteen years of the century, labored to achieve a tragic form. In an age that responded enthusiastically to the blasts of the trumpet and the declamation of the stage, such craftsmen as Kyd and Marlowe were registering significant contributions. The unity of character in *Tamburlaine;* the inner conflict of *Doctor Faustus*—accomplished by establishing the machinery of the morality play (good and evil angels, Mephistophilis, the old man, and the like) as an extrapolation of Faustus' conscience and, in effect, of the soliloquy; the development in *Edward II* of foil characters in Mortimer and the king, each existing as much to reflect antithetical qualities in the other as to act in his own right; the verge of tragic insight, recognition, and regeneration to which Edward is drawn—all are matters of extensive critical record. In Kyd's *Spanish Tragedy*, despite the lack of integration of the framing and choral action of Don Andrea and Revenge and despite the clumsy diversionary scenes set in the Portuguese court, the ghost does function as a device for establishing a pattern of anticipation, and the focus is kept constantly on the development of Hieronimo. Swearing vengeance for Horatio's murder, he is driven to madness not only by his grief and sorrow but also by the spiritual anguish arising from the conflict of his commitment (as Marshal of Spain) to public justice and his lust for private revenge. Despite all Hieronimo's grotesque antics in the last half of the play, the spectators—privy to his innermost thoughts—are prepared for the device through which, with Belimperia's aid, the revenge will be accomplished.

Certainly, by the standard of Shakespeare's later work, the structure of *Titus Andronicus* is disjointed and the results disconcerting. The tragic perspective is blurred not only by the inconsistencies of the protagonist but also by the absence of effective philosophic depth; the structural devices—by which externally, through pointer characters and character parallels to direct and focus the spectators' attention and, internally, through soliloquy and aside to probe the depths of character motivation and internal struggle—are in large measure ineffectively utilized. Nevertheless the raw material for an effective tragic perspective is present.[14] Shakespeare is apparently groping toward the philosophic dimensions of Hieronimo's struggle between public and private justice through the addition of the "fly scene" and its clumsy discussion of the ethics of murder and through the numerous references to the gods in the last two acts. Then, too, the initial scheme of revenge, which in turn provokes the major action of the plot, is more effective in *Titus Andronicus* than in *The Spanish Tragedy*. Tamora's determination to gain vengeance against Titus and all his family for the sake of her murdered son Alarbus is far more credibly motivated, if not executed, than Don Andrea's plot to strike back at Balthazar for his dishonorable tactics on the battlefield or Belimperia's decision to use her second lover Horatio as a means of revenge against Balthazar for the death of her first lover Don Andrea. Horatio, except for the brief moment of martial rivalry concerning Balthazar's capture, has no direct relationship with Lorenzo; almost accidentally he becomes the prey of the Machiavellian intriguer who is determined to see his sister wed Balthazar. By contrast Titus is directly responsible for the enmity with Tamora (and by extension Aaron); not only does he bring her captive to Rome, he also—ignor-

14. *Titus,* by contrast with the other tragedy of its day, is "on the whole, well constructed" (Sampley, p. 701), "beyond the powers of any other dramatist writing at the time" (J. C. Maxwell, ed., *Titus Andronicus* [Cambridge, Mass.: Harvard Univ. Press, 1953], p. xli). Certain scenes are "contrived with technical skill of a high order" (J. C. Adams, "Shakespeare's Revisions in *Titus Andronicus,*" *SQ*, XV [1964], 184). "As a collection of theatrical and rhetorical devices, . . . [the play was a] valuable exercis[e] for a playwright exploring new techniques and new dramatic material" (Geoffrey Bullough, *Narrative and Dramatic Sources of Shakespeare* [New York: Columbia Univ. Press, 1966], VI, 33).

ing her impassioned pleas—permits her son to be butchered in retaliation for the death of his son. Lorenzo's reasons for hatred and his desire for revenge, in other words, pale before those of the queen of the Goths. Moreover the greater emphasis on Titus' heroic capabilities and his self-pity through the numerous tragic pointers of the plot make him, through the first four acts, a far more powerful tragic figure than Hieronimo.

In the final analysis *Titus Andronicus* is an embryonic Elizabethan tragedy. But its unrealized potential anticipates the dramatic form with which Shakespeare is to experiment in his subsequent early tragedies and through which he is to achieve the more powerfully consistent tragic perspective of his major work.

If one assumes that Shakespeare is responsible in a significant way for the dramatic form of *Titus Andronicus* and that *Richard III* is (among the history-tragedies) its near successor, the direction of his efforts becomes reasonably clear. We have observed at some length that Titus, in comparison with the full tragic form that the Elizabethan age was to achieve, reflects two major flaws: the absence of a philosophic dimension (the delineation of the protagonist as a man of sensitive conscience torn between opposing values) and the failure to resolve the action in a manner logical to the perspective of the play (a meaningful development and resolution of the major emphases and expectations established at the outset). In both respects *Richard III* represents a notable improvement. Despite the constricting demands of the Tudor myth and despite Shakespeare's tendency during his apprenticeship literally to crowd his stage with incident and personae, the action of the play—along with the spectators' reaction to it—is tightly, even rigidly, controlled.[15] There are, moreover, crucial

15. Whitaker asserts that, except for Marlowe, Shakespeare was "the only dramatist who worked seriously at solving the structural problem presented by the dramatic treatment of English history" (p. 16). The play in which Shakespeare "creates great drama for the first time" (Norman Rabkin, *Shakespeare and the Common Understanding* [New York: Free Press, 1967], p. 250), *Richard III* reflects a "firm architecture of style and construction" (W. H. Clemen, *The Development of Shakespeare's Imagery* [Cambridge, Mass.: Harvard Univ. Press, 1951], p. 49). The "cyclical structure" (A. P. Rossiter,

additions to the source material by which the playwright demonstrably attempts to involve his protagonist in a full tragic experience.

There are, to be sure, structural features reminiscent of the earlier play. The spectators' response, for example, is guided in part by several characters who as in *Titus Andronicus* function rather artificially as tragic pointers through their comments or actions. The scrivener of III, vi exists solely to reveal the alarming increase in Richard's brazen callousness in moving against his enemies; the three citizens of II, iii point explicitly to the dangers of a kingdom's being ruled by a child and the ripe opportunities for the Duke of Gloucester, who is full of danger. Also as in Titus, Shakespeare constructs several specific foils to Richard. Richmond, for instance, is significant primarily as the adversary of Richard and as the antithesis of what politically and personally the Yorkist usurper represents. Richard's description of Prince Edward (son of Henry VI) is inserted for the direct comparison it affords; the sweet, lovely, "young, valiant, wise, and no doubt right royal" prince (I, ii, 244), Richard contrasts with his own halting limp and misshapen body "whose all not equals Edward's moi'ty" (I, ii, 249). Similarly, Shakespeare emphasizes the reactions of Edward IV, the second murderer of Clarence, Dighton, and Forrest to the bloody act of assassination, in order to contrast their remorse with Richard's calculating emotionlessness. Edward, shocked to learn that his countermand has come too late to save Clarence's life, recoils in horror when Stanley pleads for the life of a servant charged with murder. The distraught king exclaims that one will straightway fall on his knees to beg pardon for servants:

> But for my brother not a man would speak,
> Nor I (ungracious) speak unto myself
> For him, poor soul.
>
> (II, i 127–29)

"The Structure of *Richard III*," *Durham University Journal* [1938–1939], 46) suggests "a rhetorical symphony of five movements, with first and second subjects and some Wagnerian *Leitmotifs*" (Rossiter, *Angel With Horns*, ed. Graham Storey [London: Longmans, 1961], p. 7). Alice L. Birney examines Margaret as a representation of "the satirist at a primitive stage" (*Satiric Catharsis in Shakespeare* [Berkeley: Univ. of California Press, 1973], p. 16).

Certain dregs of conscience prompt the second murderer to fear the damnation his act will bring; he even attempts to warn his intended victim as his companion strikes, repenting of the deed as soon as it is done and refusing the money for which he has sold his peace of mind. Both Dighton and Forrest, "fleshed villains" and "bloody dogs," according to Tyrrel's report, "Melted with tenderness and kind compassion, / Wept like to children in their death's sad story" (IV, iii, 6, 7–8). By contrast, Richard asserts that he is happy in the news of the princes' death, and Clarence's death he views dispassionately as the successful completion of a task well planned. His peremptory command by which Buckingham is ordered to dispose of Hastings— "Chop off his head! Something we will determine" (III, i, 193)— provides perhaps the most effective contrast.

It is not in such external devices, however, but in the development of the protagonist that Shakespeare's dramatic progress is registered. Richard, on the one hand, is too palpably villainous, a "bottled spider," a "bunch-backed toad" who methodically and, to a large degree, unconscionably wades through blood to the throne.[16] On the other hand, measured by what has preceded rather than by what is to follow, this character is established with a structural concern not previously found on the English stage. Titus is potentially tragic—a proud and wrathful man whose atrocities win him enemies powerful enough to destroy his fame, his human dignity, and his sanity; his misfortunes, though, and even his bizarre scheme of vengeance, the spectators observe from the outside; at no time are they allowed to glimpse the inner man—his moral values, his moments of fear, his spiritual anguish. Richard, in contrast, provides the eye—albeit jaundiced—through which the spectator observes the action. Whereas

16. The symbolic significance which some critics attach to Richard limits his effective development as a tragic figure. Destroyed wholly by supernatural forces (R. Simpson, *Political Use of Historical Plays* [London, 1873], p. 423), Richard, in the operation of nemesis (R. G. Moulton, *Shakespeare as a Dramatic Artist* [Oxford, 1888], p. 110; M .M. Reese, *The Cease of Majesty* [New York: St. Martins, 1961], p. 223), is transformed from "credibly motivated villain to a symbol . . . of diabolism" (Tillyard, p. 241). He has "no suffering that we can see" (Henry Reed, *English History Illustrated by Shakespeare* [Philadelphia, 1855], p. 324).

Titus has only one soliloquy and one aside (a total of six lines), neither of which contributes a meaningful insight into his struggle, Richard delivers twelve soliloquies and four asides (a total of 186 lines). The result is a refinement for the popular stage of a Senecan device which, in part, provides the basis for the development of Shakespeare's mature tragic perspective.[17]

These soliloquies serve several major structural functions. For one thing, like those of Barabas in *The Jew of Malta* they constantly reflect the unholy vigor and callous zeal that feed Richard's ambition and provoke in the spectators, if not sympathy, an awed appreciation of his boundless energy and vitality. An Aaron moved to the center of the stage, Richard is "determined to prove a villain"; "not shaped for sportive tricks," "rudely stamped," "curtailed of . . . fair proportion," "cheated of feature," "deformed, unfinished"—he hates "the idle pleasures" of peaceful days (I, i, passim); his identity, if at all, must be established in the enforced power of the battlefield or of the court, not in the normal affections of the human heart.[18] Just as in soliloquy he broaches the action at the outset of the play, so he concludes the lengthy first scene, still obviously taking an energetic delight in the world for him to "bustle in." In the following scene he

17. In his will to resist the mounting weight of historical retribution, Richard becomes "Mankind . . . resisting oppression and being destroyed" (Nicholas Brooke, "Reflecting Gems and Dead Bones: Tragedy Versus History in *Richard III*," *CQ*, VII [1965], 134); he "dies somewhat more aware of his own troubled conscience than he was when he set out on his treacherous course" (Daniel E. Hughes, "The 'Worm of Conscience' in *Richard III* and *Macbeth*," *EJ*, LV [1966], 851). *Richard III* is "the story of how [Richard's] imagination gradually gets the better of his will" (Goddard, I, 139). For a recent analysis of Richard's terrifying dream, see Bettie Anne Doebler, " 'Despair and Dye': The Ultimate Temptation of *Richard III*," *Shakespeare Studies*, VII (1974), 75–85.

18. Richard's "many-sidedness" humanizes him (Coe, p. 24); the "consummate actor" (E. K. Chambers, *Shakespeare: A Survey* [London: Sidgwick and Jackson, 1925], p. 16), Richard "has what no Senecan villain possesses: the power of self-ridicule, the habit of ironic detachment" (Sidney Thomas, *The Antic Hamlet and Richard III* [New York: King's Crown Press, 1943], p. 15). "Destitute of virtue, he possesses ability" (W. Richardson, *Essays on Shakespeare's Dramatic Characters* [London, 1797], p. 6); he "deceives the stupid and dares the wiser sort to challenge his integrity" (Peter Alexander, *Introductions to Shakespeare* [London: Collins, 1964], p. 135).

gloats over his successful wooing of Anne, having no friends to back his suit at all but "the plain devil and dissembling looks" (I, ii, 236). Of his ability to sow dissension between the king and the queen's kindred, he inwardly boasts:

> And thus I clothe my naked villainy
> With odd old ends stol'n forth of holy writ,
> And seem a saint, when most I play the devil.
>
> (I, iii, 335–37)

Sparring verbally with Prince Edward in the middle of the play, he wryly likens himself to the formal vice, Iniquity, moralizing "two meanings in one word" (III, i, 83) even as he tosses out ominous proverbs in asides: "So wise so young, they say, do never live long" (III, i, 79); "Short summers lightly have a forward spring" (94). Assured later that his wooing of Elizabeth will proceed as profitably as that of Anne, he approaches her as a self-proclaimed "jolly thriving wooer" (IV, iii, 43).

From first to last, then, the soliloquies are utilized to remind the spectators that Richard is possessed of an almost uncanny combination of zealousness and shrewdness; like Tamburlaine he becomes more than mere tyrant, informing the stage world with his spirit as well as with his presence. Of prime significance also is the use of soliloquy to establish a perspective through which the spectator—by anticipating the events themselves—can fully appreciate the manner in which they affect the central character.[19] Step by step Richard informs the audience in advance of his plots against those who in any way limit his power; as early as the first scene he hints that the throne is his ultimate goal, the "secret close intent" which he "must reach unto" (158–59). At the same time, the soliloquy is a vehicle to exploit Richard's hypocrisy. While the result is not yet the delineation of character on the physical and metaphysical levels Shakespeare is to achieve in the great tragic figures, it is undeniably more complex and

---

19. "Tragic irony, found as a rare device here and there in pre-Shakespearean drama, becomes in *Richard III* a deliberately applied instrument of foreshadowing and cross-referencing" (W. C. Clemen, "Tradition and Originality in Shakespeare's *Richard III*," *SQ*, V [1954], 251).

more dramatically interesting than the characterization of Titus, which depends almost exclusively on choric characters or tragic pointers to suggest the growth and development in the protagonist. Through Richard's hypocrisy the spectators are drawn into the central character and share with him a rich perspective of dramatic irony. Thus they escape none of the agony as, with the victims' full confidence, he lures Clarence and Hastings to their deaths; to both he is a trusted friend and counselor, yet to Richard—as he informs the spectators—each is an obstacle in the path of his ambition to be eliminated by means of a trap sprung at the proper time. With an even greater awe they observe his ability to divide and conquer within the court of Elizabeth as her kinsmen receive the blame for Clarence's death. Similarly the spectators can anticipate Richard's egotistic joy upon winning Anne even in the presence of the corpse of her murdered father-in-law and while the memory of her murdered betrothed is still green. So also, they share with him the bitterly comic irony as, with Buckingham's aid, he woos the lord mayor and the populace by walking, prayer book in hand, between two clergymen.

The soliloquy is also of signal importance in Shakepeare's attempt to achieve a philosophic dimension for the play. More precisely, the tenth soliloquy (IV, iii, 36–43) sets the stage for Richard's first significant failure, his inability to persuade Elizabeth to rally her daughter to his side. It is at this point that the spectators begin to achieve a vision larger than Richard's—to a degree identifying with him as a result of the fascination of his ambitious energy and spirit and to a degree observing him from above as he runs headlong into the net of destruction which both history and his own character have prepared for him. The later Shakespeare will create far more powerful and complex double visions through which the spectators will be profoundly involved in the inner struggles of a protagonist with an active and sensitive conscience at the same time they observe events set in motion by a decision of passion which sweeps him to disaster. Again, however, to look backward rather than forward, the tragic perspective of *Richard III* is more fully realized than that of *Titus Andronicus*. The spectators at no point achieve a double vision in the earlier tragedy; even as Titus enacts his grisly vengeance, they in no way are allowed to anticipate either his sacrifice of Lavinia (and whatever effect that decision has had on him) or his own murder at the hands of Saturninus. In *Richard III,* although the spiritual struggle is minimal, the double vision results both from the spectators' external familiarity with the historical narrative (a narrative set in the context of a world in which God's ordinance smiles upon the emerging Tudor dynasty and presumes the destruction of Richard's demonic ambition) and from the internal structural features which provide at least a momentary glimpse of Richard's private hell. His last three soliloquies progressively force the spectators to this double vision. In Act IV he establishes the critical importance of his winning Elizabeth as bride, observing that Richmond, his primary antagonist, is aiming at the same prize (iii, 40–43). Hence, with his assumption that Elizabeth is a "relenting fool, and shallow, changing woman" (IV, iv, 431) for allowing her daughter to be won in such fashion contrasted with Stanley's assertion that the queen has readily consented to the espousal of Richmond and Elizabeth, the die is cast for the crook-backed king. Encountering deceit for the first time, he is unable to cope with it, largely because his remarkable successes and his pride have blinded him to the possibility of failure, to the possibility that someone will not acquiesce unquestioningly to his will.

Richard's only extensive articulation of spiritual anguish occurs in his final soliloquy.[20] And as Shakespeare fails to achieve a satisfactory philosophic dimension for Titus through his final soliloquy, so he ultimately fails to do so for Richard through this passage. The structural progress between the two points, however, is considerable. Titus in his three lines was simply able to assert his sanity and to announce his vengeful scheme against Tamora and her sons; nothing

20. "At this moment, crucial both in the play and in Shakespeare's career, the play turns to tragedy" (Rabkin, p. 251). Shakespeare approaches "division and self-knowledge in Richard" (R. B. Heilman, *Tragedy and Melodrama* [Seattle: Univ. of Washington Press, 1968], p. 179), forcing the spectator to "realize that Richard's hectic career is the perversion of great ability and his death a sad waste of a potentially fine human being" (O. J. Campbell, ed., *The Living Shakespeare* [New York: Macmillan, 1958], p. 118). Richard's internalization is explored extensively by William B. Toole in "The Motif of Psychic Division in *Richard III,*" *Shakespeare Survey,* XXVII (1974), 28.

in the previous scenes has meaningfully anticipated such action, and in no way does his statement suggest the previous necessity of an internal decision involving a choice of values. By contrast, Shakespeare has clearly attempted to prepare both Richard and the spectators for this climactic moment.[21]

Even Gloucester's early wit plays gingerly on matters spiritual. In the third scene, for example, as Margaret with chilling effect pronounces curses upon all responsible for the death of her husband and son, Richard quibbles with her at length, twice attempting to turn the execration back upon her by blurting "Margaret" just at the point she is to name him. On her exit he attempts to change the subject by directing the conversation to Clarence and his murderers, on whom he piously begs God's mercy and pardon. When commended by Rivers for his "Christianlike" attitude, Richard wryly responds in aside that it was well to conclude so rather than curse himself. This same turn of mind is in evidence again in Act II as Richard, following King Edward's death, feigns sorrow while requesting his mother's blessing. From the Duchess of York, who earlier accused him before Clarence's children of deceit and villainy, Richard receives a curt benison which prompts his aside:

> And make me die a good old man!
> That is the butt-end of a mother's blessing;
> I marvel that her grace did leave it out.
>
> (ii, 109–11)

On several occasions, then, the sardonic humor builds upon references to heaven, hell, blessing, and curse. While it would push the text too far to assume that Shakespeare intends to reveal an inner torment beneath this façade of wit, the spectators can hardly fail to notice that such thoughts are never far from Richard's mind.

In IV, ii the agitation is undoubtedly genuine as Gloucester for the first time is unable to conceal his emotion from those around him.

---

21. Shakespeare clearly does not intend for the final soliloquy to suggest either a "sudden and unprecedented change in Richard's character" (Rabkin, p. 251) or a "*drift*[ing]—into an unexpected deepening of [it]" (Heilman, "Satiety and Conscience: Aspects of Richard III," *The Antioch Review*, XXIV [1964–1965], 67).

Even as in a soliloquy he reacts with angry indignation to Bucking-ham's reluctance to murder the young princes (24–26), Catesby ob-serves to another that the king is angry and gnaws his lip. A few lines later Richard informs the spectators that Buckingham shall no longer be privy to his counsel, after which he orders the astonished Catesby to rumor it abroad that his wife Anne is gravely ill. His subsequent soliloquy, though he swiftly tempers himself to the task at hand, signals briefly his growing desperation and loss of confidence in his "uncertain way of gain":

> But I am in
> So far in blood that sin will pluck on sin.
> Tear-falling pity dwells not in this eye.
> (IV, ii, 63–65)

The tenor of these lines is supported by other incidents throughout the play, such as the king's addled confusion in dispatching Ratcliff and Catesby when he first hears that Richmond is landing and that many throng to the shore to welcome the invader, or his striking the third messenger, or the report of his frequent nightmares by Anne, who asserts on two occasions that she never slept a quiet hour with him because she was continually awakened with his timorous dreams.

If these moments are skillfully performed, the spectators are by no means unprepared for the spiritual despair voiced in Richard's final soliloquy. Starting from his dream, he desperately berates "cow-ard conscience" for afflicting him; his flesh trembles; he recognizes himself as a murderer and a villain and, Faustus-like, would fly from himself. His "conscience hath a thousand several tongues" as his sins "throng to the bar," proclaiming him guilty (V, iii, 194, 200). In a remark reminiscent of his earlier desire for his mother's blessing and his subsequent affiliation with Buckingham, he laments that no creature loves him; nor will anyone pity him when he dies. So pow-erful are the effects of these moments that he for the first and only time openly admits his fear to another, informing Ratcliff:

> By the apostle Paul, shadows to-night
> Have struck more terror to the soul of Richard

Than can the substance of ten thousand soldiers
Armèd in proof and led by shallow Richmond.

(V, iii, 217–20)

Shakespeare's attempt to gain a philosophic dimension for Richard involves two external structural devices as well—the numerous curses and the pattern of remorse in the individuals whose fall from prosperity precedes that of Richard. At one time or another, no fewer than sixteen characters through curses invoke God's heavy justice on Richard, eleven in the form of apparitions. Anne, for example, as she laments over the corpse of Henry VI, exclaims:

O God, which this blood mad'st, revenge his death!
O earth, which this blood drink'st, revenge his death!
Either heav'n, with lightning strike the murd'rer dead,
Or earth gape open wide and eat him quick.

(I, ii, 62–65)

In condemning to misery any wife he might have, she ironically condemns herself—a point not lost on her in Act IV as she reproaches herself anew for growing "captive to his honey words" (i, 79).

Most centrally functional to the philosophic perspective is the execration of Queen Margaret in Act. I.[22] Her comments, in addition, provide another means of foreshadowing and anticipating the action of the play. Not only does she prophesy King Richard's anguished fall, she also provides a virtual outline of the action of the drama. Twice beseeching God to intervene in order that she may accomplish her revenge (iii, 110, 136 ff.), she predicts Edward's death by sur-

22. Margaret's function, to be sure, is reminiscent of the furies of Senecan tragedy (O. J. Campbell, pp. 117-18); yet, as Clemen points out ("Tradition," p. 25), in the older tradition curses "occur . . . as conventional gestures at moments of despair and wrath"; here they represent "the principle of historical continuity within which the play achieves its meaning" (Tom F. Driver, *The Sense of History in Greek and Shakespearean Drama* [New York: Columbia Univ. Press, 1960], p. 98). She is "the one voice [Richard] quails before" (Rossiter, *Angel,* p. 13), the "prophetess of woe and doom" (G. B. Harrison, ed., *Shakespeare: The Complete Works* [New York: Harcourt, Brace, 1948], p. 224), the spokesman for "inscrutable providence" (Craig, p. 301) whose presence "involve[s] the whole scene in tenfold gloom and horror" (N. Drake, *Shakespeare and Times* [London, 1817], II, 373).

feit, the death of Edward's young son as recompense for the death of her own, the misery of Queen Elizabeth when she shall outlive her present glory, and the premature deaths of Rivers and Hastings. Her curse of Richard specifically invokes heaven's "indignation" to be hurled down on this "slave of nature and son of hell" when his sins are "ripe." Further, her plea that the "worm of conscience" torment his soul underscores Shakespeare's intention to depict a spiritual struggle within Richard. Queen Elizabeth, in Act IV, describes Margaret as "well skilled in curses" (iv, 116) and begs instruction on how to curse her enemies. Along with the Duchess of York, the three women perform almost ritualistically the Erinyes' functions of scourger and sorrower, the dual role assigned them by Dante. Their mournful wailing and lamentation (which again provides Shakespeare the opportunity to summarize the action to this point) evolves into a harrowing reiteration of curses, now made all the more chilling by the mothers' participation. Specifically, the Duchess desires to smother her "damned son" "in the breath of bitter words"; she berates herself for not "strangling" him in her "accursed womb," and, to Richard's assertion that the heavens should not hear such words, she invokes her "most grievous curse":

> Either thou wilt die by God's just ordinance
> Ere from this war thou turn a conqueror,
> Or I with grief and extreme age shall perish
> And never more behold thy face again.
>
> . . . .
>
> My prayers on the adverse party fight.
>
> (184–87, 191)

Margaret gives thanks to God for enforcing her curses and, of Richard, prophesies further that

> . . . at hand,
> Ensues his piteous and unpitied end.
> Earth gapes, hell burns, fiends roar, saints pray,
> To have him suddenly convey'd from hence.
>
> (73–76)

The ghosts—of Prince Edward (son of Henry VI), Henry VI, Clarence, Rivers, Grey, Vaughan, Hastings, Prince Edward (son of Edward IV), Anne, and Buckingham—also curse Richard's bloody ascent to the throne.[23] Indeed, the combined total of thirty-five lines spoken by these spirits who appear in Richard's dream the night before his fatal confrontation with Richmond trigger the spiritual anguish of his final soliloquy. Each apparition, after recounting the usurper's sins, chants his grisly refrain, "Despair, and die!" The spirit of Buckingham, last to appear, charges Richard to "die in terror of his guiltiness." "Fainting, despair; despairing, yield thy breath!" (V, iii, 173).

Shakespeare does not question the nature or the validity of the ghosts. These spirits, after all, represent the final stages of Margaret's curse, and Shakespeare is at some pains to establish the credibility of the supernatural machinery of the play. When Richard asserts, for instance, that Margaret's misery is the result of his father's curses upon her, Margaret responds:

> Did York's dread curse prevail so much with heaven
>
> . . . .
>
> Can curses pierce the clouds and enter heaven?
> Why then, give way, dull clouds, to my quick curses!
>
> (I, iii, 190, 194–95)

Moments later she proclaims herself a prophetess, observing that her maledictions will "ascend the sky / And there awake God's gentle-sleeping peace" (286–87). In the final act, for another instance, Richmond—whose efforts are endorsed by the spirits—is directly associated with God and the enforcement of His will for England publicly and for Richard personally; if Richard is God's scourge, clearly Richmond is His minister. The first brief glimpse of Richmond finds him addressing his followers shortly after landing in England, assail-

---

23. Both this scene (Kristian Smidt, *Iniurious Imposters and Richard III* [New York: Humanities Press, 1964], p. 168) and the earlier scene of Margaret's curse (E. K. Chambers, *William Shakespeare*, p. 301) may well be afterthoughts, but the effect in each instance is to heighten the architectonic structure of the piece.

ing Richard's yoke of tyranny and ordering his troops to advance in God's name. In the lengthy scene depicting the eve of Bosworth Field he prays to God, whose captain he accounts himself:

> Make us thy ministers of chastisement,
> That we may praise Thee in the victory.
> To Thee I do commend my watchful soul.
>
> (V, iii, 114–16)

In his final oration he proclaims that God and good cause fight upon his side. Both Blunt and Stanley, as well as the spirits of Clarence, the young princes of Edward IV, and Buckingham, bless his efforts in the name of God. By contrast Richard is consistently associated with sin and the devil. In the first act alone he is by Anne and Margaret five times branded a devil; he is "a son of hell," a "devilish slave," a "fiend," a "dreadful minister of hell." In the final act he is twice termed "God's enemy" by Richmond just prior to the battle.

Clearly, then, Shakespeare constructs a theologically affirmative world in which the omniscience and omnipotence of the divinity is assumed, even by those who experience only misfortune and misery. Equally clearly, he attempts to construct a human circle in which the conscience is alive and sensitive to the values centered on that God. More precisely, Shakespeare foreshadows Richard's final reflective moments on various occasions throughout the play as character after character, in the face of death, turns his thoughts to the state of the soul and the sinful nature of his earthly life. Grey and Rivers and Vaughan, for example, assert their innocence and embrace "until [they] meet again in heaven" (III, iii, 26). Hastings, who refuses to harken to the counsel of Stanley's dream or the omens of his stumbling horse, repents of the pride that prompted him to court the favor of mortal man more than the grace of God. King Edward on his deathbed vainly attempts to reconcile the factions at court, requesting an exchange of love before God. Buckingham, despairing for having "dallied with" the "high All-Seer," calls for the officers to lead him to his "block of shame" where his wrongs will reap their just rewards (V, i, 20, 28).

38

In this pattern of introspective moments, Clarence's final scene is the most extensively developed parallel to that of the Yorkist usurper. Like Richard, Clarence has fearful dreams that predict his destruction and, in the reflecting gems mocking the dead bones, underscore the vanity of temporal power and possession; like Richard, he faces in his troubled vision the spirits of those whom he has murdered—Warwick and Prince Edward, son of Henry VI. Like Richard, he despairs because his sins "give evidence against [his] soul" (I, iv, 67) and his prayers cannot appease God; like Richard, he is "heavy of soul" and "fain would sleep" (74); like Richard, he describes his agony to a companion who attempts to console him. And, like Richard, he is unable to achieve a full repentance.[24] Of his own spiritual state, the last the spectators hear is that his sins overwhelm the best efforts of his prayers. His last moments, far from suggesting any kind of spiritual solace, find him begging for his life, even as he loses it ignominiously with a knife in his back.

So, too, Richard's ending is passionate. His frenzied cry for a horse on the battlefield and his refusal of rescue from Catesby with the decree that he has "set [his] life upon a cast" and "will stand the hazard of the die" (V, iv, 9, 10) are surely intended to be the actions not of courage but of desperation.[25] And clearly, he has not been fatalistically manipulated into fulfilling the final stages of Margaret's curses voiced at the outset of the play and the ghosts' execrations just prior to the battle; to the contrary, he in the previous scene has clearly repudiated the promptings of his conscience even as he senses the

24. Aerol Arnold quite correctly describes Shakespeare's foreshadowing and recapitulatory uses of dreams in the play, but the text simply will not support the assertion that Clarence achieves a full repentance in contrast to the remorseless Richard ("The Recapitulation Dream in *Richard III* and *Macbeth*," *SQ*, VI [1955], 53).

25. The interpretation of Richard's final cry as an implication that "the ecstasy of the fight is worth a dozen kingdoms" (G. B. Shaw, *Shaw on Shakespeare*, ed. Edwin Wilson [New York: Dutton, 1961], p. 172) is not supported by the full context. More to the point is Goddard's observation that the final words are a desperate confession "that the worldly kingdom . . . is worth less than the few seconds by which another horse might postpone his doom" (I, 39).

vanity of human fortune and the inevitable destruction of those committed to it. The spiritual counterpart to his physical death he asserts with his final commitment to self:

> Let not our babbling dreams affright our souls;
> Conscience is but a word that cowards use.
>
> . . . .
>
> Our strong arms be our conscience, swords our law!
> March on, join bravely, let us to it pell-mell;
> If not to heaven, then hand in hand to hell.
> (V, iii, 309–10, 312–14)

In brief, Shakespeare demonstrably has labored to combine the spirit of titanic ambitions with the philosophic dimensions that would make of Richard more than a melodramatic conqueror—through the protagonist's numerous asides and soliloquies, through the supernatural machinery that anticipates both his external and internal struggles, and through the parade of characters across the stage who, in their own moments of truth, provoke the spectators' attention to the metaphysics of Richard's personality. It is in the combined effect of these structural devices that Shakespeare's achievement must be measured. Such features are missing entirely in *Titus Andronicus* and are only imperfectly realized in *Tamburlaine* and *The Jew of Malta*.

In *Tamburlaine*, more specifically, Marlowe makes a similar use of character foils to enhance the titanic stature of the central figure; he also develops, especially in Part I, an elaborate series of individuals who fall victim to Tamburlaine; in fact, Tamburlaine's adversaries appear in a rigidly ascending order of power and importance. As in Shakespeare's play, numerous characters are used to point the spectators' attention and attitude to the protagonist through references to his fated glory as "scourge and wrath of God," and Tamburlaine himself engages in several flights of rhetoric which assert his defiance of the gods, especially Mahomet, and imbue the drama with the spirit of his destined accomplishments. There is even a suggestion of an internal struggle in Tamburlaine's soliloquy in Part I, Act V, as he sets the thirst for martial glory against his love for Zenocrate. The moment is brief, however, and no such quality is found in the manner in which he confronts death in Part II. Even so, the spirit and the external shape of *Richard III* may well owe much to *Tamburlaine*. But with the internal glimpses into Richard's wit, his fear, even his momentary remorse, Shakespeare has produced a more complex characterization than that of the Scythian conqueror. In the same way, by imbuing the Machiavellian protagonist with a semblance of moral sensitivity in the twelfth soliloquy and by placing the narrative within the moral framework of God's ordinance in human history, Shakespeare has created a character of more compelling human interest than Barabas.

To this end Shakespeare has made significant alterations from the several sources he presumably utilized. In none of them does Margaret, who actually died in 1482, return to England after she is ransomed. In none is Hastings imprisoned at the instigation of his enemies at court, the queen and her kinsmen; and in none does he naively miscalculate his fortunes with Richard just prior to his condemnation. The details of Clarence's murder are borrowed primarily from Hall's description of the murder of the two young princes—previously dramatized both in Legges' *Richardus Tertius* and the anonymous *The True Tragedy of Richard III*. Admittedly, Shakespeare does not basically reshape his central figure; he inherits the tradition of a guilt-ridden Richard in whom vaulting ambition has overleaped itself and whose mind, according to Polydore Vergil, was "enflamyd with desire of usurping the kingdom, [and] was trubblyd by gultynes of intent to commyt so haynous wickednes." Hall describes Richard's dream before the battle as "a punccion and pricke of his synfull conscience" in which he "sawe diverse ymages lyke terrible develles which pulled and haled hym, not sufferynge him to take any quyet or rest." In *The Mirror for Magistrates* these devils have become all those "murdered Ghostes whome I / By death had sent to their untimely grave"; and in *The True Tragedy* Richard relates to Lord Lovell that the ghosts of those whom he has slain in reaching for the crown—whether he wakes or sleeps—come gaping for revenge." But if Shakespeare does not create his Richard whole cloth, he is the first actually to dramatize the ghosts and to provide them the extensive dialogue by which they function as an extrapolation of Richard's conscience. Moreover, in none of the sources does Shakespeare find the elaborate Machiavellian strategy which the soliloquies provide in methodically mapping out Richard's designs on the throne, or his nervous blessings on Clarence's murderers lest he spiritually indict himself, or his anxious concern for not receiving his mother's full blessing, or his frenzied anger when Buckingham balks at the command of murder.

The True Tragedy anticipates, to be sure, the moral sensitivity of the Yorkist usurper. At one point in that play a page describes the deep sighs and fearful cries that come from the depths of Richard's heart. On three occasions Richard himself bemoans the kingdom gotten by murder of his friends; he fears "the severe judge" and for a brief moment would repent and appeal for mercy to a righteous God; the "horror" of his "bloodie practise" strikes terror to his "wounded conscience." Twice his comments point beyond his physical death: though his enemies would kill his body, yet they shall leave a "never dying" mind; having spoken his final words, he asserts, "What more I have to say, ile make report among the damned souls."

Shakespeare's dramatic contribution, in relation to *The True Tragedy,* is one of subtlety and refinement. The earlier play contains not a single line of soliloquy, Richard's remorse being voiced not in the inner recesses of the human spirit but in open conversation with those about him. Furthermore, the Richard of *The True Tragedy* is a relatively simplistic character, fluctuating throughout between the poles of temporal ambition and spiritual anguish. By contrast, Shakespeare's Richard is at the outset a dedicated and calculating Machiavel whose slow erosion of self-confidence will eventually precipitate the frenetic disillusionment of his final soliloquy; only then does he overtly admit his fear to another, even as he falls victim to the despair that controls his actions on the battlefield.

Nevertheless, apprentice qualities are not difficult to find in this play. It may well be, for example, that the presumed inevitability of Margaret's curses tends to diminish the impression of Richard's free will, as does the consistent barrage from the surrounding characters of images equating him with the devil. By the same token, Richmond, God's captain, is highly stylized, as are several of Richard's victims such as the young princes and Anne. Even the ghosts, which function as a metaphysical device by which we gain insight into Richard's soul, lose impact through extension into the dream of Richmond; with the rhetorically balanced condemnation of Richard and praise of Richmond, the apparitions become too obviously a stage device for ordering the final events of the play. It may well be also that Shakespeare is guilty of redundancy, that the moral design comes close to being tedious at times as Margaret's prophecies in Act I are reiterated in Act IV with the help of Elizabeth and the Duchess of York, and as the spectators view the seriatim destruction of nine characters, each of whom to some degree recalls the design of the action.[26] And it certainly is true that Richard is not a totally convincing tragic character in comparison with Shakespeare's later figures. Like Titus, he at no point reflects a concern for the consequences of an act before he commits it, and his momentary remorse is relatively superficial, the result more of fear than of contrition or spiritual insight.[27]

Admitting all such deficiencies, one can still assert that the construction of *Richard III* is an exceptional accomplishment for the early 1590s; indeed the play in all probability was Shakespeare's first major stage success. It is not at all surprising that in his early years in London he turned his efforts to chronicle material so much in vogue, but the strong historical traditions imposed certain inescapable limitations. Shakespeare obviously was not free to depict Richard as a sympathetic and misunderstood ruler; the basic political facts of the recent past which weighed so heavily upon the present could not be altered beyond reason; Richard's defeat clearly had to carry the conviction that an era of greater stability was ushered in, establishing on the throne a ruler of finer moral sensibilities and of larger capacity to unite the many factions of a divided kingdom; consequently, the final scene had to emphasize Richmond's assumption of power rather than Richard's loss of life and any tragic implications inherent to it.

26. H. Ulrici in 1876 criticized the "internal uniformity of the play" (*Shakespeare's Dramatic Art* [London], II, 276). More recently, Reese has described the "rigidly paralleled" action and the redundancy of the "symbolic episodes" (pp. 208, 210). As Driver observes, "a primary fault" is that "the audience knows so much so soon" (p. 88).

27. See Roland Mushat Frye, *Shakespeare and Christian Doctrine* (Princeton: Princeton Univ. Press, 1963), p. 151.

Shakespeare was free, however, to shape the events concerning Edward IV, Edward V, and Richard III to the life of a single figure —a focus painfully absent in the Henry VI plays. He was free to emphasize Richard's thirst for power and the physical infirmities for which the Machiavel was determined to compensate. He was free to treat the various incidents so as to give the impression of mounting tension resulting from an ambition that was never sated, to reveal the moments at which such obsession cost Richard control both of others and of self, to depict in the king's moments of weakness his fear of the moral order he had violated. Above all, he was free to infuse the action with dramatic tension by placing in conflict Richard's towering ambitions and the historical fate that dooms him to ignominious defeat. Both the curses and the pattern of remorseful falls underscore the philosophic dimensions of the play by emphasizing in turn the macrocosmic divine control and the microcosmic spiritual reflection preceding death. Thus are established the environment for and the anticipation of Richard's spiritual anguish triggered in the final soliloquy. In a word, whatever the play's flaws, Shakespeare has consciously shaped his material in an attempt to construct a tragic perspective that aesthetically accommodates the historical fate.

Although Richard II is not essentially a dynamic character, Shakespeare's development as a tragic dramatist is remarkable in the play setting forth the origins of England's fifteenth-century internecine political struggle. For one thing, whereas Titus' actions in the first four acts in no effective way prepare the spectators for his sudden emergence as a manipulator and revenger in Act V, Richard II is dramatically coherent. Like Richard III, whose soliloquies carry the spectators through the various stages of his overreaching ambition and thus force them to anticipate his destruction at Bosworth Field, Richard's characterization points inevitably to his confrontation and deposition by Bolingbroke and to the necessity of his extermination in the name of King Henry. At the same time, this Richard is dramatically more interesting than his earlier namesake. The Yorkist king who wades through blood to the throne which is his obsession is limited in dramatic appeal. Like Tamburlaine he can feel only hate and greed—though, more so than the Scythian titan, he can experience the chilling shock of fear. But he is incapable of repentance, and he is oblivious to affection, whether familial or societal. The spectators, consequently, can never fully perceive the human being beneath the Machiavellian cloak; they can sit in awe of his calculated inhumanity and of the single-mindedness of purpose that permits him to sacrifice affection for achievement, but they cannot share from within the full range of human emotions which in the later tragedies to come will produce pity as well as fear.

Richard II, by contrast, is a man for whom pity—if not terror—comes easily, both because of the poetic eloquence that stylizes his suffering and turns it into a "thing of beatuy"[28] and because of his own capacity for sorrow. Granted, most of this sorrow is self-pity. Nonetheless, there are moments when the emphasis on his suffering blinds us to the woeful shortcomings as a king that precipitate his downfall; moreover, he has at least fleeting moments of concerned affection for those around him who share his fate.[29] For the spectators, then, there is an emotional dimension in Richard II that Richard III does not possess and that the narrative inconsistencies in Titus never allow to develop. The full tragic experience is not yet realized, to be sure; there are no final insights that produce wisdom concomitant with destruction and death. By the same token, Richard lacks something of the

28. Chambers, A Survey, p. 91. Richard "was a sonneteer's king" (G. B. Harrison, Shakespeare At Work, 1592–1603 [London: Routledge, 1933], p. 90), Shakespeare's first central figure who is "introspective, imaginative, and eloquent" (M. W. Black, ed., The Tragedy of King Richard II [Baltimore: Penguin, 1957], p. 15). Through his "moving and subtle" verse (Raleigh, p. 184) he lends "to sentimentality the momentary might of passion" (H. B. Charlton, Shakespearian Tragedy [Cambridge: Cambridge Univ. Press, 1949], p. 45).

29. While it may be extreme to assert that the queen "is merely a reflector to emphasise . . . the loving-kindness of [Richard's] devotion" (Lionel Aldred ed., King Richard II [London: Macmillan, 1935], p. xxxvi), Richard's "relations with his friends and his wife" do, as Irving Ribner writes, "reveal him as not lacking in private virtue" (The English History Play in the Age of Shakespeare [London: Methuen, 1965], p. 153). Recently Robert R. Reid has maintained that Richard's love affair was "with his kingdom"; rejected, he "instinctively turns on himself" ("Richard II: Portrait of a Psychotic," JGE, XVI [1964], 63).

physical stamina and the demonstrative assertiveness against his adversaries that we come to expect in Shakespeare's tragic protagonists
(and that Marlowe was able to depict somewhat more effectively in
Edward). But Shakespeare's overriding concern for the relationship
between character and spectator is clearly emerging.

For our present purposes, the most significant measure of this concern lies in the structural experimentation. In both *Richard III* and
Richard II the playwright seems to be attempting to provide the psychological depth that will foster a meaningful rapport. In the earlier
play the protagonist is manipulated from within; despite the rigidity
of character that constrains the degree of success, Richard III's numerous soliloquies and asides do compel the spectators to relish the savor
of victory and suffer the agony of defeat through his eyes. Perhaps
consciously, Shakespeare traces a different path in *Richard II* in
which the protagonist delivers only a single soliloquy moments before
his assassination.[30] Here the character is manipulated from without, as
a procession of characters emphasizes at one moment Richard's heinous
mismanagement of his office coupled with his moral latitude, at another moment the sanctity of the kingship which forbids a subject to
oppose the divinely ordained monarch, and at still another moment
Richard's personal distress. The result is a powerful ambivalence in
the figure of Richard. God's vicar on earth capable through sensitivity
of evoking the aura of mystery that surrounds medieval royalty as
envisioned by an Elizabethan audience, he at the same time is thoroughly decadent in his self-centeredness; intent upon catering to his
personal pleasures, he lacks the vital concern for the security of his
kingdom as well as the masculinity and decisiveness that characterize
an effective leader.

To compound the ambivalence, Bolingbroke's development as a foil
is far more powerful than that of Richmond in the earlier play.
Whereas Richmond for all intents and purposes is not introduced until the fifth act, Bolingbroke figures in the play from the opening

---

30. It is true, as F. E. Halliday observes, that many of Richard's passages
are quasi-soliloquies, since he "rarely talks to people; he talks to things, to the
earth, to the crown" (*The Poetry of Shakespeare's Plays* [London: Duck-
worth, 1954], p. 81).

scene, and his eventual struggle with the king is inevitable by the end of Act I. Moreover, Bolingbroke is not, like Richmond, a simplistic figure of virtue acting as the hand of God rendering justice to a tyrant and bringing peace to a strife-torn land. Not only is he a political usurper against God's anointed, his own motives are ambiguous from the beginning. The spectators, never able flatly to condemn him for moving in defense of his inheritance and in defiance of the parasites who surround Richard, are yet never able to make an emotional commitment to him; they perceive Bolingbroke as one who, whatever the justification, defies the value structure established in the stage world and are thus thrown all the more powerfully back upon Richard, albeit both in sympathy and in disdain.

Richard, in brief, is clearly Shakespeare's most complex character to date.[31] But, as with Romeo and with Juliet, it is a complexity imposed from without, not—as later in Brutus and more powerfully in Hamlet—a quality that boils up from within. It is the result of setting a dissipated king in the religio-political context of divine right, of juxtaposing to him an ambiguous figure who seems to possess all the monarchical traits the ruler lacks, and then of surrounding them with numerous pointer characters who in a variety of ways call constant attention to the king's dilemma.

The authority of God is flatly assumed in the play. The hand of divinity operates directly through His anointed, and this relationship is alluded to time and again by Richard and his supporters and tacitly

---

31. J. A. Bryant sees Richard as *"microchristus"* and *"microcosmos,"* as the "Lord's anointed" and as "Everyman" ("The Linked Analogies of *Richard II*," *Sewanee Review*, LXV [1957], 425) while J. W. Draper analyzes him as the mercurial type ("The Character of Richard II," *PQ*, XXI [1942], 230). Leonard F. Dean argues that Shakespeare depicts an ironic version of the tragic hero, in whom "tragic qualities . . . are constantly undercut and thwarted" ("From *Richard II* to *Henry V:* A Closer View," in *Studies in Honor of De Witt T. Starnes* (1967), rpt. in *Shakespeare: Modern Essays in Criticism*, ed. Leonard Dean [New York: Oxford Univ. Press, 1967], p. 192). To the contrary, both Travis Bogard in the king's suffering ("Shakespeare's Second Richard," *PMLA,* LXX [1955], 208) and P. G. Phialas in the nature of the tragic process ("*Richard II* and Shakespeare's Tragic Mode," *TSLL*, V [1963], 344) view Richard as a significant step in Shakespeare's development of tragic character. For a similar view, see Harold F. Folland, "King Richard's Pallid Victory," *SQ*, XXIV (1973), 390, 398.

acknowledged through King Henry's "guilt of conscience" in the final scene. Bolingbroke admittedly defies the political power of the king. But he is no Richard III who delights in evil for its own sake; nor does he, like Iago or Edmund, ever challenge the power of heaven. To the contrary, he refers to his "divine soul" (I, i, 38) and to "God's grace" (iii, 37), and he later ascends the throne in "God's name" (IV, i, 113). This value structure is further enforced through the elaborate emphasis on knighthood, an order founded in service to God and king—as both Mowbray and Hereford frequently reiterate.

Richard's position as king by divine right, then, is not at issue.[32] Instead, the complexity of the play arises from the manipulation of the spectators' attitude toward Richard the man. In the opening scene, for example, their first impressions are of a king who attempts with dignity and equity to moderate a vicious quarrel between two of his subjects, Mowbray and Bolingbroke.[33] Before the conclusion of the scene, however, the seeds of suspicion are sown concerning Richard's

32. Rabkin, p. 81. F. W. Moorman claims that Shakespeare viewed divine right with "mordant irony" ("Plays Attributed to Shakespeare," in *Cambridge History of English Literature*, V, 278), and Kott (p. 37) asserts that to Shakespeare "history has no meaning" in the repetition of "its cruel cycle." To the contrary, Shakespeare utilized the "publicly acknowledged morality" (Robert Langbaum, *The Poetry of Experience* [New York: Random House, 1957], p. 161) to depict the "dichotomies" in the human interpretation of this moral order (E. W. Talbert, *The Problem of Order* [Chapel Hill: Univ. of North Carolina Press, 1962], p. 200). In other words, he "develops the political issue in all its complexity, and leaves judgment upon it to the spectator" (J. D. Wilson, ed., *King Richard II* [Cambridge: Cambridge Univ. Press, 1951], p. xxxv); "no one can tell whether Bolingbroke or Richard II is in the right" (Hardin Craig, *The Enchanted Glass* [Oxford: Blackwell, 1950], p. 157).

33. In what Leonard Dean describes as a good example of the "theatricality of politics" ("*Richard II:* The State and Image of the Theater," *PMLA*, LXVII [1952], 214), Richard is "capable enough . . . in his official role of ceremonialist" (Theodore Weiss, *The Breath of Clowns and Kings* [New York: Atheneum, 1971], p. 210). The act slowly reveals, however, the "nature of Richard's exercise of power" (Norman J. Jeffares, "In One Person Many People: King Richard II," in *The Morality of Art*, ed., D. W. Jefferson [London: Routledge and Kegan Paul, 1969], p. 54), and the unfinished tournament is a "reflection of Richard's character . . . as well as his love of ceremony" (P. G. Phialas, "The Medieval in *Richard II*," *SQ*, XII [1961], 306).

complicity in the murder of his Uncle Gloucester, the Protector during his minority, and the remainder of the act confirms this royal involvement. Thus, Richard's character is intentionally sketched slowly in the initial scenes. Only after the favorable impressions are registered are the flaws revealed, at first obliquely, then directly—even as the spectators confront a specific defense of the royal prerogative along with the first hints of Bolingbroke's possible ulterior motives.

The key to Shakespeare's ambivalence in this first act is the figure of Thomas Mowbray, Duke of Norfolk, an enigmatic character for many a commentator on the play. The problem centers primarily on Mowbray's response to Bolingbroke's assertion that he is responsible for the death of Thomas, Duke of Gloucester:

> For Gloucester's death,
> I slew him not, but, to my own disgrace,
> Neglected my sworn duty in that case.
>
> (I, i, 132–34)

Perhaps, it has been suggested, Norfolk means that he has failed to reveal a plot against Gloucester's life, or to protect him from physical danger, or to avenge the murder immediately, or to report fully his knowledge of the murder.[34] Or, possibly the passage is intentionally vague and ambiguous, a part of Shakespeare's design in blurring Richard's involvement with the debate, at least during the first scene.[35] Obviously, the significance of this or any other passage is subject to the determination of the individual actor or armchair reader. The actor may delete the lines altogether or deliver them in a manner that fails to provoke any reaction from the auditor. On the other hand, he may choose—by well-placed pauses and assertive glances at both

34. A. P. Rossiter (ed., *Woodstock: A Moral History* [London: Chatto and Windus, 1946], pp. 48–49) explains the passage through reference to the older play.

35. A. F. Watt (ed., *King Richard II* [New York: Clive, 1907], p. xix) calls Mowbray Richard's "scapegoat." More recently Wilson (p. 126) has written that Mowbray's lines are "embarrassed and ambiguous," that the issue of the murder "is left quite obscure." Similarly, Tillyard (p. 297) has observed that Shakespeare "leaves uncertain the question of who murdered Woodstock and never says that Richard was personally responsible," and M. W. Black that "Mowbray speaks ambiguously" (ed., Penguin, p. 32).

Bolingbroke and Richard—to provide striking dramatic emphasis. So delivered, Mowbray's words need not be explained away as vague or as a loose end that is further evidence that this is Shakespeare's early work. To the contrary, they are pivotal to the developing relationship between Richard and Mowbray, and—more important—between Richard and Bolingbroke. As a small but significant modification of Holinshed's account, the lines reveal Shakespeare's growing determination to mold the material of the *Chronicles* into the stuff of drama.

To be sure, there is no open proclamation of Richard's personal commitment or involvement in Bolingbroke's accusations concerning Gloucester's death.[36] In the following scene, however, the widowed Duchess of Gloucester pointedly accuses Richard of responsibility for her husband's murder and urges Gaunt to seek vengeance and justice, to which Gaunt replies that he may not "lift / An angry arm against [God's] minister" (I, ii, 40–41). Thus, when Hereford and Mowbray meet to pursue their challenge by duel-combat in scene iii, the spectator—aware of the possible alliance in murder between Mowbray and the sovereign—now will rivet his attention on Richard's treatment of Mowbray and the king's attempts to maintain in public an image of equity and objectivity.

Since the protatic emphasis in *Richard II* is clearly the crucial struggle between Richard and Bolingbroke, a struggle that takes final shape from Bolingbroke's unlawful return to England in open defiance of Richard's proclamation of banishment, one of Shakespeare's principal objectives in the first act is to make dramatically credible the scene in which Bolingbroke is banished. Holinshed obviously provides the lead with the description of the struggle between Hereford and Mowbray, but he is altogether silent concerning Richard's specific motives for moving against them. The historian says only that the king "waxed angrie"[37] when Hereford first stated his charges against Mowbray, a remark vaguely suggesting latent antagonism between Bolingbroke and his king. As for the defendant, Mowbray does not

36. Shakespeare's intention was "to show Richard playing the part of majesty with a fair efficiency in these first scenes" (Peter Ure, ed., *Richard II* [London: Methuen, 1956], p. lxv).

37. *Holinshed's Chronicles of England, Scotland, and Ireland* (London, 1807), II, 845.

in Holinshed reply to Hereford's charge of responsibility for Gloucester's murder; he at no time invokes the king's name in self-defense. He simply denies that he has misused eight thousand nobles from the king's treasury in failing to "pay the souldiers that keepe . . . Calis" (p. 845). When later pronouncing eternal banishment upon the Duke, Richard asserts that Norfolk "had sowen sedition in the relme by his words" (p. 847) and that the troops in Calais had indeed not been paid. Both points Shakespeare apparently rejects as unsuited to a scene in which the focus must remain sharply on the developing relationship between king and cousin.

Shakespeare, in short, must provide the motivation for the banishments at the same time he draws clear lines of contention between the two principals. It is not sufficient for Richard to banish Bolingbroke (as well as Mowbray) merely for the refusal to be reconciled by royal mandate. Richard must come to believe that Bolingbroke already is directly challenging the power of the throne and "undermining [his] authority and the very basis of his survival."[38] The banishment of both must be integral to this growing conviction.

The most obvious motivation is provided in the brief scene (I, iv) following the banishment. Even as the king decides to sell the right to taxation and suggests that Gaunt's death will result in additional coffers to underwrite his war in Ireland, Bolingbroke clearly emerges in Richard's mind as a personal foil. In conversation with his courtiers, Richard decries the audacity of "high Hereford" and demands to know how much of an emotional show there was at the parting. He scoffs with obvious jealousy at Hereford's

> courtship to the common people;
> How he did seem to dive into their hearts
> With humble and familiar courtesy.
>
> (I, iv. 24–26)

The more significant point for the present discussion is that Shakespeare subtly but firmly establishes the grounds for this dissension through the character of Mowbray and his "enigmatic" lines in the

38. H. M. Richmond, *Shakespeare's Political Plays* (New York: Random House, 1967), p. 124.

first scene. Richard, in other words, is by no means suddenly obsessed with Bolingbroke's personality in scene iv; he is merely giving verbal expression to an animosity that has been growing and festering since the opening moments.

Specifically, the turning point in the relationship between Richard and Mowbray—and, in turn, between Richard and Bolingbroke—is Mowbray's choleric retort that he did not kill Gloucester, but in that case neglected his "sworn duty."[39] Richard, at the outset presumably unaware of the charges Bolingbroke is to bring against Norfolk (even Gaunt tells the king that he has not been able to sift the argument), acts with magnanimity and grace as he addresses each of his subjects, warmly calling Bolingbroke "cousin" at the same time he observes that it will take a serious matter indeed to provoke "a thought of ill" in Norfolk. When Bolingbroke states his charges against Mowbray, Richard retorts, "How high a pitch his resolution soars!" (I, i, 109). While he may indeed suspect at this point that the attack is really leveled against him, he is careful to maintain his posture of objectivity, assuring Mowbray that the hearing will be fair despite Bolingbroke's royal kinship. Mowbray, however, pushes the issue to the critical stage with his reference to "sworn duty"; with more gall than discretion, he appears overtly to implicate the king as ultimately responsible for the murder, a fact which a significant reaction from Richard can make indelibly clear. To make matters even worse, he then roundly protests the king's efforts to silence the whole matter before it gets out of hand:

> My life thou shalt command, but not my shame.
> The one my duty owes; but my fair name,
> Despite of death that lives upon my grave,

39. W. G. Clark and W. A. Wright, eds., *The Cambridge Shakespeare* (Cambridge, 1864), IV, and C. H. Herford, ed., *The Works of William Shakespeare* (London, 1899), VI (see M. W. Black, ed., *The Life and Death of King Richard The Second: A New Variorum Edition of Shakespeare* [Philadelphia: Lippincott, 1955], p. 29)—though not considering the effects on the total scene—have accepted the lines as indicative of Richard's complicity. So also, more recently, have Craig, ed., *The Complete Works*, p. 648, and G. L. Kittredge, ed., *The Tragedy of King Richard II*, rev. Irving Ribner (Waltham, Mass.: Blaisdell, 1966), p. 5.

To dark dishonor's use thou shalt not have.

.   .   .   .

     Take but my shame,
And I resign my gage.
              (I, i, 166–69, 175–76)

Mowbray assumes no doubt that Bolingbroke—realizing where his charge now falls—will not dare pursue the issue further. This, of course, is Mowbray's cardinal error; his unbridled tongue will shortly cost him the price of perpetual banishment. Specifically, Richard speaks not one kind word to the duke after this moment. He is furious when Norfolk refuses the royal reconciliation. Likewise, at the lists in Coventry, when Mowbray formally requests the king's blessing prior to his encounter with Bolingbroke, he receives only a curt two-line response: "Farewell, my lord. Securely I espy / Virtue with valor couchèd in thine eye" (I, iii, 97–98). In contrast, Richard—mere moments earlier in reaction to his cousin's request—descends histrionically from his platform and embraces Bolingbroke in his arms, a point not present in Holinshed. Surely the response to Mowbray is no "touch of affectionate approval,"[40] but instead a sharp rebuff delivered with a cold and formidable stare. A few lines later Mowbray is facing the exile from which he will never return, a turn of events that seems abrupt only to the spectator who has missed the significance of Richard's reaction to Mowbray's careless words and the growing alienation stemming from that instant. Mowbray, apparently having acted as virtual henchman for the king, may well claim that this sentence was "all unlooked for from your highness' mouth" and that he has deserved more, but it is hardly likely that the irony of his final words—"Within my mouth you have enjailed my tongue"—is unintentional on either Shakespeare's part or the duke's.

Mowbray's words are, of course, no less critical to the relationship between Richard and Bolingbroke. For, from this moment, if not from the outset, Bolingbroke's charge of murder extends to the king, and he now realizes that his refusal to "throw up his gage" (and thus

40. John Palmer, *Political Characters of Shakespeare* (London: Macmillan, 1945), p. 130; see also Wilson, p. 139.

retract his charges against Norfolk) Richard must now take as a direct affront to the royal prerogative, indeed as treason itself. The king's subsequent blessing for Hereford at Coventry is a rather obvious attempt at overcompensation for the sake of the public image. But what follows should surprise no one. Bolingbroke's banishment is as dramatically credible as that of Mowbray, even without the subsequent scene (iv) in which Shakespeare draws the more specific foil relationship between the royal cousins.

The narrative from Holinshed that describes Richard's abuse of royal power and Bolingbroke's illegal return from banishment with demands arising from this abuse is not, in the particulars leading to this situation, primarily concerned with either focus or motivation. Shakespeare in Mowbray's words is consciously molding this material to create the interest in character and the conflict of the individual wills that are essential to effective drama. As C. H. Herford in his edition of 1899 was among the first to observe, the playwright in devising Mowbray's reply draws on two additional passages from the *Chronicles,* one before the actual encounter between Mowbray and Bolingbroke and the other following it. Holinshed reports that, when Mowbray first received instructions to do away with Gloucester, "the earle prolonged time for the executing of the kings commandment, though the king would haue had it doone with all expedition" (II, 837). The historian later records that Sir John Bagot, at his trial following the deposition of Richard and the assumption of power by Bolingbroke, reported that Mowbray claimed he had not murdered Gloucester, that "he had saued his life contrarie to the will of the king, and certeine other lords, by the space of three weeks" (III, 5). In both passages Richard's guilt is clear; in fact, in the latter passage Shakespeare found the words of Mowbray, which he has transferred to a crucial moment in the play. As a consequence, Mowbray's actions both emphasize the growing hostility between Richard and Bolingbroke and also provide credible motivation for the banishments which otherwise would seem to be triggered by sheer impetuosity.

By the end of Act I, then, although the balance of sympathy by slow degrees has been tilted against him, Richard is a thoroughly ambivalent character. Through the remainder of the play the numerous

54

pointer characters pull the sympathies of the spectators first in one direction, then in the other.[41] In four further scenes, for example, the dominant emphasis is on Richard's flagrant abuses of office. The strongest condemnation occurs in II, i, as the dying Gaunt proffers his counsel to a king whose will mutinies against reason and whose "shameful conquest" (66) of England has resulted in his leasing the nation like a tenement or paltry farm. He proclaims Richard to be sicker than he:

> Thy deathbed is no lesser than thy land,
> Wherein thou liest in reputation sick;
>
> . . . .
>
> A thousand flatterers sit within thy crown,
>
> . . . .
>
> Landlord of England art thou now, not king.
> (II, i, 95–96, 100, 113)

His finishing thrust names Richard directly as murderer of his brother Gloucester. The charge is confirmed by York as, in the face of the King's seizure of Gaunt's "plate, coin, revenues, and moveables" (161) that rightfully should descend to Bolingbroke, he decries the monarch's violation of the law of primogeniture by which Richard himself holds the throne. The nobles, too, in the same scene reproach Richard for a host of ills ranging from the flatterers who basely lead him to the exorbitant taxation and the general dissolution. In the following scene, York as Lord Governor of England bemoans the "sick hour" that Richard's "surfeit" has made (84), the "tide of woes" (98) as the nobles flee and the commons grow cold; torn between his duty to his sovereign and love for his kinsmen whom the

---

41. Richard becomes "man and martyr" (Karl F. Thompson, "Richard II: Martyr," *SQ*, VIII [1957], 160) as the scenes "are played against each other for effect" W. B. C. Watkins, *Shakespeare and Spenser* [Princeton: Princeton Univ. Press, 1950], p. 80) to force the spectators to "see the unfolding story through the eyes now of one character, now of another" (Francis Fergusson, *Shakespeare: The Pattern in His Carpet* [New York] Delacorte, 1970], p. 94.) Most recently, see Paul A. Jorgensen, "A Formative Shakespearean Legacy: Elizabethan Views of God, Fortune, and War," *PMLA*, XC (1975), 232.

king has wronged, he openly comments on the king's responsibility for Gloucester's death, preferring such a fate for himself to his present misery.

Bolingbroke, in scene iii, voices similar charges against the ruler who plucked his rights and royalties from his arms. Similarly, in IV, i Richard's complicity in political murder is flatly assumed as the nobles quarrel among themselves over who wrought noble Gloucester's death "with the king" (3–4).

At the same time, in eight of the fifteen scenes of the last four acts these pointer characters divert the spectators' attention from Richard's faults. Both York and Carlisle, for example, continue to stress the religious nature of the royal office which renders immediate judgment on rebel and rebellion alike.[42] At Berkeley Castle York denounces Bolingbroke's unlawful return to England as "deceivable and false" to the "anointed king" (II, iii, 84, 96), just as later at Flint Castle he warns his nephew not to take more than he should from the "sacred king" because the "heavens are over [their] heads" (III, iii, 9, 17). The strongest affirmations of divine authority are voiced at Westminster Hall at the moment Bolingbroke informs the courtiers that he will ascend the throne. The Bishop of Carlisle proclaims Hereford a "foul traitor" as is any subject who dares "give sentence on his king" (121):

> the figure of God's majesty,
> His captain, steward, deputy elect,
> Anointed, crowned. . . .   (125–27)

At the same time, the characters who observe his anguish and misery compel the spectators to pity the king who seems so unaccustomed to suffering. The queen's affection, for example, on three occasions underscores Richard's finer qualities. Apprehensive for his safety in Ireland, she makes a "guest" of grief in recompense for "bidding

42. S. C. Sen Gupta brands York, who later supports Bolingbroke as king, a "spineless, vacillating old man" (*Shakespeare's Historical Plays* [Oxford: Oxford Univ. Press, 1964], p. 117). The opposite view, held by J. M. Murry, is that York's "loyalty (perfect in kind) is to royalty as the fount of Order. . . . For him royalty is divine, only so long as it fulfills a divine purpose" (*Shakespeare* [London: Cape, 1936], p. 147).

farewell to so sweet a guest" as her "sweet Richard" (II, ii, 8, 9).
This grief intensifies six scenes later as she is forced to overhear the
gardeners converse of her husband's deplorable state. And it is most
poignant during her final meeting with her lord in the streets of
London. She is her "true king's queen" (V, i, 6), he her "fair rose"
(8), her "map of honor" (12), her "most beauteous inn" (13); on
parting from her husband and her king, she strives to kill her heart
"with a groan" (100). Northumberland, one of his most outspoken
opponents, is touched at Flint Castle by the king's sorrow and grief.
Certainly the most gripping moment is York's tear-filled description
of Richard's ignominious plight in Bolingbroke's victory procession
in London, in which there was no man to cry "God save him!" and
no joyful tongue to welcome him home. When dust was thrown upon
his head, only with smiles, the badge of patience, did he manage to
combat the tears of grief. The groom in the final act reflects a similar
affection in visiting his erstwhile master in prison to voice his anguish
over Bolingbroke's riding during his coronation parade "on roan
Barbary," the horse on which Richard so often rode.

Shakespeare, then, scatters his tragic pointers in order to force the
spectators to view Richard as rightful king, dissolute reprobate, and
suffering man. The character at the center is also vocal about his woes,
and, interestingly enough, his comments help to maintain the ambivalence. On the one hand, the audience tends to react sympathetically to his outspoken grief, both because of the natural tendency to
respond to pain when it is introspectively depicted on stage, and because of Richard's magnificent gift of poetic utterance. Certainly, for
example, the spectators react sympathetically to Richard's almost pa-
rental concern for his native land as he returns from Ireland in III, ii.
He salutes the "dear earth" (6), greeting it like "a long-parted
mother with her child" who eagerly mixes her tears and smiles (8–9).
But respect wanes with his naive assumptions that nature will protect
him and his comparison of himself with the sun whose rising in the
east Bolingbroke will not be able to endure.[43] So also they are stirred

43. Samuel Kliger ("The Sun Imagery in *Richard II*," *SP*, XLV [1948],
197–98) traces Richard's passage from noonday to eclipse, and K. M. Harris
("Sun and Water Imagery in *Richard II:* Its Dramatic Function," *SQ*, XXI

by his wrath when he believes that his attendants Bushy and Green have defected and touched by his grief when he discovers they are dead. Certainly, too, they are stirred by his lyric eloquence as he determines to "sit upon the ground / And tell sad stories of the deaths of kings" (155–56). But the moment turns sour when, in despair, and refusing to defend his title or his kingdom, he announces his intention to go to Flint Castle and there to "pine away" (209). The situation is similar in III, iii. Richard's initial posture in confronting Bolingbroke is firm and admirable as he demands the obedience due to the lawful king and stresses the sacred nature of his office. But, as so often he "begins with a strong denunciation only then to weaken and give in altogether,"[44] he capitulates in sentimentality before Hereford has to demand anything, glibly comparing himself to "glist'ring Phaethon" and calling for night owls to "shriek where mounting larks should sing" (183). Again later, in Westminster Hall, the spectators' sympathy goes out to the oppressed ruler who so poetically can express his grief and his disdain. To compel him publicly to read his list of grievances is cruel, however wise politically; when forced to insinuate, flatter, and bow, he indeed seems painfully out of character; to demand that he personally hand over the crown is to render his grief most poignant even at the moment Bolingbroke's fortune is at its height. Ultimately, however, he sacrifices full sympathy through his histrionic display of self-pity. The dignity of suffering is transformed

---

[1970], 162) describes the transfer of the sun imagery to Bolingbroke. Other studies stress the imagery of the earth (Richard D. Altick, "Symphonic Imagery in *Richard II*," *PMLA*, LXII [1947], 339–65), of the crown (Allan S. Downer, "The Life of Our Design," *Hudson Review*, II [1949], 242–63), of rise and fall (Paul A. Jorgensen, "Vertical Patterns in *Richard II*," *SAB*, XXIII [1948], 119–34; Arthur Suzman, "Imagery and Symbolism in *Richard II*," *SQ*, VII [1957], 355–70), of negligence, excess, and waste (R. J. Dorius, "A Little More Than a Little," *SQ*, XI [1960], 13–26), and of trees, plants, and planting (C. F. E. Spurgeon, *Shakespeare's Imagery* [Cambridge: Cambridge Univ. Press, 1935], p. 220). For a general discussion of the image patterns, see Kenneth Muir, *Shakespeare the Professional and Related Studies* (Totowa, New Jersey: Rowman and Littlefield, 1973), p. 90.

44. Robert Hapgood, "Shakespeare's Thematic Mode of Speech: *Richard II* to *Henry V*," *Shakespeare Survey*, XX (1967), 42.

into maudlin sentimentality when, for example, he claims that his eyes are so "full of tears" that he "cannot see" (IV, i, 244), then examines his face for "deeper wrinkles" now that sorrow has "struck / So many blows" (277–78), afterward dashing the mirror to the ground even as he declares that thus sorrow has destroyed his face.[45]

Through each of these scenes, in effect, Richard's poetic eloquence is undeniable, but the moments of excessive sentiment tend to hold the spectators at arms' length, limiting their sympathetic engagement with what otherwise could be construed in the protagonist as a kind of wisdom gained through adversity. He may perceive, at least dimly, that kingship provides only a "hollow crown" in which man has but "a little scene" to "monarchize" (III, ii, 160, 164–65), that he should be as great as his name, that in considering the course of his downfall he must brand himself "a traitor with the rest" (IV, i, 248). But the full impact of such potential insight dissolves in tears. So, also, do his final pronouncements just prior to his death, though here Shakespeare certainly brings the protagonist as close to an anagnorisis as Brutus and far closer than Titus, Richard III, or Romeo. Here too the spectators' rapport with Richard is most nearly complete as in his lone soliloquy—his single performance without an audience—he muses on the many roles a person is forced to play in life. So also, overhearing discordant music, he compares his own life to broken time and unkept proportion, admitting that he had no ear to recognize the "true time": "I wasted time, and now doth time waste me" (V, v, 48–49). Although from this point he again laments excessively the sighs, tears, and groans that mark his present time, and although he dies with the conviction that his soul will mount and that his seat is on high, the moment is not without power; coupled with his anomalous moment of physical valor as he slays two assassins before receiving his fatal

45. Lacking "the virtue of passive fortitude" (Hudson, p. 55) to control his "consciousness of his own nullity, which descends, at certain times, almost to baseness" (F. P. G. Guizot, *Shakespeare and His Times* [New York: 1852], p. 310), Richard on occasion "reduces tragedy to melancholy" through his juxtaposition of "hysteria, emotional excess, and of true tragedy" (Derek Traversi, *Shakespeare From Richard II to Henry V* [Stanford: Stanford Univ. Press, 1957], pp. 30, 32).

wound, the scene elevates Richard as close to tragic stature as any figure in Shakespeare's early plays.[46]

One of the fundamental necessities of maintaining a delicate ambivalence in the protagonist is that Bolingbroke must not emerge as a clear villain (for artistic as well as political prudence), thereby casting the audience's sympathy totally upon Richard despite his flaws.[47] Certainly by the end of Act I the worst possibilities are established— though through the biased mouth of Mowbray, who warns that the king will to his sorrow all too soon discover Bolingbroke's true nature. Moreover, the gnawing question of timing lingers in the back of the mind when, soon after Gaunt's death and Richard's seizure of the

46. Richard's final words have been branded as "attitudinizing" (Whitaker, p. 122) and as "the merest of lip-service" (Willard Farnham, *The Medieval Heritage of Elizabethan Drama* [Oxford: Blackwell, 1956], p. 417), his final actions as "boyish . . . impetuosity" (A. C. Swinburne, *Three Plays of Shakespeare* [New York: Harper, 1909], p. 83) and as the "fury of desperation" (Goddard, I, 159). To the contrary, Michael Quinn avers that Richard "dies as Somebody, a lion overpowered, a king deposed" (" 'The King is Not Himself': The Personal Tragedy of Richard II," *SP*, LVI [1959], 184) who has learned to "distinguish in himself shadow from substance" (D. H. Rieman, "Appearance, Reality, and Moral Order in *Richard II*," *MLQ*, XXV [1964], 40). If Richard falls just short of the tragic (Rossiter, *Angel*, p. 36), with no "final impression that transforms all that has gone before" (Alexander, *Introductions*, p. 105), there is unmistakeably a move "toward self-knowledge, and even repentance" (Ure, p. lxxxii), a "developing away from self-serving despair" (R. L. Montgomery, "The Dimensions of Time in *Richard II*," *Shakespeare Studies*, IV [1968], 82). On the significance of Aumerle's shifting loyalty as a means of creating a compassionate view of Richard, see Warren J. MacIsaac, "The Three Cousins in *Richard II*," *SQ* XXII (1971), 139.

47. On the one hand, Bolingbroke is seen as "a manifestation . . . of the actual Machiavellian philosophy" (Ribner, "Bolingbroke, A True Machiavellian," *MLQ*, IX [1948], 178), a "schemer" whose "speeches . . . betray calculation in their over-humility, over-sweetness" (R. F. Hill, "Dramatic Techniques and Interpretation in *Richard II*," in *Early Shakespeare*, ed. J. R. Brown and Bernard Harris [New York: St. Martin's Press, 1961], pp. 115, 106). On the other hand, he is an "instrument in the hands of Providence" (Georges A. Bonnard, "The Actor in Shakespeare," *SJ*, LXXXII [1951], 89), an opportunist (Brents Stirling, "Bolingbroke's Decision," *SQ*, II [1951], 30) who thought of deposition only when Richard suggested it to him (A. L. French, "Who Deposed Richard II?" *Essays in Criticism*, XVII [1967], 424). There is guilt in Hereford, to be sure, yet he "is certainly meant to be admired" (Patrick Cruttwell, *The Shakespearean Moment* [New York: Random House, 1960], p. 197).

Duke's estate (the same scene in F1 and in all modern editions), Northumberland announces that Bolingbroke with a large group of supporters is returning to England in defiance of banishment. Shakespeare seems through the telescoping of time almost consciously to be clouding Bolingbroke's claim, voiced later by Northumberland, that his coming is only to claim his own dukedom. As A. C. Sprague aptly observes, Shakespeare, "with the chronicles before him, . . . must have been aware that Bolingbroke's weeks were becoming hours."[48]

But the possibility of villainy never becomes a certainty—as it does with Mortimer in *Edward II*—both because the ambiguity of motive is sustained throughout and because Bolingbroke, the foil of the king, possesses those qualities of pragmatism and leadership so painfully lacking in Richard that they tend to be accepted as virtues almost without question. Admittedly, though, Bolingbroke's first words on English soil sound strange for a man of limited ambition; he promises recompense for his friends as his "fortune ripens" with their "love" (II, iii, 48) and as his "treasury" grows richer (60). Also, without anyone's questioning his right to do so, he swears to "weed and pluck away" the king's parasites (167); and later he seizes the royal prerogative of execution, judiciously washing their blood from his hands by a public hearing of their crimes in misleading Richard. He is careful, though, to send a pledge of allegiance to Richard at Flint Castle. The offer of peace, to be sure, is conditional. He demands his estate, else a "crimson tempest" (46) will stain the fair land. For the second time, Northumberland reports that Bolingbroke "swears" his coming is "for his lineal royalties" (105, 113). But Richard gives all, in effect, and Bolingbroke is not forced to reveal his full motive; he becomes the king's captor without the need for explanation.

In the final acts Bolingbroke displays the specific qualities of leadership that Richard lacks. By permitting no one to accept a challenge pending a day of further trial, for example, he firmly contains the developing quarrel among his nobles so reminiscent of the struggle which Richard at the outset bungles so badly. Again unlike Richard, he decisively puts down a budding rebellion, rendering immediate judg-

48. *Shakespeare and The Audience* (Cambridge, Mass.: Harvard Univ. Press, 1935), p. 50.

ment on the conspirators among the nobility. At the same time he gives evidence of political sagacity sorely absent in his predecessor. On the one hand, he accepts the necessity of condemnation though his heart rejoices—in the perfunctory banishment of Sir Pierce of Exton moments after Richard's assassination. On the other hand, he also realizes the pragmatic value of selective mercy though his heart thirsts for vengeance—in his not forcing Richard to read publicly the scroll listing crimes against the people or in his pardon granted to Aumerle for the sake of his aunt as well as his cousin.[49] Interestingly enough, in suppressing the Oxford conspiracy such Lancastrian policy breaks for this drama (if not for history and for Shakespeare's future chronicle plays) the mounting waves of progressively successful agitation against the royal office—from the Duchess of Gloucester's powerless defiance, to the nobles' conspiracy in Bolingbroke's usurpation. The sanctioned king obviously could bring no peace and order to his realm; for Bolingbroke—though he pays judicious public token attention to a guilty conscience—and perhaps for the spectators as well, victory and stabilization appear to be ample justification for the outrage inflicted upon the spirit.

Shakespeare, in short, effectively creates a chameleon in the character of Bolingbroke; a reading of his actions at any particular point depends upon one's momentary attitude toward Richard, to whom he is the direct foil. Yet, his intentions are always vague until the very minute he accepts the crown—and even then the spectators may choose to believe that he has had greatness thrust upon him without actively and methodically seeking it. Thus, though their relationship with him constantly shifts, it is always Richard who determines that relationship.

49. Henry immediately crushes the Oxford plot despite "the fact that his own brother-in-law is among the conspirators" (James Winny, *The Player King* [New York: Barnes and Noble, 1968], p. 73). Equally decisive, he acts to pardon Aumerle; Robert Hapgood contends that the decision is made "before the elder Yorks arrive but for the sake of public relations [he] goes along with the Yorks as they act out their old-fashioned rite of pardon" ("Three Eras in *Richard II*," *SQ*, XIV [1963], 283). "This entire episode has been carefully planned to infuse Bolingbroke's . . . judgment scene with a confidence of royal power great enough to admit a divine virtue" (McIsaac, p. 144).

More effectively than Richmond, then, and more extensively than Mercutio, Bolingbroke is the shadow against whom the principal figure is illuminated.

In establishing the perspective for Richard's ambivalence, Shakespeare inserts freely throughout his plot passages which create for the spectators a pattern of anticipated action. This material is by no means as heavy-handed as is the case in *Richard III*, in which Margaret's curses at the outset literally outline the events to come and the spirits of Richard's victims appear in the final act to recapitulate the incidents and announce Richard's imminent overthrow. Although still repetitious and on occasion artificial, such passages in *Richard II* are for the most part more effectively integrated in the action, "more subtle, less obtrusive."[50] Most significantly, they serve a more varied function, at times enriching the ambiguities of Bolingbroke, at times anticipating from various angles the decline and fall of Richard, and at times strengthening the philosophic dimensions of the play. Concerning the antagonist, for instance, Mowbray's prediction that Bolingbroke's true colors will shortly be revealed (I, iii, 204–5) has already been noted. A scene later the suspicion is strengthened by Richard's observation that, when Bolingbroke returns from banishment, it will not be as a friend (iv, 20–22).

Far more extensively, the anticipatory devices prepare the spectators for Richard's ill fortunes. Both uncles, for example, emphasize the flaws that will lead to destruction. The dying Gaunt flatly proclaims that the king's "rash fierce blaze of riot cannot last" (II, i, 33); his vanity like an "insatiate cormorant" will soon "prey . . . upon itself" (38–39). York's warning is directed to Richard himself, who invites untold dangers upon his head and loses countless followers by appropriating Gaunt's estate. More emotionally charged are the queen's intuitive apprehensions just prior to news of Bolingbroke's return concerning some unborn sorrow, "ripe in fortune's womb," that is approaching her, and Bagot's ominous conviction a few lines later, on parting from Bushy and Green, that the three shall never meet again. Two further passages are admittedly more artificial. In II, iv the

50. Clemen, *The Development of Shakespeare's Imagery*, p. 31.

Welsh forces loyal to Richard refuse any longer to await his return from Ireland because of withered bay trees, meteors, a pale moon, and whispering prophets—various signs that foretell the death or fall of kings. Richard's glory crashes to earth "like a shooting star" (19); his "sun sets weepingly in the lowly west" (21). More elaborate still is the scene in which the queen overhears the conversation of the gardeners at Langley. Here certainly Shakespeare sacrifices credibility for the sake of an extended comparison of Richard with an incompetent gardener whose failure to "root away" the "noisome weeds" (III, iv, 37–38) and to prune the "fast-growing sprays" (34) has produced his "fall of leaf" (49). Though too contrived, like Margaret's curses, this scene positioned midway through the play does glance both backward to Richard's misuse of the royal office and forward to the deposition and death that will be its consequence.

In the last half of the play Shakespeare on four separate occasions directs the spectators to an anticipation of the War of the Roses which Richard's overthrow ignites. At Flint Castle Richard himself first mentions the "pestilence" which will strike the "children yet unborn and unbegot" (III, iii, 87, 88) if usurping hands are lifted against his crown. Twice the Bishop of Carlisle lends the dignity of religious office to a similar prophecy. At the moment of Bolingbroke's ascension at Westminster, he declares that if Bolingbroke is crowned the "blood of English shall manure the ground / And future ages groan for this foul act" (IV, i, 137–38). And he reiterates the point following the coronation: "The woe's to come. The children yet unborn / Shall feel this day as sharp to them as thorn" (322–23). Finally, Richard voices the same concern to Northumberland as he is being conveyed to the Tower, predicting that the earl will shortly not be satisfied with half the kingdom, that the time shall not be many hours of age before foul sin will gather head and new rebellion spread corruption through the land.

These passages obviously fortify the religious dimensions of the play because they suggest God's ordinance beyond Bolingbroke's successful usurpation. That is, though the violation of religious sanction wreaks no disaster within the scope of the play, the spectators are assured that God's inexorable justice will ultimately prevail. The prophecies also enable Shakespeare to set the play within the fifteenth-century political-historical context with which his spectators were familiar and, as recent criticism has suggested, to allow those in the audience to draw certain analogies between Richard's reign and that of Elizabeth.[51] Thus, these anticipatory devices function within the play to heighten the tension and to suggest the power of heaven inextricably bound to the kingship; they also function beyond the play to broaden the scope of the issue and thereby provoke a richer emotional and intellectual response.

It is likely also that Shakespeare, now preparing his fifth play involving the War of the Roses, was coming to envision the dramatic treatment of Henry IV and Prince Hal.[52] If so, these passages serve the additional function of providing narrative links with the work to follow; and, while this matter is not in itself pertinent to the evolution of his tragic technique, it does further reflect the growing concern for

51. "Each of Shakespeare's histories serves a special purpose in elucidating a political problem of Elizabeth's day" (L. B. Campbell, *Shakespeare's Histories: Mirrors of Elizabethan Policy* [San Marino, Calif.: Huntington Library, 1947], p. 125). Evelyn M. Albright weaves an elaborate explanation for the play as political allegory ("Shakespeare's *Richard II* and the Essex Conspiracy," *PMLA*, XLII [1927], 686–720; "Shakespeare's *Richard II*, Hayward's History of *Henry IV*, and the Essex Conspiracy," *PMLA*, XLVI [1931], 694–719). Alfred Hart claims that a medieval concept of the divine right of kings is "historically false" and that Shakespeare and his colleagues "drew their allusions to the doctrines" from the Tudor-inspired *Book of Homilies* (*Shakespeare and the Homilies* [Melbourne: Melbourne Univ. Press, 1934], pp. 68, 73). J. W. Figgis points out, however, that Wycliffe's writings in defense of imperialism and the general struggle over the papacy did lead Richard to "claim for himself the position of an absolute monarch by Divine Right" (*The Divine Right of Kings* [Cambridge, 1896], p. 73). By contrast, the driving force in the development of divine right during the Tudor era was not the need for anti-papal theory but the desire for an omnipotent crown in parliament (J. W. Allen, *A History of Political Thought in the Sixteenth Century* [London: Methuen, 1928], p. 169).

52. Tillyard writes, for example, that *Richard II* is "only the prelude" of a "great new epic attempt" (299), and Chambers calls it the "first act in the trilogy which leads up to . . . *Henry V*" (*Survey*, p. 89). Recently, John R. Elliott has examined the material in Acts IV and V which "look[s] forward to the continuing historical events that Shakespeare is to depict in the remainder of the *Richard II–Henry IV–Henry V* tetralogy" ("History and Tragedy in *Richard II*," *SEL*, VIII [1968], 269).

structural control in the early plays that is central to the present study. Certainly the prophecies anticipate Henry IV's struggles to consolidate his power at Shrewsbury and at Gaultree Forest. So also, as various critics have noted, Henry's first mention of his "unthrifty son" in V, iii, anticipates Hal's legendary wildness, which is to be more extensively developed in the future play: " 'Tis full three months since I did see him last / . . . Inquire at London, 'mongst the taverns there" (1, 2, 5). The remainder of this scene, however, most critics would explain away as immature, even unintentionally ridiculous. But quite probably the playwright, though without total success because the relationship remains vague, was attempting to anticipate Hal's equally legendary true repentance. For at the very moment in the scene when King Henry remarks that he sees some sparks of better hope in his son, Aumerle bursts into the king's chambers proclaiming his abject repentance for his part in the conspiracy against the new king. Proclaiming fealty to Bolingbroke, he begs for a pardon on his knees and swears that his heart and hand were not confederate in his earlier treasonous plotting.

Aumerle's action has every justification within the individual stage world of *Richard II*. For one, the father's discovery of the son's conspiracy against Bolingbroke provides a basis for the display of York's fierce loyalty to the crown despite his abhorrence of the method by which Henry ascended the throne. For another, as previously noted, Henry's pardon of Aumerle reveals his disposition to mercy as a means politically of consolidating the power of his command and personally of atoning for the guilt he harbors concerning the deposition of Richard. Nevertheless, it is difficult to assume that the juxtaposition of Aumerle's present repentance with Henry's expectations of a future repentance in Hal is mere coincidence.

There is, moreover, an analogy between the reaction of York and that of King Henry in the following plays. The extent of this analogy suggests further that the dramatist in *1 Henry IV* was quite conscious of the link provided in this earlier scene of *Richard II*. Both situations construct a twofold contrast between father and son. First, in both the parent is envisioned as loyal and efficient, the son as treacherous and digressing; secondly, in both the father fears that his reputation, his ambition, and his estate will be destroyed through the actions of his offspring.

In *Richard II*, Aumerle's disloyalty is described in Henry's words to York:

> O loyal father of a treacherous son!
> Thou sheer, immaculate, and silver fountain,
> From whence this stream through muddy passages
> Hath held his current and defil'd himself!
> Thy overflow of good converts to bad,
> And thy abundant goodness shall excuse
> This deadly blot in thy digressing son.
>
> (60–66)

In the initial scene of the following play, Henry proffers a similar denunciation of his own son: "I . . . see riot and dishonor stain the brow / Of my young Harry" (*1 Henry IV*, I, i, 84–86). Later, he condemns Hal's low "desires" "grafted" to the "greatness of [his] blood" (III, ii, 12, 15, 16). References to Hal's "base inclination," his disloyalty to his ancestors, and his alienation from "the hearts of the court and princes of [his] blood" suggest parallels with the earlier condemnation of Aumerle.

More important to the dominant conflict between father and son in *Henry IV* is the analogy suggested by York's fears that Aumerle's deeds threaten to destroy the father's reputation and Henry's similar apprehensions in the later play.

> So shall my virtue be his vice's bawd,
> And he shall spend mine honor with his shame,
> As thriftless sons their scraping father's gold.
> Mine honor lives when his dishonor dies,
> Or my shamed life in his dishonor lies.
> Thou kill'st me in his life.
>
> (*Richard II*, V, iii, 67–72)

It can hardly be coincidental that Henry, in lamenting Hal's delinquency, draws upon precisely the same figures of the son motivated by the desire for the father's gold and the father's symbolic death in the son's misdeeds.

> See, sons, what things you are!
> How quickly nature falls into revolt
> When gold becomes her object!
>
> (*2 Henry IV*, IV, v, 64–66)

> Give that which gave thee life unto the worms.
> Pluck down my officers, break my decrees,
> For now a time is come to mock at form.
>
> (116–18)

Branding Hal his "nearest and dearest enemy," Henry is convinced that the future reign will be unguided and rotten (*1 Henry IV*, III, ii, 123).

Shakespeare, then, in the final act is apparently anticipating specific events in his next chronicle play just as in the predictions of civil strife he is mindful in general of the eighty-six years he was tracing in a number of plays. In the present tragedy, he would make his spectators mindful in particular of the ultimate price of usurpation. As in *Richard III*, he is constantly providing the narrative guideposts to achieve coherence of plot by arousing in the spectators anticipations concerning both theme and character which the action will then satisfy. He is also obviously attempting to establish a double vision by which the spectators will experience Richard's dilemma sympathetically in part at least and at the same time sit in judgment on him as they perceive the forces of power that his failures allow to emerge and the subsequent destruction they will wreak in the context of history. Admittedly Richard has several rhetorical flurries when action is virtually suspended and drama suffers despite the poetic eloquence; admittedly, also, Richard is essentially a static character who never achieves true tragic insight. In his soliloquy in Act V, however, the spectators are compelled to believe that he is bordering on such wisdom. Like Edward II, he is remarkably engaging despite his deeply flawed nature. Indeed, among Shakespeare's protagonists he is the first whom the spectators seem to know thoroughly and consequently to care about emotionally. While this familiarity does not arise from a delineation of the inner man, there is—as in *Romeo and Juliet*—a significant structural achievement in the perspective resulting from the numerous angles and attitudes with which they are invited to view him. Significant also is the skillful manipulation of Bolingbroke as an antagonist whose motivations remain sufficiently ambiguous not to force the reader into a firm judgment on him and in turn on Richard. Thus, whereas Marlowe makes the spectators almost oblivious to Edward's faults in drawing them to pity for the king's physical torments and to condemnation for the heinous ambition that is revealed in Mortimer, Shakespeare is able to maintain a delicate balance throughout the play, keeping ever before the audience both the best and worst in Richard's personality. Equally important, through references to Bolingbroke's ultimate destiny, Richard's downfall is accommodated within the philosophic context of the play. With its emphasis on a protagonist of potential merit who freely engages in decisions and actions that violate the values established in the stage world and in turn produce waste and destruction, both individual and general, *Richard II* points directly toward the major Shakespearean tragedy to come.

Critics have argued *ad nauseam* over whether *Romeo and Juliet* is a tragedy of destiny or free will. It is neither—if by destiny one means a dominant emphasis on an inanimate cosmic force that impels the young lovers to disaster and death[53] and if by free will one means a dominant emphasis on a responsible agent who makes conscious choices of passion for which he can predict the consequences and for which the spectators hold him morally accountable.[54] It is instead a

53. Chambers, for instance, describes the characters as "puppets" subject to a force of destiny that renders inconsequential "any deliberate act or abstention of their own" (*Survey*, p. 74). John W. Draper makes a case for literal astral determinism, arguing the principals "are the puppets of the stars and planets and of the days and times of day" (*Stratford to Dogberry* [Pittsburg: Univ. of Pittsburg Press, 1961], p. 88).

54. Romeo's love has been characterized as an " 'ulcerate' condition of soul" leading to a "slow disintegration" (H. Edward Cain, "*Romeo and Juliet*: A Reinterpretation," *SAB*, XXII [1947], 186). Romeo "*loses* himself in love" (M. A. Goldberg, "The Multiple Masks of Romeo," *Antioch Review*, XXVIII

tragic narrative in which Shakespeare holds the contradictory assumption in constant tension and in which he frankly favors the young lovers, however immoderate their passion may be, provoking sympathy for them through the structural devices by which with remarkably increasing effectiveness he controls the spectators' perspective. Admittedly, as a consequence, the philosophic depth of the later tragedies is markedly absent—a depth growing from the central concerns for individual responsibility which presume man to be in a limited way master of his own destiny.

Certainly the prefatory statements in Shakespeare's source, Arthur Brooke's *The Tragicall Historye of Romeus and Juliet*, set the fundamental blame in a promiscuous, irrational love and its Catholic counselor. In "To The Reader" the author tells us that the story is intended

> to describe unto thee a coople of unfortunate lovers, thralling themselves to unhonest desire, neglecting the authoritie and advise of parents and frendes, conferring their principall counsels with dronken gossyppes, and superstitious friers (the naturally fitte instruments of unchastitie) attempting all adventures of peryll, for thattaynyng of their wished lust, usyng auriculer confession (the kay of whoredome, and treason) for furtheraunce of theyr purpose, abusyng the honorable name of lawefull mariage, the cloke of shame of stolne contractes, finallye, by all means of unhonest lyfe, hastyng to most unhappye deathe.

There is little to suggest in Brooke's poem, however, that the preface is anything more than the conventional ploy of catering to the high didactic purposes of poetry which the Renaissance found morally reassuring. Except for occasional allusions to the sinfulness and lustfulness of Romeus' infatuate love (primarily in the first five hundred lines), the narrative stresses the piteous overthrow of young lovers far

---

[1968], 425); they "idolize each other, and in doing so make a religion of their passion" (R. W. Battenhouse, *Shakespearean Tragedy* [Bloomington: Indiana Univ. Press, 1969], p. 103). "Romeo is guilty of something approaching a *hubris* of love" (M. B. Smith, *Dualities in Shakespeare* [Toronto: Univ. of Toronto Press, 1966], p. 94).

more sinned against than sinning. The muse commands Brooke to describe a woeful tale in mourning verse of two unhappy families whom Fortune has pleased to strike; from their black hate and rancor grows the "most wofull Tragedy" (2908) of "poore lovers in distress" (2910) to whom a monument is erected in "memory of so *perfect, sound,* and so *approved* love" (3012, italics mine). Romeus and Juliet are not, in short, made to sense a guilty passion which displeases God or endangers their spiritual health.

The mixed evidence is similar for Shakespeare's dramatic poem. In the ecstatic anxieties of young love crossed in various ways Romeo and Juliet are not without some apprehension of the dangers attendant to their ardent affection, but Shakespeare does not in any serious fashion choose to focus upon their individual culpability. Most important, he in no way attempts to suggest the slightest internal struggle. Passages from the play are frequently cited out of context at the cost of at best distorting and at worst destroying the original meaning. Many, for example, in the heat of conversation reflect little more than the hyperbole of young love; that Romeo is lost in the sweet madness of love, that Juliet is his soul, that she would kill him with cherishing—in context these are frothy and lighthearted exclamations with no obscure or symbolic intentions on the part of the speaker. Benvolio's insistence on replacing one infection with another is a part of his comic badinage with his histrionically love-sick friend whose mistress refuses to reciprocate; the context of old Montague's concern for Romeo's humor can hardly be one of high seriousness when, moments after he declares that his son absolutely refuses to reveal to anyone the cause of his tears and sighs and secret, close retirement, Romeo readily blurts to Benvolio that he is in love. Nor does the choral sonnet in Act II stigmatize Romeo's love for Juliet as sinful or diseased; instead we are made to sense the sheer intensity of their love, by whatever definition, and their frantic determination to meet, whatever the social barriers. Juliet's reference to her lover as the "god" of her "idolatry" (ii, 114) is the result of her comic insistence that he swear his devotion by himself and not by the inconstant moon; youth also humorously runs the gamut of extremes in the juxtaposition of her fear that their love is too rash with her insistence that it will "prove a beauteous flow'r" (122).

Other references divorced from context produce more serious distortions. Juliet's only specific allusions to sin, orisons, and repentance, for instance, are deliberately simulated; at one point, after having agreed to use the friar's potion, she needs to convince her father of her apparent willingness to marry Paris, and at another she needs to convince the nurse of her sincere desire to be alone on the eve of her wedding. When Romeo berates his effeminacy (i.e., disease) as a result of Juliet's beauty and calls for "fire-eyed fury" now to be his conduct (III, i, 122), we can hardly assume that his violence is in some enigmatic way morally superior to his earlier attempts to avoid battle with Tybalt or to stay the duel between Tybalt and Mercutio. In other words, this reference *in context* does not function as a condemnation of the power which love has exercised upon him. And surely Romeo's intervention with Mercutio is an act of affection, not cowardice on the one hand or a prideful and naive assumption that now he can re-draw the lines of feudal hatred on the other. Moreover, Romeo's later statement about the sin upon his head refers, in his own mind, not to a causal pattern of events stemming from what he knows to be sinful infatuation, but solely to his previous altercation with Tybalt, and the thought of moral error never seems to enter his head again—even after he has dispatched Paris.

The centrally significant passage concerning the struggle of passion and reason is, of course, Friar Lawrence's soliloquy in Act II.[55] Clearly the friar describes the two "opposèd kings" (iii, 27)—"grace and rude will" (28) which dwell in men as well as plants, observing

---

55. G. G. Gervinus (*Shakespeare Commentaries*, in *Variorum*, p. 455), Whitaker (p. 113), and F. M. Dickey (*Not Wisely But Too Well* [San Marino, Calif.: Huntington Library, 1957], p. 106), consider these lines spoken by the "wise" Lawrence the "leading idea of the play"; the ecclesiastic exemplifies "grace," Romeo "rude will" (T.P. Harrison, "Hang Up Philosophy," *SAB*, XXII [1947], 208). On the other hand, G. I. Duthie (ed. [with J. D. Wilson], *Romeo and Juliet* [Cambridge: Cambridge Univ. Press, 1955], p. xix) maintains that the play simply does not bear out such an assumption; and Theodore Spencer, that for all his comment the friar does not "increase an understanding of the protagonists" (*Shakespeare and the Nature of Man* [New York: Macmillan, 1942], p. 92). R. O. Evans questions the friar's competence for such "intellectual pursuits" (*The Osier Cage* [Lexington: Univ. of Kentucky Press, 1966], p. 48).

that "where the worser is predominant, / Full soon the cankered death eats up that plant" (29–30). Certainly the lines again register upon the audience the dangers of passionate action; and, pointedly inserted between Romeo's betrothal within mere hours of his meeting Juliet and his frantic request that Friar Lawrence marry them posthaste, their application is hardly in question. Like a kind of moral undersong, they counterbalance the numerous assertions of star-crossed fatalism.

Whether Romeo ever hears and reacts to this counsel is quite another matter. One may obviously argue that Romeo walks on stage behind the friar, evesdrops on the final lines, and in some physical way signals his comprehension to the audience. But the assumption of one character's overhearing the soliloquy of another is a contradiction in stage convention. The single occasion in Shakespeare is in this play —as Romeo overhears Juliet speaking from her balcony in II, ii. Their subsequent dialogue clearly builds upon this interaction, however, whereas neither the friar nor Romeo ever suggests such is the case. Moreover Romeo never once registers the slightest symptom of any such microcosmic struggle. And, perhaps most significantly, the friar tends to defeat his own purpose; Romeo can hardly be expected to assume that his impetuosity has been condemned when moments later the friar himself has agreed that the Holy Church will "make short work" (iv, 35) of their ceremony.

In short, though the spectators may well sense the moral dilemma involved in one's succumbing to inordinate haste, the various lines that on occasion are paraded as evidence of Shakespeare's concentration on protagonists consciously struggling with diseased love and actively alert to the spiritual dangers of uncontrolled passion fail under contextual scrutiny to carry the emphasis claimed for them. In actual fact, Shakespeare time and again alters his source in small ways in order to achieve a more sympathetic relationship between the spectator and Romeo and Juliet and at the same time to minimize any sense of guilt that might attach to the young lovers.[56] Gone, for instance, is

---

56. Harry Levin describes the love of Romeo and Juliet as "the one organic relation amid an overplus of stlyized expressions and attitudes" ("Form and Formality in *Romeo and Juliet*," *SQ*, XI [1960], 9); "however slender the experience afforded by [such] love, it can in its brief span create values other-

Brooke's suggestion that Romeus is a spiritually impoverished infatu-ate—an implication arising from a description of Romeus' first love (Rosaline in Shakespeare) as one who peremptorily repulsed his amorous advances because she was fostered from her youth with vir-tue's food and wisdom's skillful lore or of Romeus' friend (Benvolio in Shakespeare) as one of riper years arid mature counsel who sharply rebuked him for a love characterized by vice and error. Gone too is Brooke's description of Romeus' love at first sight for Juliet as love's sweet bait and deadly pains which spread poison throughout his bones and veins and eventually banishes "health and fredome from eche limme." Gone is any suggestion that the nurse contaminates Juliet's mind with wicked words. And gone is Romeus' prayer moments be-fore his suicide, in which he begs pity on his sinful and afflicted mind and on his body which is "but a mass of sinne . . . subject to decay."

In several alterations involving more extensive adjustments, the in-tention of strengthening the spectators' sympathy for Romeo is equally clear. For one thing, both the prince and the friar are made to assume a greater responsibility for the tragic events than is the case in Brooke's poem. In Shakespeare, Prince Escalus with a strong hand issues a de-cree of death to anyone who again breaks the peace, an order he later disregards in banishing Romeo; his own vacillation, he himself ad-mits, is partially responsible for the deaths of Juliet and Paris.[57] The friar in Brooke is forever acting out of fear and desperation; in Shake-speare, except for his frenetic flight from the tomb and from Juliet in the final act, Friar Lawrence is a much firmer character, and he as-sumes a far more significant image as he manipulates the young lovers

---

wise forever obscure" (Joseph S. M. J. Chang, "The Language of Paradox in *Romeo and Juliet," Shakespeare Studies,* III [1967], 38). The lovers alone "are possessed of a light incomprehensible to the rest of Verona's citizens" (Ruth Nevo, *Tragic Form in Shakespeare* [Princeton: Princeton Univ. Press, 1972], p. 40. On the significance of Romeo's journey to Mantua, see Mark Rose, *Shakespearean Design* (Cambridge, Mass.: Harvard Univ. Press, 1972), p. 9.

57. Barry B. Adams sees Escalus as the central character for the audience, exhibiting rational prudence but also subject to irrational fortune ("The Pru-dence of Prince Escalus," *ELH,* XXXV [1968], 47), while Lodwick Hartley frankly blames the prince for "not summarily and cruelly ending the feud" and thus avoiding the tragedy ("Mercy But Murders," *PELL,* I [1965], 263).

to what he trusts will be a Christian solution both to their dilemma and to the feud. For another thing, through Mercutio's involvement in the quarrel with Tybalt, Romeo's culpability in the Capulet's death is mitigated; Romeus is enraged into direct confrontation with his taunting adversary, while Romeo is persuaded to fight only after (through a gesture of peace) he feels himself directly responsible for his friend's death. Shakespeare, as H. C. Goddard (I, 125) has observed, "goes out of his way to prove that the guilty party in the death of Tybalt is Mercutio." Similarly, Shakespeare's addition of Paris at the Capulet tomb in Act V further stresses the circumstances to which Romeo is victim; again he wishes to avoid the fight, and again his intentions are grossly misunderstood.

Alterations that enhance the spectators' sympathetic attachment to Juliet are also not far to seek. One of the most significant, certainly, is the manner in which Shakespeare motivates the establishment of her wedding date with the County Paris. In Brooke, Juliet—separated for a considerable period of time from her banished Romeus—grows so melancholy that her mother encourages the father to select a husband for the distraught daughter; prompted to action out of a concern for his daughter's health, he reacts with indignant anger to her refusal of cooperation. In Shakespeare, Juliet is far more the victim as her father, without the slightest attempt to consult her even in the midst of family mourning for Tybalt, sets her wedding date three days hence; all too clearly old Capulet acts out of concern, not only for his daughter, but also for his estate and family name. Another modification that prompts a stronger rapport between Juliet and the audience concerns the nurse's role at the time of Tybalt's death. Brooke's nurse attempts to calm the distraught girl, whose first thought is to turn viciously on the husband as murderer of her cousin, by stressing the fact that Romeus at least is alive and that it was either his life or Tybalt's. Shakespeare depicts a much stronger character in Juliet, forcing her to confront the nurse's lamentation for Tybalt and—in the face of it—to reason through the dilemma on the strength of her love alone to the support of her husband. Also, Shakespeare—by eliminating the prince's judgments handed down on the nurse, Romeus' man, the apothecary, and the friar—achieves a more poignant emotional emphasis on the sacrificial death of Juliet as the culminating stroke in a long series of disastrous mischances.

Once we agree that an unambiguous sympathetic depiction of Romeo and Juliet is intended, the development in Shakespeare's dramatic skill becomes clear—development not in this play in the incipient complexity of the tragic protagonist but in the progressively more powerful utilization of structural devices firmly to control the spectator's attitude toward this central character. For one thing, the chorus, appearing before Acts I and II, establishes a pattern of anticipation. In the first appearance, the spectators are clearly informed of the play's outcome and of the social conditions that will determine it; in the second, with Romeo's affection for Rosaline dead, the ardent intensity of his new commitment is declared. The chorus, then, in the feud and in the love which insists on crossing it sets forth the lethal ingredients for what it proclaims will be "misadventured piteous overthrows," deaths that will bury the parents' strife. As a stage device the chorus makes pronouncements that obviously must be accepted without question; even more omnisciently than Margaret's prophecy in *Richard III*, it sets a general narrative frame within which the action is to take place. In *Richard III*, one of the disadvantages of such a rigid device is that it undermines the sense of inner conflict which Shakespeare suggests at other moments in his depiction of the Yorkist king. In *Romeo and Juliet*, on the other hand, this device complements the other structural features that minimize the internal struggle and cast the guilt upon the hostile social conditions.

Far more significant is the nature of the devices of internalization. Romeo and Juliet soliloquize more than Hamlet, with nineteen soliloquies and one aside (a total of 237 lines) as compared with Hamlet's eight soliloquies and one aside (223 lines). If one assumes that Shakespeare through these devices is consciously striving to establish a vital level of the dramatic conflict within the hearts and consciences of the young lovers, then the only possible conclusion is that Shakespeare has far indeed to develop before his delineation of the melancholy Dane. For here, though the soliloquies do establish a close rapport, a sense of intimacy, between the audience and the principals, they make no attempt at self-analysis—no attempt to reveal an inner struggle along with the philosophic dimensions vital to the decision-making process.

Again, a comparison with the technique of *Richard III* is helpful. In that early history-tragedy—in which Shakespeare externally emphasizes the tyrant king who must be destroyed for the sake of God's will and the Tudors—the soliloquy works somewhat at cross-purposes; at times it is purely expositional, serving to underscore Richard's wit or his cruelty or his fearlessness or his crass indifference to God and fellow man in his developing ambition and schemes; at other times it signals moments of apprehension and concern; on one occasion it is an attempt to reflect the gnawing pain and apprehension of a conscience alive to God. Certainly Richard has both his public and his private face; but, with the soliloquy (which by convention depicts the true personality) used to reflect both faces, the design of the play on occasion at least is blurred. In *Romeo and Juliet* the consistent use of soliloquies and asides as devices of emphasis rather than analysis admittedly does not result in the most profound tragedy, in which the individual's struggle reaches the twilight regions of the soul. But in Romeo Shakespeare does create the most engaging personality of his early tragedies, and the power of this engagement would leave most spectators totally unconvinced by the argument that the philosophic perspective is blurred and that the resulting power of the play is thereby sorely diluted.[58]

Specifically, each of Romeo's soliloquies serves either for rhetorical or narrative emphasis. The first five, for example, all occurring in the first two scenes of Act II, rhetorically reiterate the intensity of his newfound love for Juliet; they are in no way concerned with any struggle that may have been involved in his coming to this decision. Significantly, his first soliloquy (II, i, 1–2) occurs moments after his meeting Juliet at the Capulets' ball. Along with two additional passages (II, ii, 1–25, 25–32), it provides him the opportunity to affirm her his "heart," his "center," his "sun," and his "bright angel." He is utterly

---

58. Stauffer (p. 55), for example, suggests that the play "may fail as serious tragedy" because Shakespeare was unable to decide whether to place the "causes of tragedy" outside or inside "the sufferers."

oblivious to political dangers as his affection draws him to her orchard following the dance. Two further passages (II, ii, 139–41; 156–58) emphasize his delirious joy as he takes leave of her after their forbidden conversation. Emotional outbursts which signal to the spectators the sincerity—and hence the potential danger—of his love, these flights of speech serve no self-analytic function whatever.

In his remaining soliloquies the function shifts to narrative emphasis. The sixth, for instance, announces his intention to reveal all to Friar Lawrence and to request immediate marriage. Again he does not, even for a moment, ponder the immediate or future consequences of such a request and weigh one value against another. But the soliloquy does force the spectators to accept his intentions as honorable, and their disapproval on either moral or pragmatic grounds is further disarmed. Similarly, the eighth, ninth, and tenth soliloquies serve to support the narrative element; one (V, i, 1–11) establishes painful dramatic irony as Romeo awakens from a dream which he is convinced presages some joyful news at hand mere moments before Balthasar's arrival with news of Juliet's presumed death.[59] The other two (V, i, 34–57; iii, 45–48) simply announce his determination to lie in death beside Juliet—as, in one, he recalls an apothecary from whom poison is obtainable and as, in the other, he forcibly removes the stones at the entrance of the tomb. The seventh and eleventh soliloquies are the most significant perhaps in approaching something akin to self-analysis. In the former, he ponders Mercutio's death suffered in his behalf (III, i, 108, 109) and in the latter, as he gazes around the Capulets' tomb, he reflects regretfully on the slain Paris and asks forgiveness of his cousin Tybalt (V, iii, 101).[60] In neither, however,

59. That the joyful dream is not ironic but instead a "premonition that does come true in the ultimate happiness of the lovers' reunion beyond death" is suggested by Warren D. Smith ("Romeo's Final Dream," *MLR*, LXII [1967], 579). N. N. Holland reads the scene as indicative of Romeo's sexual arousal, but he admits that only an audience "composed entirely of psychoanalytic critics" would agree ("Romeo's Dream and the Paradox of Literary Realism," *Literature and Psychology*, XIII [1963], 100, 102).

60. Paul N. Siegel attaches great significance to this moment at which Romeo is able to love even his enemies. ("Christianity and the Religion of Love in *Romeo and Juliet*," *SQ*, XII [1961], 390).

is there significant emphasis on a sense of culpability, and there is no trace whatever of insight gained through agony and error; instead, the primary purpose of each passage is to provide the immediate motivation for an especially critical action—the furious retaliation against Tybalt, and the drinking of the potion which enables him to "shake the yoke of inauspicious stars" (V, iii, 111) from his "world-wearied flesh" (112) and gain reunion with Juliet at the tomb.

Juliet's soliloquies are consistently rhetorical. While the first three passages (II, ii, 25; 33–36; 38–49) are not soliloquies in the technical sense but rather lines spoken to herself and overheard by Romeo, the effect is privately to affirm her affection just following Romeo's initial soliloquies. She acknowledges the family enmity but claims the greater power for love, naively suggesting that Romeo can doff his name to gain her. The middle soliloquies (II, v, 1–17; III, ii, 1–33; v, 60–64) underscore her youthful agitation, as she frantically awaits the nurse's return with Romeo's plans for marriage or Romeo's arrival on his wedding night or at his leave-taking as she apprehensively calls on fickle Fortune quickly to send him back. Her seventh soliloquy (III, v, 237–44) confirms her love despite even the nurse's betrayal and her willingness to die for it unless the friar has a remedy. And her final soliloquy (IV, iii, 14–58), like Romeo's, reflects no significant awareness of a flawed and passionate love, as she concentrates instead upon the possible horrors in the tomb which could result from the friar's potion.

Soliloquies, in short, abound; but without exception they are utilized not to slice into the heart of a protagonist and reveal the conflict of a divided mind but to provoke a sympathetic rapport by signaling to the audience the integrity of the youthful romantic vows or by providing vital narrative links.[61] The most striking example is in Act II. Certainly, in the early scenes it is diffcult to take Romeo seriously as (like Lysander with the flower in *A Midsummer Night's Dream* or like Proteus in *The Two Gentlemen of Verona*) he is wrenched from

61. Shakespeare simply does not depict what Ruth Nevo asserts to be the major conflict in the play—Romeo's attempt to avoid a fight with Tybalt on the one hand and his code of honor which prompts him to avenge Mercutio's

one object of adoration to another. The spectators are presumably to see one as fatuous dotage and the other as devoted affection and to see Juliet's love at first sight as unfaltering. To be sure, there is humor in these affairs of the heart, especially in Romeo's traumatic transition. But, as we have noted, Shakespeare concentrates ten soliloquies in Act II—overwhelming the spectators with ardent statements of devotion in order to convince them of the sincerity of the young lovers.

Shakespeare also constructs foils who enhance Romeo's personality in these early acts: Mercutio he creates whole cloth, drawing the name from a rival wooer for Juliet's attention at the Capulets' ball in Brooke's poem; Tybalt he adapts from his source. Both are dead by the end of III, i (the twelfth of the twenty-four scenes of conventional editorial division); Mercutio appears in four scenes, speaking a total of 270 lines, while Tybalt appears in three scenes, speaking only thirty-six lines. Each, however, significantly affects the spectators' attitude toward Romeo. Tybalt, for example, whose importance to the plot is out of all proportion to his handful of lines, is living testimony to the hatred sparked by the feud. Testy, irascible, and ever primed for a fight, he is what Coleridge (II, 96) has called "a man abandoned to his passions." That is, he seeks no cause for hating the Montagues, but simply delights in the opportunity. And, it would appear, he has a particular aversion to Romeo—perhaps because Romeo is the only Montague recognized at the ball, perhaps because he has the audacity to converse with Capulet's daughter, perhaps even because he has been particularly active in the previous fracases which roaming groups must have experienced in Verona. In any event, Tybalt's every line is angry and vicious, peppered with "draw," "hate," "coward," "strike," and "villain" (the most frequently used word in his vocabulary). Mercutio best captures his character in labeling him the Prince of Cats who "fights as you sing pricksong—keeps time, distance, and proportion; . . . the very butcher of a silk button, a duellist, a duellist" (II, iv, 20–22, 23–24). Certainly, by comparison Romeo's dotage for Rosaline is far less objectionable to the spectators than the bellicosity of

---

death on the other ("Tragic Form in *Romeo and Juliet*," *SEL*, IX [1969], 245–46); see also John Lawlor, *"Romeo and Juliet,"* in *Early Shakespeare*, p. 138.

Tybalt, whose determination to provoke a fight forces them virtually
to leap to uncritical—if unexamined—support of Romeo's subsequent
love for Juliet.

Shakespeare exercises further control upon the spectators' attitude
through the creation of Mercutio, whose mockery is as incessant as
his doubles entendres.[62] At one moment, he advises Romeo to play
the field and not to get emotionally attached, to prick love for
pricking:

> Give me a case to put my visage in.
> A visor for a visor! what care I
> What curious eye doth quote deformities?
>
> (I, iv, 29–31)

At another, he conjures Romeo by Rosaline's "fine foot, straight leg,
and quivering thigh, / And the demesnes that there adjacent lie" (II,
i, 19–20), claiming not that he wishes to "raise a spirit in his mistress'
circle" (24) but only "to raise up him" (29). A man like Romeo,
who is "for the numbers that Petrarch flowed in" (II, iv, 38–39), is
constrained to "bow in the hams" (52), to "hit" the "very pink of
courtesy" (54, 56). Mercutio's bawdiness halted by Benvolio, he
retorts that he already "was come to the whole depth of [his] tale,
and meant indeed to occupy the argument no longer" (93–94). But
the nurse enters and is subjected to his description of the time of day,
that the "bawdy hand of the dial is now upon the prick of noon"
(106–7), and his suggestive serenade about "an old hare hoar)
(126). There may well be more than an ounce of truth in Dryden's
assertion that Shakespeare had to kill Mercutio in the third act or be
killed by him; certainly the jester's wit and his general mockery of
romance do work at cross-purposes with the high seriousness of the
theme. But structurally his purpose has been served; his light banter
provokes an atmosphere of levity which contributes to the spectators'

62. Surely he is not—as Charlton would have it—the one man who "might
have understood the depth of Romeo's love for Juliet" (p. 62). To the contrary, he has no "real comprehension of or use for the spiritual element in
romantic love" (Duthie, p. xxxvii); to him, "swords are real, and the power
of love is not" (John Vyvyan, *Shakespeare and the Rose of Love* [London:
Chatto and Windus, 1960], p. 169). H. McArthur sees him as a device for

approval of Romeo's romance and, combined with the function of the chorus, the early soliloquies, and the characterization of Tybalt, helps Shakespeare to control the perspective in the first half of the play.

Although the chorus and both foils are gone by III, i, the play is also structured in the final acts to provoke maximum sympathy for the lovers as their tragedy culminates. Regardless of the extent of their guilt to the point of Tybalt's death, both Romeo and Juliet—in the action which follows—confront reversals in companionship, creating dilemmas in the face of which they are woefully inept. Juliet, for instance, sees her emotional and physical support methodically stripped away. Her first shock comes from her father. Capulet, in his initial appearances, has been characterized by temperance and moderation: in I, ii he urges Paris to be patient and to endeavor personally to win Juliet's love; in I, v he firmly insists that Tybalt restrain his anger against Romeo and keep the peace; in III, i, with an amazing gesture of compassion and reconciliation, he encourages the prince not to seek Romeo's life in exchange for Tybalt's since Mercutio was the Montague's friend.[63] Certainly, the spectators as well as the daughter react with amazement and shock as, in III, iv, he peremptorily announces her wedding date to Paris and then, in the following scene, reacts with awesome fury to her opposition. Next, the nurse betrays Juliet by capitulating to the father's demand that Juliet wed the County Paris.[64] Romeo is betrayed; Paris is available; the father is insistent: to the nurse the only solution, spoken she claims from her soul, is for Juliet to be "happy in this second match" (III, v, 224). Finally, the friar's desertion in the tomb leaves Juliet totally without support, and the spectators cannot deny that the steadfast devotion to Romeo that prompts her to join him in death excels any fidelity which she has found outside the tomb.

---

prefiguring Romeo's destruction ("Romeo's Loquacious Friend," *SQ*, X [1959], 44). Similarly, see Raymond V. Utterback, "The Death of Mercutio," *SQ*, XXIV (1973), 116.

63. It is not necessary to assume, as most editors do, following Q4, that the speech (11. 186–88) must be assigned to old Montague.

64. Charles Williams (*The English Poetic Mind* [Oxford: Clarendon Press, 1932], p. 25) brands her apostasy the first "appearance of spiritual evil"

Romeo's predicament is even more pathetic. He leaves Juliet and Verona assured that Friar Lawrence will

> find a time
> To blaze [his] marriage, reconcile [his] friends,
> Beg pardon of the Prince, and call [him] back.
> (III, iii, 150–52)

The friar promises further to seek out Romeo's man and send him news from time to time. Never again, though, does Romeo have conversation with Juliet, the friar, or any of his kin; and he is utterly oblivious of the events that transpire after his banishment. The only news he receives is that Juliet is dead, and, with no message from the friar, he can only presume he has been deserted. His suicide in the tomb—provoked by mistaken assumptions of Juliet's death and providing no redeeming qualities of insight or self-analysis—is ultimately the most painful moment for the spectators.

Shakespeare, then, methodically constructs and maintains a sympathetic portrayal of Romeo and Juliet. The spectator is by no means blind to the excesses of passionate love, and on brief occasions both principals anticipate the worst possible consequences; but, with no internal struggle and with other figures manipulated to reflect the admirable characteristics of the young lovers, the structure of the play literally does not permit the audience to develop a critical posture. Instead, the greater antipathy is directed against what at one moment is branded as destiny and at another is depicted as a deadly feud. In the final analysis the two are synonymous; the destructive force that converges on them is no malevolent or sadistic deity but an all-too-human hatred and envy which divides society into two armed camps admitting no commerce of affection.

More specifically, the terms "star-crossed lovers," "death-marked love," and "misadventured piteous overthrows" in the Prologue must be seen in the context that defines them. Numerous surrounding ref-

---

in the play. Martin Stephens has recently described the pattern of her increasingly misleading advice which here culminates in her rejection as confidante ("Juliet's Nurse: Love's Herald," *PLL*, II [1966], 205).

erences clearly describe the fate which limits human freedom in this society as the rivalry of two rich families:[65] "two households," "alike in dignity," "ancient grudge," "new mutiny," "civil blood," "civil hands," "fatal loins of these two foes," "parents' strife," "parents' rage." And the feud is the subject of the first 118 lines of Act 1 as the struggle involves, in turn, the servants, the youth, the aged, and the prince in a mounting crescendo of senseless terror. The servants fight from sheer habit, not from cause, asserting that this quarrel between their masters and the servants is "all one" to them. They know nothing of motive and are not concerned to know, questioning only whether the law is "of our side" in provoking an altercation. Nor is young Tybalt capable of greater reflection; to him it is sufficient that swords are drawn and that he hates all Montagues. Cruel humor is added as old Montague and old Capulet, each restrained by his wife, hobble on stage determined to leap into the fray. The prince denounces the lot of them as "rebellious subjects, enemies to peace" (i, 79), "beasts" (81) whose "pernicious rage" (82) and "cank'red hate" (193) has bred "civil brawls" from an "airy word" (87).

Verona's fate, in brief, is the human condition. To be sure, references to destiny in the play suggest a strong confluence of malignant coincidences and no effort of human logic can minimize the sense of an ominous design that seems to control the lives of the young protagonists. At the same time, each incident is clearly seen as the fruit not of the stars but of human hatred. Romeo obviously steers his own course to the Capulets' ball, and the "consequence . . . hanging in the stars" (I, iv, 107) is what he might well expect from his discovery in the enemy fold. A later day's "black fate" (III, i, 117) makes him "fortune's fool" (134) because Tybalt's insistence on upholding the

65. Romeo and Juliet are victims of the evil of Verona, not because they share in it, but because they "represent an opposite principle" (G. A. Bonnard, "Romeo and Juliet: A Possible Significance," RES, II [1951], 325). Their "fate" is the "inappeasible hatred of the two houses" (H. T. Rötscher, Romeo and Juliet Analyzed, in Variorum, p. 453). G. M. Matthews observes that the feud is "an 'expanded metaphor' for the conflict in Elizabethan sex-relations," reflecting the antagonisms toward arranged marriage ("Sex and the Sonnet," Essays in Criticism, II [1951], 134). To Herbert Howarth, the issue reflects the "Elizabethan apprehension of a city divided against itself" (The Tiger's Heart [New York: Oxford Univ. Press, 1970], p. 32).

wronged honor of the Capulets forces him into a fight from which there is no escape short of death. And what Romeo sees as inauspicious stars which he defies and whose yoke he shakes in the final act, the spectators see in large part as the pitiful results of old Capulet's insistence on a marriage of economic and aristocratic convenience for his daughter; significantly, Prince Escalus' final judgment falls not upon the immoderate lovers who lie dead before him but upon the families. The spectators, in the final analysis, then, are prone to condemn cruel circumstance rather than the dead lovers, to exclaim with Mercutio "a plague o' both your houses."[66]

All things considered, *Romeo and Juliet* is something of an anomaly among Shakespeare's early plays, in which the action normally tends to center on a single individual who asserts himself and his values against society. In most cases this character is possessed of an ambition, either noble or awesome or both, which is at least partially responsible for his position of leadership and social responsibility. But this ambition is also stained with a moral flaw which, if only loosely in the early plays, is responsible for his disasters. The horrendous sufferings of Titus, for example, are the direct consequences of his enormous pride, even though he fails to realize it. While Shakespeare's early protagonists never weigh the moral consequences prior to their actions, they do—with the exception of Titus—experience sporadic moments of internal struggle which the spectators view through soliloquy and aside. Above all, each is clearly the dominant force in a conflict that his personality and his choices determine.

The plot of *Romeo and Juliet* involves no such protagonist. No figure grows through tragedy to a greater knowledge either of his own nature or the nature of society. One can argue, to be sure, that Romeo

---

66. According to Irving Ribner, "We are made to see that through the suffering of individuals the social order is cleansed of evil" (*Patterns*, p. 34), and L. E. Bowling ("The Thematic Framework of *Romeo and Juliet*," *PMLA*, LXIV [1949], 220) speaks of the Montagues and Capulets as "growing up . . . in their attitudes toward love and hate." Yet, Shakespeare fails to be totally convincing in this respect. As Marvin Spevack points out, this tragedy is "in some ways more severe than anything else Shakespeare was to write. . . . A whole generation—and the possibility of generation—is wiped out" (ed. *Romeo and Juliet* [Dubuque: Brown, 1970] p. xv).

grows in love—from his infatuation with Rosaline to his pure devotion to Juliet, from his bawdy jests with Mercutio to his sincere vows with Juliet, from his frenzied despair at the thought of banishment from her to his calm determination in the tomb to join her in death. So also, one can maintain that Juliet is the immature youth as she impatiently awaits the nurse's return with news from her new-found lover, the harried youngster as she must confront the sudden report of Tybalt's death at Romeo's hands, the distracted child in the face of her father's marital mandate, but the mature and resolute woman as she agrees to drink the friar's potion and later as she refuses to leave her dead lover's side. In this sheer determination, then, they do indeed become more intense. But so convincingly has the sincerity of their love been established through the soliloquies in Act II that there is a sense, not of growth, but of constant reaffirmation of the affection sworn at the Capulets' ball.[67] Furthermore, growth in determination and growth in insight are not synonymous, and Shakespeare nowhere provides internal glimpses of a conflict of values between Romeo's personal devotion to Juliet on the one hand and family and social responsibilities on the other or of a realization of the fundamental ambivalences involved in a total dedication to romantic love. Such moments, which could have revealed the protagonist's growing awareness of the true nature of the social values and his commitment to transcend them through love whatever the price, separate this tragedy from those Shakespeare is shortly to write.

Moreover, no single figure provides the central unity of the play through the exertion of his will upon those around him; instead the only significant public force is the collective hatred that the feud represents. As a result, the basic thrust of the play is the narrative intrigue, and the characters are caught in a web not essentially of their own making. This type of story, the source of which is probably the

---

67. To claim that the lovers "come together in the flesh" with the help of the nurse, move beyond it with the help of the friar, and move beyond him in their deaths (Philip Parsons, "Shakespeare and the Mask," *Shakespeare Survey*, XVI [1963], 127) is flatly to disregard the spiritual intensity of their dialogue and their soliloquies in the second act. On the significance of the style in this play to Shakespeare's development, see R. F. Hill, "Shakespeare's Early Tragic Mode," *SQ*, IX (1958), 467.

Italian *novelle* or contemporary Italian drama, is—as Madeleine Doran observes—"on the whole more suitable for romance than for tragedy. . . . A romantic intrigue plot may by a clever turn be brought to a happy conclusion. Indeed that is the inevitable direction of this sort of tragedy, as seen in the tragi-comedies and romances of the later Jacobean and Caroline dramatists."[68] Even among such companion pieces, though, *Romeo and Juliet* strongly emphasizes innocent central characters swept to destruction by action prompted neither by themselves nor by any single human adversary. Only in the academic play *Gismonde of Salerne* (1567–1568), written by five authors from the Inner Temple, does one find a similar passive heroine who, in the face of her father's murder of her lover, takes her own life; even here, however, the authors stress the unlawful love (the guilt of Gismonde) which provokes the disaster. In Kyd's *Solyman and Perseda,* Solyman clearly emerges as the tyrant who, by murdering his rival for Perseda's love, prompts both his own death at Perseda's hands and her subsequent suicide. Certainly, in the remaining "tragic romances" —such as Marston's *The Insatiate Countesse,* in which Isabella practices both desertion and murder to satisfy her lust, or Beaumont and Fletcher's *Cupid's Revenge,* in which the old Duke Leontius dotes on the strumpet Bacha and, after marriage, permits her to scheme against the virtuous son and legitimate heir—the firm lines are drawn on the villain who instigates the intrigue and who, along with the innocent, is subsequently destroyed. In *Romeo and Juliet,* on the contrary, the lines of guilt are vaguely sketched. If it is at best only a half-truth to assert that in this play there is "neither crime nor vice of any kind to serve as a contrast to the two young lovers . . . except the fatality . . . which sets a snare for them,"[69] it is true that Shakespeare fails to make the feud a "vital and effective element in the plot";[70] by developing the spectators' unqualified sympathy for Romeo and Juliet, he forces their sympathies to "culminate in pity for the lovers" rather than in the "larger conception"—"the blindness of the elders to the

68. *Endeavors of Art* (Madison: Univ. of Wisconsin Press, 1954), pp. 132–33.

69. A. De Lamartine, *Shakespeare et son oeuvre,* in *Variorum,* p. 440.

70. J. M. Nosworthy, "The Two Angry Families of Verona," *SQ,* III (1952), 225.

consequences of their hatred until it is too late."[71] And, since there is no tragic guilt except the plague of both the houses, numerous critics are understandably led to the conclusion that the play "has pity only, no purgation by pity and terror."[72]

The structure of *The Rape of Lucrece* poses several interesting parallels. While analogies between genres obviously can be pressed only so far, the poem (almost certainly composed within a year or so of the tragedy of Verona's young lovers) does involve a tragic situation, and the factors which shape it and the nature of the consequences upon character reveal something of Shakespeare's general concept of the tragic experience at this point. For that matter, the stage was apparently never far from the poet's mind; at one point he suggests that the full impact of tragedy requires more than mere narration:

> To see sad sights moves more than hear them told,
> For that the eye interprets to the ear
> The heavy motion that it doth behold,
> When every part a part of woe doth bear.
>
> (11. 1324–27)

In any event, the causes of disaster set forth in the poem hover— as in *Romeo and Juliet*—between the personal and the impersonal. To Lucrece, on the one hand, tragedy has no apparent causal explanation. Guiltless and innocent, unless she is to be blamed for entertaining Tarquin as her husband's friend and colleague, she decries the "giddy round of Fortune's wheel" (952), the chance, the "dreadful circumstance" (1703) that has robbed her of her honor and purity. Night, Time, and Opportunity she addresses as metaphoric extensions of the conflux of events before which she was a helpless pawn. Each bears the guilt for her "cureless crime" (772, 876, 923–24, 930–31). She asserts, in brief, that only in her suicide can she be "mistress of [her] fate" (1069) and "cancel" her cruel destiny (1729).

71. H. S. Wilson, *On the Design of Shakespearean Tragedy* (Toronto: Univ. of Toronto Press, 1957), p. 29.

72. Brents Stirling, *Unity in Shakespearean Tragedy* (New York: Columbia Univ. Press, 1956), p. 17; see also D. A. Traversi, *An Approach*, p. 17; Charlton, p. 63.

Tarquin, on the other hand, provides one of the clearest pronouncements in Shakespeare that tragic action is the direct consequence of
human choice. Sensitive to the shame that a military man should be
slave to fancy and to the virtual certainty that his fleeting joy will
carry the price of a curse on his posterity, he admits that his will is
stronger than reason. Affection is his "captain" (271), desire his
"pilot" (279). His "eye" provokes a "mutiny" (426), an "uproar"
in his "veins" (427). Reiterating that with earlier counsel he has
"debated . . . in [his] soul" (498) and cognizant of the repentance
that will ensue, he commits himself to love's course: "Will is deaf
and hears no heedful friends" (495).

To be sure, Tarquin as ravisher and Lucrece as victim might quite
understandably view the act of violence from different poles. Even
so, with no controlling focus upon a single character throughout the
piece, the reader is left with more conflicting evidence than his imagination is able to reconcile effectively. More specifically, the reader
sees the events leading to the rape only through Tarquin's thoughts,
the subsequent events exclusively through Lucrece, her husband, and
his friends. Given the emphasis on self-will in the first half of the
poem, the readers are not likely to agree with Lucrece that all is the
result of crass destiny in which the individual plays no determining
role; nor is there any real indication that imprudence in her entertainment of a young man during her husband's absence has prompted the
lustful response. One perhaps might as easily lay the blame on Col-
latine for boasting in Tarquin's tent of his wife's matchless beauty,
though again there is no meaningful development of this possibility.
Certainly most readers accept the responsibility which Tarquin so
readily assumes, probably at the same time experiencing some degree
of sympathy for him as a consequence of his prolonged internal struggle. Yet, except as an object of Lucrece's vengeance, they never read
of him following the rape. Thus, the agonies of conscience and the
consequences of fear which they are led to anticipate in his development form no part of the remainder of the poem beyond the lustful
moment.

In effect, the structure of the poem reflects apprentice qualities
similar to those of the early tragedies. Both principals, indeed, are

powerfully drawn. Tarquin, for example, in the first half of the poem is an intensively introspective individual; although limited in development, he appears to be as painfully cognizant of his failures as Richard II and far more sensitive to human values than Richard III. Lucrece, in the second half, projects the kind of character most effectively realized later in Brutus. Suffering, while sincere enough, provokes a sense of self-righteousness that seems to preclude the possibility of meaningful insight and self-examination.

Neither character, however, furnishes a perspective that effectively relates the total action of the poem, and it is in this respect that the structural similarity with *Romeo and Juliet* is most significant. In the drama, as well, the experience of no single character provides a convincing rationale for the profound suffering and waste. Nobody, in fact, can fit all the pieces together—Romeo is oblivious of the events in Verona after Act III; Juliet is unaware of Romeo's agonizing reflections in Mantua, even of the actual nature of his suicide in dedication to her; those remaining alive when it is all over have access to the facts, but they have no knowledge of the emotional intensity of the lovers' commitments.[73] Only the spectators, in other words, have a full view of the tragedy. And, in the final analysis, this perspective involves a double vision in which the disparity is too great between their comprehension and that of the protagonists.

The significant feature of *Romeo and Juliet,* in the final analysis, is the strong bond of sympathy which Shakespeare establishes between the spectators and the protagonists. One must readily admit that, in comparison with his greatest drama, the play is seriously flawed. The protagonists suffer the consequences of tragedy rather than acting as its causal center, and neither principal possesses sufficient knowledge of the total pattern of events to provide an effective and coherent perspective; certainly, too, the young lovers are inchoate as tragic characters, without sufficient recognition of flaw or passion to create the internal ambivalence that comes to be a hallmark of Shakespeare's mature work. Nevertheless, through the foils, the characters who betray the principals' trust, and the carefully placed solilo-

73. On the sheer bewilderment of those left alive in the final lines, see Bertrand Evans, "The Brevity of Friar Lawrence," *PMLA*, LXV (1950), 850.

quies, Shakespeare creates the most engaging and sympathetic characters of his early tragedies. Far more so than in *Titus* or in *Richard
III,* these structural devices lead the spectators genuinely to care about
the central figures, their suffering, and their fate. It remains, then, for
Shakespeare to apply these skills in Brutus and in Hamlet to a depiction of the tragic experience within the protagonist, an experience
in which man clearly exercises a major degree of responsibility for
his own destiny.

III

THE PRIVATE DIMENSIONS OF TRAGEDY:
JULIUS CAESAR, HAMLET, OTHELLO

The writing of *Julius Caesar,* which to Granville-Barker is the "gate-
way through which Shakespeare passed"[1] to the writing of his greatest
plays, reveals a major advancement in the delineation of the tragic
process. In *Richard III*, as we have noted, numerous soliloquies force
the spectators to share the perilous joys of the Yorkist king's rise to
power even as they react with horror to the bloodletting and judge
him morally through the perspective of Margaret's curses and the
Tudor myth. Success in convincing the spectators of Richard's turbulence of soul is limited, however; and, for the most part, they view
him with detachment, as a villain in the role of protagonist. Hence
the tragic experience is aborted, though the careful concern for the
relationship between the audience and the character is clearly registered. In both *Richard II* and *Romeo and Juliet*, this concern leads
Shakespeare to generate the spectators' interest in the protagonist and
control their attitude toward him essentially from the outside; the
focus is on the central figure, to be sure, but we view his personal
flaws and his tension largely through the surrounding characters. In
the first, Shakespeare juxtaposes scenes emphasizing Richard's sensitivity and his religious sanctions as king with scenes revealing his
criminal abuses of the royal prerogative. Thus, the audience is in a

---

1. *Prefaces to Shakespeare* (Princeton: Princeton Univ. Press, 1946), II,
160. While the play reflects the "methods and insights" of the histories, it also
"anticipates . . . the distinctive features of the plays which follow" (Moody E.
Prior, "The Search for a Hero in *Julius Caesar*," *Renaissance Drama*, II
[1969], 100). Brutus may die recognizing the irony of man's inability to
control his fate (Myron Taylor, "Shakespeare's *Julius Caesar* and the Irony
of History," *SQ*, XXIV [1973], 307), but the play hardly depicts history as
a cruel mechanism (R. H. Yoder, "History and Histories in *Julius Caesar*,"
SQ, XXIV [1973], 315). Brutus, as J. Leeds Barroll observes, cannot comprehend the complexities of the external political realities "through the mental
persona which he adopts" (*Artificial Persons: The Formation of Character in
the Tragedies of Shakespeare* [Columbia: Univ. of South Carolina Press,
1974] p. 14).

position to perceive, albeit externally, the tragic dilemma of a man of potential merit destroyed by his inability to meet the demands of his position, and to a degree they are provoked to suffer with him at the same moment they judge him. So also, with familial hatred as a vague but powerful antagonist in *Romeo and Juliet*, a situation which mutes the spectators' judgment on the passionate nature of youthful affection, the audience is again encouraged to sympathize with the lovers— in this instance largely by emphasis on the external forces that block their happiness and render pitifully inevitable their ultimate destruction.

Building on the techniques employed in these early plays, Shakespeare in *Julius Caesar* for the first time effectively combines the external pointers with the devices of internalization to produce a perspective inviting rich emotional rapport simultaneous with objective judgment. There are difficulties, to be sure. For one thing, on occasion the focus is blurred.[2] The dominant interest unquestionably is Brutus, who as a result of a naive idealism which blinds him to his own egotistical nature is manipulated in the first half of the play by Cassius and in the later acts by Mark Antony.[3] Yet there are moments —such as the passages depicting Caesar's defiance of danger in Act II, or Antony's apparent heart-rending lamentations over Caesar's body

2. Several critics see the effect as deliberate. This "experiment in point of view, intended to reveal the limitations of human knowledge" (Rene Fortin, "*Julius Caesar:* An Experiment in Point of View," *SQ*, XIX [1968], 322), operates on the basis of "suspended judgment" (Adrien Bonjour, *The Structure of Julius Caesar* [Liverpool: Liverpool Univ. Press, 1958], p. 3). The "divided, complex, and often ambiguous response" (Ernest Schanzer, "The Problem of *Julius Caesar*," *SQ*, VI [1955], 299) creates problems of interpretation which Shakespeare "did not intend . . . to be resolved" (Mildred H. Hartsock, "The Complexity of *Julius Caesar*," *PMLA*, LXXXI [1966], 58).

3. Brutus is a "reformer . . . without a cause or motive" (E. E. Stoll, *Shakespeare Studies* [New York: Macmillan, 1927], p. 110); "pompous, opinionated, and self-righteous" (T. S. Dorsch, ed., *Julius Caesar* [London: Methuen, 1955], p. xxxix), an "intellectually limited do-gooder" (W. R. Bowden, "The Mind of Brutus," *SQ*, XVII [1966], 67), he attempts to operate within "the closed circle of his own integrity" (D. A. Stauffer, *Shakespeare's World of Images* [Bloomington: Indiana Univ. Press, 1949], p. 115). Brutus' vision is necessarily limited by the Christian concept of Roman history (J. L. Simmons, *Shakespeare's Pagan World* [Charlottesville: Univ. Press of Virginia, 1973], p. 14).

in Act III, or Cassius' conflicting emotions when he is forced to swallow his pride in Act IV—which tend to dilute the spectators' interest by diverting their attention from the evolving tragedy of Brutus. For another thing, there is still no anagnorisis. Indeed, following Caesar's assassination, sympathy for Brutus is manipulated purely by external methods in a manner quite similar to that of *Richard II.*

The true indication of the nature of Shakespeare's maturing tragic artistry, however, is in the first half of the play. Through Cassius, Caesar, the tribunes, and Portia, he both projects the spectators' sympathy strongly upon the central character and also provides a measure by which to judge Brutus' fatal flaw.[4] And, for the first time, he makes massive use of the devices of internalization, with eight characters delivering thirteen soliloquies and four asides totaling one hundred fifty-four lines. Again several of the speeches are purely expositional. In Brutus, however, Shakespeare creates the first protagonist with whom the spectators achieve a carefully controlled yet profoundly absorbing emotional identification; through glimpses into his spiritual struggle they share his agony as well as trace the inner corrosion that leads to his ultimate commitment to destructive passion.

Cassius is the primary figure through whom Shakespeare establishes this perspective of double vision. In the first half of the play the spectators see him as a man bent on personal vengeance. "Resentment raised to the status of a social cause,"[5] he is concerned not with the

4. The "liberal intellectual in a world of *Realpolitik*" (David Daiches, *Literary Essays* [London: Oliver and Boyd, 1956], p. 3), Brutus is trapped "between political necessity and normal human feeling" (D. A. Traversi, *An Approach to Shakespeare* [New York: Doubleday, 1956], p. 214). He is "ineffectual" (John Palmer, *Political Characters of Shakespeare* [London: Macmillan, 1945], p. 1), caught between his "loyalty to the traditions . . . of the republic on the one hand and loyalty to his friend and benefactor on the other" (Peter Alexander, *Introductions to Shakespeare* [London: Collins, 1964], p. 157), and lapsing at moments "into Machiavellianism" (T. J. B. Spencer, *Shakespeare: The Roman Plays* [London: Longmans, Green, 1963], p. 25) inevitable to such a cultural elitist (Marvin L. Vawter, " 'Division 'Tween our Souls': Shakespeare's Stoic Brutus," *Shakespeare Studies,* VII [1974], 192); see also Ruth M. Levitsky, "The Elements Were So Mixed . . . ," *PMLA,* LXXXVIII (1973), 240–45.

5. Margaret Webster, *Shakespeare Without Tears* (New York: McGraw-Hill, 1947), p. 156. His anger arises, not from the fact that "old civic ideals

protection of Rome's civil liberties but with the gratification of his petty and spiteful hatred of the man Caesar. Equally significant, he is a realistic politician who is not above the use of trickery and deceit to achieve his goals. Above all, he is a clever judge of human nature; and, while he seems to have a genuine admiration for Marcus Brutus' noble qualities, he also perceives the manner by which such self-conscious integrity can be manipulated to serve a baser design. Hence, as he methodically twists Brutus to his own selfish ends, the spectators are forced to realize how gullible idealism is when not grounded in a fundamental understanding of human nature and how dangerous when the idealist himself is unaware of the baser aspects of his own nature that lie just below the surface of the brilliant rhetoric and the selfless goals.[6]

In other words, as his motives become clear, Cassius underscores both the best and the worst in the protagonist. And he pinpoints these polar qualities in the opening scenes, thereby preparing the spectators for the ambiguous experience of both sharing and judging during Brutus' soliloquies. Appropriately, as Cassius broaches the conversation about Caesar's return to the city in triumph, Brutus' pride is the point of entry. The conspirator's main concern is to turn Brutus' "hidden worthiness" into his "eye" (I, ii, 57) and to assure him that many of the noblest Romans, groaning under the oppression of the age, have wished that noble Brutus could see clearly his own merits. Since Brutus admits that one can see himself but by reflection—in itself perhaps an indication of a dangerous tendency indiscriminately to read his worth through the evaluation of others—Cassius will be

> your glass,
> Will modestly discover to yourself
> That of yourself which you yet know not of.
>   (I, iii, 68–70)

. . . should be set at nought," but from chagrin that "he personally should be an underling" (E. K. Chambers, *Shakespeare: A Survey* [London, Sidgwick and Jackson, 1925], p. 152).

6. Francis Fergusson writes that there "is really no 'hero'" (*Shakespeare: The Pattern in his Carpet* [New York: Delacorte, 1970], p. 181). "We are meant to accept both sides as true to life and to modulate from approval to

Admittedly, Cassius has not planted in Brutus the seeds of suspicion against Caesar; Brutus readily acknowledges that he is vexed of late with passions proper for himself alone to know, and a few moments later he admits that he already knows what Cassius would counsel. But that Cassius is finding in pride the fertile ground to nourish the seeds is obvious when Brutus—naively equating Caesar's proffered kingship with loss of honor—avers that, since he loves honor more than he fears death, he will put himself in the hands of the gods. Cassius methodically hammers on the physical infirmities of this Caesar who—and note how subtly he has shifted tenses—has now become a god. Describing the moment when Caesar boastfully provoked a swimming match only to have to call for help lest he drown and the occasion of a fever in Spain which caused him to shake and groan, Cassius berates this "man of such a feeble temper" (129) who would "bear the palm alone" (131). Again he drives the point home upon the pride of Brutus, whose name is as fair: "What should be in that 'Caesar'? / Why should that name be sounded more than yours?" (142–43). With cunning audacity he implies that Brutus lacks the honor of his ancestors:

> Men at some time are masters of their fates.
> The fault, dear Brutus, is not in our stars,
> But in ourselves. . . .
> There was a Brutus once that would have brooked
> Th' eternal devil to keep his state in Rome
> As easily as a king.
> (I, ii, 139–41, 159–61)

The spectators' suspicions of Cassius' ulterior motives are confirmed in his soliloquy at the conclusion of the scene in which, as D. A. Traversi observes, he signals his conviction that even the noblest of men may be perverted to a base end.[7] He delights in the fact that Brutus' "honorable mettle may be wrought / From that it is dispos'd" (306–

---

disapproval" (Geoffrey Bullough, *Narrative and Dramatic Sources of Shakespeare* [London: Columbia Univ. Press, 1964], V, 57).

7. *Shakespeare: The Roman Plays* (Stanford: Stanford Univ. Press, 1963), p. 29.

7) and determines to feed him false reports concerning the "great opinion" that "Rome holds of his name" (315–16). His personal malice is strongest in his admission that, were he loved of Caesar, he would not be so easily deceived by flattery (311–12). Ironically, Caesar himself a few lines earlier has provided a signal clue to Cassius' nature in describing him as morbidly spiteful and jealous, a man who can never be content so long as he beholds one greater than himself. In the following scene the charges against Caesar grow bolder as he works frenetically with Casca and Cinna to generate the enthusiasm vital to the insurrection. Again Caesar's absolute power he assumes as an accomplished fact in his charges that they are governed with their mothers' spirits; "Our yoke and sufferance show us womanish" (iii, 83–84). The Romans "are but sheep" (105), "hinds" (106), "trash" (108), "offal" (109) to follow "so vile a thing as Caesar" (111). His trump card is the proclamation that Brutus, "three parts theirs already," will yield himself entirely during their next encounter. His concern now is not Brutus' noble honor but their "great need of him" (161), whose worth, as Casca observes, "like richest alchemy," will change all to "virtue and to worthiness" (159–60).

In drawing Brutus to his moment of violence, then, Cassius functions as an external pointer whose devious manipulations and clearly selfish values provoke sympathy from the spectators for Brutus as the unwitting victim. At the same time, the subtle revelations of pride as Brutus' true motive undermine the asseverations of honor, forcing them to sit in judgment on his participation. Portia, who appears in two scenes, serves a similar function. She would be acquainted with the cause of grief which has forced him from his bed, covered his face with "ungentle looks" (II, i, 242), and provoked him to discourtesy. She would have him explain the visit of the six or seven men who hid their faces even from darkness. Once knowledgeable of their plan, she prays that the heavens will speed him in his enterprise; fearful for his safety on the appointed morning, she frantically sends Lucius to observe whether he is well and nervously questions a soothsayer about events at the Capitol. At the same time she draws sympathy for her husband through such concerns for his health, however, she also reinforces the spectators' condemnation of the conspiracy through her charge that Brutus has some "sick offense" within his mind (268). An obsession which will let him neither eat nor talk nor sleep, it has sorely affected his entire condition.

Caesar, too, is apparently a character through whom Shakespeare intends the double vision to be grounded. Certainly his pride is insufferable, and the spectators on occasion cannot avoid sympathy with Brutus' aversion to Caesar's apparent desire for absolute power.[8] The fate of Marullus and Flavius attests, by Casca's implication at least, to his political ruthlessness. In the initial scene they berate the citizens for rejoicing in Caesar's civil victory over Pompey; these "blocks . . . stones, . . . worse than senseless things" (35)[9] who decorate the "images" with "Caesar's trophies" (68–69) fail to realize, the tribunes assert, that he desires to "soar above the view of men" and keep them all in "servile fearfulness" (74–75). The two are never heard

8. Extreme views brand him a "piece of puff-paste" (H. N. Hudson, *Shakespeare: His Life, Art, and Characters* [Boston, 1872],II, 224), a "Roman Tamburlaine" and "monstrous tyrant" (J. D. Wilson, ed., *Julius Caesar* [Cambridge: Cambridge Univ. Press, 1949], p. xxv), a "silly braggart" (G. B. Shaw, *Shaw on Shakespeare*, ed. Edwin Wilson [New York: Dutton, 1961], p. 110). To the contrary, one need not quibble with L. L. Schucking's assertion that Caesar "is meant to possess dignity [and] self esteem" (*Character Problems in Shakespeare's Plays* [New York: Holt, 1922], p. 39); after all, the "strength of his character is seen in the impression he makes upon forceful and strong men" (R. G. Moulton, *Shakespeare as a Dramatic Artist* [Oxford, 1893], p. 176). And, ironically, Shakespeare will make it "abundantly clear that the rule of the master-mind is the only admissible solution to the problem of the time" (M. W. MacCallum, *Shakespeare's Roman Plays and Their Background* [London: Macmillan, 1910], p. 214). But Shakespeare— as G. G. Gervinus aptly observes—had to "present that view of him which gave a reason for the conspiracy" (*Shakespeare Commentaries*, trans, F. E. Bunnett [London: 1863], p. 719)—hence the emphasis on Caesar's "temerity [which] gives the conspirators their final provocation" (G. A. Starr, "Caesar's Just Cause," *SQ*, XVII [1966], 77) and on his supreme overconfidence, "a character flaw invented by Shakespeare to account for his vulnerability to the conspirators' plot" (D. L. Peterson, "Wisdom Consumed in Confidence: An Examination of Shakespeare's *Julius Caesar*," *SQ*, XVI [1965], 20).

9. As Northrop Frye observes, the people "represent nothing but a potentiality of the response to leadership" (*Fools of Time* [Toronto: Toronto Univ. Press, 1965], p. 18). Their shouts heard offstage and ambiguous in intent are "a good example of presentational images that are not visual" (Maurice Charney, *Shakespeare's Roman Plays* [Cambridge, Mass.: Harvard Univ. Press, 1961], p. 68.

from again; within one scene they are put to silence and, along with them, all such overt opposition to the Roman conqueror. With mounting intensity as his assassination approaches, Caesar's "wisdom . . . consumed in confidence" (II, ii, 49) is calculated to provoke the audience's disdain. In his opening lines, for example, he haughtily brushes aside the soothsayer's warning to beware the ides of March, peremptorily branding him a dreamer and refusing to ask the questions which normal curiosity—not fear—would prompt. With similar fanaticism he later brushes aside his own premonitions about Cassius, informing Brutus that he would rather explain what is to be feared than what he in fact fears; "for always I am Caesar" (212). So also, proclaiming to Calpurnia that he "shall forth" (II, ii, 10) despite the portentous events of the previous night, he histrionically proclaims that he is more dangerous than danger itself:

> The things that threatened me
> Ne'er looked but on my back; when they shall see
> The face of Caesar, they are vanished.
> (II, ii, 10–12)

Eagerly he listens to Decius Brutus' false report that the senators have today decided to give a crown to mighty Caesar, and he reacts instantly to the insinuation that his failure to appear might be construed as fear. At the Capitol his pride reaches its most repulsive heights. After once more flouting the soothsayer and the sophist, both of whom attempt to warn him further of impending disaster, he dismisses with incredible pomposity the suit to repeal the banishment of Publius Cimber. His blood cannot be fired like that of ordinary men; Caesar does no wrong; as "constant as the Northern Star" (III, i, 60), as firm as Olympus itself, he "unassailable holds on his rank, / Unshaked of motion" (69–70).

Caesar, in sum, seems at certain moments almost to invite the audience's sanction of the violence that strikes him down, especially when it is couched in terms of freedom and liberty. At other moments, however, Shakespeare inserts humanizing touches which by drawing sympathy to Caesar force the spectators to view Brutus' actions from a more sharply critical angle. His first words, for instance, reflect his desire for children as he reminds Antony to touch his wife while running the footrace of the Lupercalia and thereby shake off her sterile curse.[10] It is a passing moment, to be sure, but it establishes a significantly human quality in this man who publicly would appear so invulnerable. So also do his physical infirmities—both the deafness of his right ear and the epilepsy that seizes him in the public gathering. His three-line soliloquy in II, ii reveals a deep-seated apprehension concerning the turbulence of nature and the ominous indications of Calpurnia's dream, which he will admit only to himself. Again, the moment is brief, but the fleeting glimpse into the inner man is enough to reinforce the spectators' suspicions that the courage and confidence that he flaunts before others is but the bravura of a tormented man who has committed himself to a particular political stance. If the role is skillfully performed, the spectators have harbored such suspicions at least since his ambiguous comments about Cassius' lean and hungry look which he would fear were he not Caesar. Now the scene with his wife and with Decius Brutus becomes painful when he is pushed into a decision against his better judgment for the sake of his public image, and his heroics in the Capitol have the exaggerated ring of one who is out to convince himself as much as anyone else. At such moments Caesar's struggle is primarily with himself and his public posture; Brutus is at best only peripherally involved, and thus the spectators' attention is diverted from *his* developing tragedy. In the larger view, however, these passages encourage the spectators to condemn Brutus' conspiratorial plot, while the passages underscoring Caesar's hubris encourage them to condone it. Hence, Shakespeare presumably was by no means attempting to construct a double tragedy or to make Caesar the protagonist,[11] but to develop yet another external pointer through whom

10. Maynard Mack argues that this episode "dramatizes instantaneously the oncoming theme of the play: that a man's will is not enough" (*"Julius Caesar,"* in *Essays on the Teaching of English,* ed. E. J. Gordon and E. S. Noyes, rpt. in *Modern Shakespearean Criticism,* ed. Alvin B. Kernan [New York: Harcourt, Brace and World, 1970], p. 291).

11. Admittedly the play concerns the "process by which a new Caesar emerges from the wreckage of the conspiracy" (J. W. Velz, " 'If I were Brutus now . . .'. Role-Playing in *Julius Caesar,"* *Shakespeare Studies,* IV [1968], 152), a "tyranny of the triumvirate . . . far more terrible than those of which the conspirators could accuse Caesar" (J. E. Phillips, *The State in*

to create a powerful perspective of double vision for Brutus' dilemma.

The central feature is Brutus' spiritual struggle which the spectators are forced to share through the devices of internalization. Of the seven soliloquies and one aside, totaling seventy-three lines, only two soliloquies totaling ten lines occur after Caesar's assassination. These final soliloquies, moreover, are relatively insignificant. Framing the appearance of Caesar's ghost which appears to Brutus in his tent near Sardis, they function primarily to provide the emotional tension for the scene. In the sixth (IV, iii, 267–74), specifically, Brutus muses affectionately over the boy Lucius who has fallen asleep while performing for his master; carefully removing the instrument, he speaks almost apologetically of the good boy whom he has driven to exhaustion. This emphasis on his gentle nature does indeed provoke sympathy for Brutus at the moment his fate in effect is sealed by the "monstrous apparition" which, claiming to be his evil spirit, will see him again at Philippi. But neither here nor in the final soliloquy—in which he merely exclaims that he would talk more with the spirit— is there meaningful introspection for further revelation of the inner man.

The strength of the characterization is found in Act II, essentially in the lengthy first scene in which the audience perceives in Brutus the transformation of political idealism into the ideology of violent revolution. Actually he verbally commits himself in his first soliloquy; through the psychic struggle which then ensues, his spirit too will eventually assent.[12] In this initial statement (II, i, 10–34), prompted

---

Shakespeare's Greek and Roman Plays [New York: Columbia Univ. Press, 1940], p. 186). It is quite another thing, however, to maintain that Shakespeare "undoubtedly meant to focus interest on . . . Caesar" (Louis B. Wright, ed., *Julius Caesar* [New York: Washington Square Press, 1960], p. x), that Julius is "the real as well as the nominal protagonist" (Roy Walker, "Unto Caesar: A Review of Recent Productions," *Shakespeare Survey*, XI [1958], 132).

12. In this soliloquy his "virtue and his intellect work . . . together to produce only rationalization" (G. R. Smith, "Brutus, Virtue, and Will," *SQ*, X [1959], 373). We watch "Brutus' attempt to defend his decision before the court of his conscience" (Ernest Schanzer, *The Problem Plays of Shakespeare* [New York: Schocken, 1963], pp. 54–55). With the decision already made, Shakespeare is "directing our attention more to the nature of Brutus'

and goaded by Cassius in the earlier scenes, he observes that Caesar
must die; he must be attacked for the general good; to give him a
crown is to give him a "sting" (16); an absolute ruler forgets the
meaning of remorse; an ambitious man looking in the clouds will
scorn the "base degrees" (26) by which he made his ascent; a serpent
is best killed "in the shell" (34). Certainly at this point, however, he
is capable of separating fact from fancy, and his whole being seems
to well up in rebellion against the sophistry of his rationalization. He
admits, for example, that he knows no personal cause to spurn Caesar,
that the crown *might* "change his nature" (13), that he *may* "do
danger" with the sting (17). He admits also that he has never known
Caesar in the past to allow his reason to be swayed with affection.
Again, though, "Caesar *may*, . . . augmented, . . . run to . . . extremi-
ties" (27, 30, 31). Clearly, Brutus' case against Caesar is pitifully
weak and problematical—and no one, at this particular moment,
knows it better than he.

The second soliloquy (44–58), shifting the grounds of his reflection to himself, projects the egocentricity that will blind him to these
distinctions between what Caesar is and what he may be. Gullible victim to the messages Cassius has planted in his home, Brutus all too
willingly pieces out the implications of the plea for him to awake,
speak, strike, and redress. With a touch of smugness he recalls the
feats of his ancestors in driving Tarquin from the streets. And the
touch is but prelude to full seizure as, envisioning himself as Rome's
present savior, he pledges himself to the city and vows that she shall
receive her "full petition" at his hand (58). In the space of an incredibly few moments, then, pride has converted concern into an opportunity for heroics, and it is no longer convenient to consider
Caesar's guilt as mere possibility.

The misery and torment of Brutus' inner hell reaches its height in
the third soliloquy (61–69). Describing such agitation as "a phan-
tasma or a hideous dream" (65), he likens the struggle in the state

---

judgment, than to the issues themselves" (D. J. Palmer, "Tragic Error in
Julius Caesar," *SQ*, XXI [1970], 404).

of a man between the "Genius and the mortal instruments"—the spiritual and the physical—to an insurrection" suffered by "a little kingdom" (66, 68, 69). Similarly, in the fourth soliloquy (77–85) he is plagued by the guilt that attaches to the covert and stealthy movements of the conspirators. The plot will show its "dangerous brow" only by night, when "evils are most free" (78–79). Either by day it must find a dark cavern within which to mask its "monstrous visage" (81), or it must cloak true intent "in smiles and affability" (82). If for the moment he can manufacture the courage of desperation in the assurance that hypocrisy, skillfully practiced, is incapable of perception, certainly he has lost it in the fifth soliloquy (229–33) as—like Henry IV obsessed with a commitment inherently tainted—he laments that he is deprived of "the honey–heavy dew of slumber" (230) which comes so naturally to a mind uncharged with "figures," "fantasies," and "busy care" (231–32). In his aside, before Caesar is struck down, this hypocrisy is the focus of Brutus' particular agony; to Caesar's remark that they like friends will go together, he can only mutter in remorse that his heart aches to think upon the deception that festers behind the cloak of friendship.

In no other play does Shakespeare cluster soliloquies so thickly within a single scene, a point even more remarkable in light of the fact that this work presumably follows two tragedies in which the devices of internalization are of minimal significance. Through the juxtaposition of these frequent glimpses within the soul, which are arranged to produce a steady growth in intensity, with the external pointers, who underscore the virtuous as well as the vicious in Brutus' character, Shakespeare demonstrably is probing for ways to create a convincing perspective involving both sympathy and condemnation. In this respect the structure of Acts I and II reveals Shakespeare's maturing artistry and points directly to the powerful perspective of the tragedies to follow.

Granted, there is a general falling off in the last half of the play. Brutus' additional soliloquies, as we have noted, are insignificant, and no further substantial development occurs in his character. At the moment of Caesar's murder, Brutus' delusion is complete; both Caesar's guilt and his own right to judge this guilt are no longer questioned.[13] Hence, he expects any momentary agitation among the populace to be quickly dispelled as he assures them that there is no cause for alarm now that ambition's debt is paid. Similarly, he proclaims to Antony that his action has been provoked out of "pity to the general wrong of Rome" (III, i, 170), assuring him that the

> reasons are so full of good regard
> That were [he], Antony, the son of Caesar,
> [He] should be satisfied.   (III, i, 224–26)

So also, the conspirator—in an oration filled, in R. W. Zandvoort's words, with "euphuistic prose" markedly different from Antony's verse "for the emotions"[14]—exhorts the citizens to hear him for his cause and to believe for his honor that he rose against Caesar not because he loved Caesar less but because he loved Rome more.

This conviction that he acted on pure, altruistic grounds is never really shaken.[15] Certainly the most unpleasant evidence is provided in

13. Brutus attempts to bury his guilt in the ritualistic manner of the assassination, "ending in kneeling, by one conspirator after another until the victim is surrounded" (Brents Stirling, *Unity in Shakespearian Drama* [New York: Columbia Univ. Press, 1956], p. 48). Similarly, as Leo Kirschbaum notes, Brutus' proposal that the entire group bathe "their hands in the blood of Caesar's body . . . emphasizes the disorder in the man" ("Shakespeare's Stage Blood and its Critical Significance," *PMLA*, LXIV [1949], 524).

14. "Brutus' Forum Speech in *Julius Caesar*," *RES*, XVI (1940), 65–66.

15. Several critics insist that Brutus has gained significant insight: he "comes to see the error of his choice in his consequent suffering, and before his death renounces it" (Irving Ribner, *Patterns in Shakespearian Tragedy* [London: Methuen, 1960], p. 53); he realizes that he has erred in "assum[ing] the divine prerogative of God" (Anne Paolucci, "The Tragic Hero in *Julius Caesar*," *SQ*, XI [1960], 333); "there is resignation here, a knowledge of failure" (G. Wilson Knight, *The Imperial Theme* [Oxford: Oxford Univ. Press, 1931], p. 79). Insist as one might, however, Brutus simply never articulates such insight; nor does he ever seem to realize that Pompey and Caesar in their turn probably also conceived of themselves as "saviors of Rome" (M. N. Proser, *The Heroic Image in Five Shakespearean Tragedies* [Princeton: Princeton Univ. Press, 1965], p. 14). His final assertion that all men have been true to him reveals, as Bernard Breyer observes, a "monumental" ignorance ("A New Look at *Julius Caesar*," in *Essays in Honor of Walter Clyde Curry*, ed. R. C. Beatty *et al.* [Nashville: Vanderbilt Univ. Press, 1954], p. 167); and his claim that he will have glory by this losing day "is simply non-

Act IV in the complacent assumption of impeccability during his confrontation with Cassius, who he remarks has given him "cause to wish / Things done undone" (ii, 8–9). While he has the good sense to avoid public wrangling before the soldiers, in private he is quick to see the fault in Cassius despite the beam in his own eye. Cassius, obviously, is not blameless; no doubt he has taken bribes from the Sardians and sold his offices for gold. How insufferably illogical is Brutus, however, to condemn such practices for sustaining an army in his assertion that he is incapable of raising money by vile means, then to berate Cassius for failure to send him "certain sums of gold" (iii, 70) wherewith to pay his legions. Refusing Cassius' explanations, he invokes the gods to "dash him to pieces" (82) when he grows so covetous that he will not share with his friend. With the assertion that he is "armed so strong in honesty" that threats and charges pass by him "as the idle wind" (67–68), he scoffs at Cassius' furious rage, branding him a "slight man" (37) and a "madman" (40) who must fret till his "proud heart break" (42) and "digest the venom of his spleen," even if it splits him (47).

Admittedly, his arrogant posturing is short-lived. Within moments he is reconciled with Cassius, admitting that his friend's anger "shall have scope" (108) and apologizing for being ill-tempered with him. At Philippi, moreover, Brutus eulogizes Cassius as the "last of all the Romans" (V, iii, 99). But he is persistently oblivious to his own complicity in the whole affair; never once does he make a meaningful association of Cassius' greed and dishonesty with the probable motivations for striking down Caesar in the first place or with any possible ways in which his own better nature could have been misled by such a design. He never perceives, in other words, that he has been used by another who has hidden dishonest intent behind his courage and integrity. At other moments, too, he is blind to his own limitations.

sense" (H. M. Richmond, *Shakespeare's Political Plays* [New York: Random House, 1967], p. 216). Indeed, the "end of *Julius Caesar* shows, among other things, how unchanged Brutus is by all that has happened" (H. S. Wilson, *On The Design of Shakespearian Tragedy* [Toronto: Univ. of Toronto Press, 1957], p. 95). Essentially he recognizes only that "the end is known when the day has ended" (Norman Rabkin, "Structure, Convention, and Meaning in *Julius Caesar*," *JEGP*, LXIII [1964], 253).

Insisting on his battle strategy which in large part leads to the defeat of the entire group, for example, Brutus self-assuredly proclaims to Cassius that good reasons must "give place to better" (IV, iii, 203), the same attitude evident in his leading the conspirators to bathe their hands ritualistically in Caesar's blood or in his timely silence when the Plebeians yelled for Brutus to "be Caesar" and "be crowned" (III, ii, 50–51). At Philippi he boasts to Octavius that no death is more honorable than one on his sword. In the same scene he asserts that he "bears too great a mind" ever to "go bound to Rome" (V, i, 112, 111), and later in the battle he announces himself as his country's friend. And moments before his suicide he claims that he "shall have glory by this losing day" (V, v, 36).

Despite, then, the powerful internal development of the early acts, Brutus in the final analysis is only slightly closer to true self-knowledge at the conclusion of the play than are Shakespeare's earlier protagonists. He can muse philosophically about the uncertain end of this day's business and, since night hangs upon his eyes and his bones would rest, of the desirability of leaping in the pit himself rather than waiting to be pushed in. He can even relate the catastrophic events to the spirit of Caesar which walks abroad and turns their swords into their own entrails and which appears to convince him that his hour is come. And in his most affecting moment, as he runs on his sword, he can exclaim that he killed not Caesar with "half so good a will" (V, v, 51). Not for a moment, though, does he seem to realize the spiritual price he has paid for participation in the murder of a Caesar whose ambition *might* have produced a tyrant. In this respect, perhaps the weakest moment of the play occurs when Caesar's spirit appears to him at Sardis. Instead of a dialogue that would force Brutus to admit pride's role in his personal tragedy, there is only insipid repetition of the fact that Brutus will meet the spirit again at Philippi—a confrontation not dramatized and not centrally significant to the action of the final scenes.

By the standard of the plays to come, this static characterization of Brutus in the last acts presents a rather strange contrast with the powerfully developing figure of Acts I and II. An equally striking inconsistency is noticeable in the character of Cassius. The Cassius of

Act II is a practical and hard-headed schemer who through consummate self-control is able to manipulate Brutus by masking selfish interest behind selfless cause. The rebel leader of Act IV, on the other hand, is a more openly emotional figure who—though furious—must bite his tongue time and again to avoid total alienation from Brutus. Certainly the one character could incorporate the other—in a sense his conduct here could be simply another facet of the practical man who at this point must resort to other means to accomplish his goal— but Shakespeare nowhere provides the information and insight that would make such development effective.

Obviously this shifting personality in Cassius, along with Brutus' fundamentally static characterization in the final acts, tends to weaken the spectators' concern for the protagonist. Shakespeare, does, however, strive to maintain sympathy through external devices similar to those employed in *Richard II* and *Romeo and Juliet*. For one thing, Mark Antony emerges as a clear antagonist in Acts III through V; as his actions in the name of Caesar become more obviously perverted to his own particular purposes, the spectators are thrown back upon Brutus as the single character not consciously motivated by selfish interests at whatever price. At the point of the murder Antony, apparently sincerely grieved and shocked, threatens to drain all remaining sympathy from Brutus' cause by offering his own life beside Caesar's in this hour "so fit" for death (III, i, 153). Although he makes his political peace with the assassins, assuring them that he does not doubt their wisdom and is friends with all concerned, he also speaks affectionately over his slain leader and requests permission to

> Produce his body to the market place
> And in the pulpit, as becomes a friend,
> Speak in the order of his funeral.
>
> (III, i, 228–30)

His indignation bursts forth anew in his first soliloquy as he begs pardon from Caesar for being "meek and gentle with these butchers" (255) and prophesies that shortly "Caesar's spirit, ranging for revenge," will "let slip the dogs of war" (270, 273). Moreover, his subsequent oration, which R. M. Frye has described as the climax and turning point of the play,[16] is a masterfully subtle attack upon those who have killed in the name of honor, a word he ironically uses ten times in provoking the citizens against Brutus and the fellow conspirators.

During the funeral oration, the first suspicions of something less than honorable in Antony's intentions arise from his producing Caesar's will and implying that he dare not read it for fear of inflaming the Plebeians and making them mad. From this moment he harps increasingly on the idea of forceful retaliation. Though at one point he avers that he would not stir them to mutiny, at another he claims that Caesar's wounds should move the stones of Rome to rise up in rebellion. Suspicion turns quickly to reality as in his second soliloquy he irresponsibly observes that mischief is afoot and that he cares not what course it will take. When he hears that Brutus and Cassius are ridden like madmen through the gates of Rome, he takes an almost sinister pleasure in the way he has moved the people. Also, his own material interests are clearly registered for the first time in his observation that fortune in such a merry mood will give anything to him, Octavius, and Lepidus. The subsequent brief scene in which the mob mistakes Cinna the poet for Cinna the conspirator and hales him off to be torn to pieces graphically illustrates the mindless fury that Antony has unleashed and attests to the high stakes for which he is willing to gamble so wildly.[17]

Through the crystallization of Antony's ambitions in the fourth act Shakespeare directs strong sympathy toward Brutus, who stands in opposition to the emerging triumvirate. It becomes all too clear that

16. "Rhetoric and Poetry in *Julius Caesar*," *Quarterly Journal of Speech,* XXXVII (1951), 44.

17. The incident illustrates how "language deteriorates into the disembodied and crudely physical" when the "social order is no longer there to mediate" (Sigurd Burckhardt, "The King's Language: Shakespeare's Drama as Social Discovery," *Antioch Review*, XXI [1961], 375). According to Manfred Weidhorn, it is a reflection and mimicking of Brutus' attempt to kill the name of Caesar, not the man ("The Rose and Its Name: In *Othello, Romeo and Juliet,* and *Julius Caesar*," *TSLL*, XI [1969], 684); as an "echo to Caesar's" death, it "sets a sharp limit to any notion that Brutus and the rest of the conspirators are 'honourable' men" (Norman Holland, "The 'Cinna' and 'Cynicke' Episodes in *Julius Caesar*," *SQ*, XI [1960], 441).

Antony's rule will be far more tyrannical and arbitrary than was Caesar's. He casually pricks the names of those who must die, including that of his own nephew. And he has sheer disdain both for the general populace, whom he must find some way to cut out of Caesar's will, and for his colleague Lepidus, whom he spurns as "a slight unmeritable man" (IV, i, 12) fit only to "be taught, and trained, and bid go forth" (35); if the man is useful for the moment, he may be turned off at will; he merits being spoken of but as a "property" (40). Later reports of a bloody purge reveal that scores of senators, including Cicero, have been put to death.

Sympathy for Brutus is further reinforced by two additional external devices—the death of Portia and the comments of those surrounding Brutus at his death. The two reports of his wife's death may well be the result of textual corruption, but they do serve effectively to underscore individually his grief and his courage.[18] His sorrow is poignant as, "sick of many griefs" (IV, iii, 144), he reports to Cassius that Portia has fallen "distract" (155) and swallowed fire as a result of her desperate concern for his absence and fear for his well-being in the face of Octavius' and Antony's growing power. Soon after, Brutus accepts news of her suicide with stoic fortitude, observing that he can now endure such information patiently since he has been fortified with meditation on her death. Certainly, too, his finest qualities are emphasized by Lucilius' willingness in V, iv to permit himself to be captured in order to give his friend additional moments to achieve his escape through death. Similarly, his servants had rather

18. Brents Stirling ("*Julius Caesar* in Revision," *SQ*, XIII [1962], 187–205) has joined an eminent array of scholars—including Granville-Barker, Chambers, Harrison, Kittredge, and J. Dover Wilson—in arguing for textual revision. One commentator lays the blame on Brutus' "incipient insanity" (H. Somerville, *Madness in Shakespearian Tragedy* [London: Richards, 1929], p. 56), an argument not unlike those which see Portia as "an unstable, impulsive, dependent individual . . . inclined to self-mutilation" (M. D. Faber, "Lord Brutus' Wife: A Modern View," *Psychoanalytic Quarterly*, LII, no. 4 [1965], 110) and her swallowing fire as indicative of a "pathologically intense wish to be loved" (K. Menninger, *Man Against Himself* [New York: Harcourt, Brace, 1938], p. 56). Recently, W. B. Smith has argued that Brutus, when Messala broaches the topic of his wife's death, desperately hopes for a brief moment that the earlier report of her death has been false ("The Duplicate Revelation of Portia's Death," *SQ*, IV [1953], 154).

kill themselves than strike their master. And, in the final lines both Antony and Octavius praise Brutus as the "noblest Roman of them all" (68), one who will be honored according to his virtue with all respect and rites of burial. Antony's observation that Brutus alone joined the conspiracy not in envy of great Caesar but "in a general honest thought / And common good to all" (V, v, 71–72) appropriately describes the idealism that prompted him to action. It leaves unsaid, of course, that which could have made Brutus Shakespeare's first fully developed tragic protagonist—that Brutus himself came to understand the nature of his fellow conspirators and to acknowledge that pride misled him into association with them.

Despite the absence of these further significant glimpses of the inner man, then, Shakespeare maintains the spectators' sympathy for Brutus through the characters surrounding him. Since there is never a moment of full insight, the predominant feeling is admittedly one of tragic waste; but Shakespeare has structured his materials in an attempt to intensify the spectators' interest as the protagonist approaches his final moments at Philippi.

Shakespeare further enhances the power of Brutus' characterization by setting him in a context that provides significant philosophic depth. The stage world is not Christian, to be sure, but it is nonetheless a world in which the existence of the gods is unquestioned.[19] The play opens, for example, at the feast of Lupercal, a day on which the tribunes direct the citizens to pray to the gods to stop the plague.

19. The outer conflict "serve[s] to order the human action by relating it to some hinted outerness" (R. H. West, *Shakespeare and the Outer Mystery* [Lexington: Univ. of Kentucky Press, 1968], p. 97). Though admittedly "they do not determine anything" (H. S. Wilson, p. 55), they do "represent Shakespeare's attempt to symbolize his belief that the social order is part of the order of nature, in that a breach of nature's order will produce convulsions throughout the whole" (V. K. Whitaker, *The Mirror Up To Nature* [San Marino: Huntington Library, 1965], p. 125). The storm, which "mark[s] the fatal night" (Marvin Felheim, "The Problem of Time in *Julius Caesar*," *HLQ*, XIII [1950], 405), also reflects the "moral *dereglement* . . . when the forms of friendship are exploited for political ends" (L. C. Knights, "Shakespeare and Political Wisdom: A Note on the Personalism of *Julius Caesar*," *Sewanee Review*, LXI [1953], 47).

Caesar also takes note of the religious day and its "holy chase" (I, ii, 8). From this point, references to the Roman deities are scattered freely throughout the action. It is also a world in which the intervention is subject to diverse interpretation. The events of the night preceding the murder provide a ready example: Casca, labeled Shakespeare's "mouthpiece" by V. K. Whitaker,[20] believes, for instance, that the "tempest dropping fire" (I, iii, 10) and the strange sights such as the lion in the Capitol and men "all in fire," walking up and down the streets (25), are "portentous things" (31) to a world that has incensed the gods "to send destruction" (13); Cassius, to the contrary, would read the "strange impatience of the heavens" (61) as "fear and warning" of "some monstrous state" to come (70–71) if Caesar remains unchecked; or, at another moment, he compares the tempest to the "bloody, fiery, and most terrible" work which the conspirators have in hand (130); Calpurnia sees the tumult as a forewarning to Caesar; Caesar, as the gods' test of his courage. The spectators, however, who see beyond the limited vision of the individual, are aware of the impending disaster for Rome, for Casca, and for Brutus; and they inevitably tend to associate the turbulence with some teleological power, however inscrutable, which not unconcernedly observes the human condition.

Such association is encouraged time and again by particular events within the play that appear to involve a metaphysical dimension. The soothsayer, for example, twice attempts to warn Caesar. Artemidorus, also, presumably with divinatory insight, possesses full knowledge of the conspiracy and of those involved in it. He too intends to forewarn the victim, observing in a soliloquy that, if Caesar reads his message, he may live; "If not, the Fates with traitors do contrive" (II, iii, 15–16). Caesar disregards the advice of both men, just as he defies the priests who, unable to find the heart in their beast of sacrifice, would not have him stir from his home on the fateful day, and Calpurnia, who dreams in vivid detail that her husband's statue runs pure blood "like a fountain with an hundred spouts" (II, ii, 77).

20. *Shakespeare's Use of Learning* (San Marino, Calif.: Huntington Library, 1953), p. 246.

The appearance of Caesar's spirit, which few critics would claim to be purely hallucinatory, also betokens a level of existence beyond mortality. It is on stage on only the single occasion at Sardis, but its activity is anticipated by Antony's prophecy that the spirit will come hot from hell with Ate by his side, and further confirmed by Brutus over the dead Cassius and again just before his own suicide.

The spectators are free, of course, to deny the divinatory nature of any of these passages. None, however, fails to predict accurately, and even Cassius, who earlier scoffed at the idea of heavenly prerogative, admits at Philippi that he has changed his mind and now partly credits "things that do presage" (V, i, 78). In any event, each passage, through establishing a pattern of anticipated action, serves to intensify the spectators' interest and, at the same time, to focus their concern more firmly upon the characterization of Brutus.

Shakespeare, then, has combined the anticipatory devices with events that provide significant philosophic depth. As in the great tragedies to come, the precise nature of the supra-human power is ambiguous, and human lives are left sufficient flexibility through free will to attempt to choose the tide which, "taken at the flood, leads on to fortune" (IV, iii, 219). Whatever the degree of ambiguity, however, the sense of a moral order is firm, and Brutus' religion of honor is based upon a commitment to integrity in his relations with his fellow man and to courage in defense of his country and her republican principles. Pride indeed distorts these goals; and, as we have noted, since Brutus never fully perceives this distortion, his tragic experience is limited. The focus of the play is also uncertain; attention is diverted on occasion from Brutus to Caesar, to Mark Antony, and to Cassius. Also, admittedly, the play loses much of its impact in the last half through Shakespeare's failure to develop further the spectators' vision of the inner man and, consequently, his dependence almost entirely upon the manipulation of the external pointer to maintain their interest and sympathy. And, R. B. Heilman has noted, the tragedy misses its greatest potential because, as in *Romeo and Juliet*, "the antecedent fact is the public situation . . . and we see the private life in this context" whereas, "in the later tragedies, the commotion within the state is secondary to the turmoil within the individual, to actions that have been taken in answer to some personal need or passion."[21]

On the other hand, for the Brutus of the first two acts the subtle use of the soliloquy and of the choric comments of surrounding characters, in combination with the frame of values arising from the religious dimensions of the play, establishes a perspective that forces the spectators simultaneously to emotional commitment and to ethical judgment. In this respect, *Julius Caesar*, whatever its weaknesses, contains Shakespeare's first genuine double vision and among the early plays most clearly points in structure to his tragedies following the turn of the century.

Shakespeare, in *Hamlet*, was apparently recasting a gory old melodrama that had provoked no little attention in the 1580s. In doing so, and in placing the concepts of obligatory blood revenge within the framework of Christian ethics, he was at the same time creating a dilemma which in after years would provoke incredible intellectual ferment among literary scholars, actors, theologians, and medical doctors. Certainly the power of the drama results in part from the exciting plot in which a murderer-usurper confronts a son-avenger prompted to action by a chilling ghostly apparition. Far more significant are the structural features that focus the spectators' attention on Hamlet's inner struggle. The devices of internalization, for example, are extensive; more important, the clue to Hamlet's personality is to be found in the unique manner in which the playwright utilizes these devices to reveal the complexity of the inner man.

Throughout the early and middle tragedies, the soliloquy serves two fundamental purposes. On the one hand, it is an expository device that establishes for the spectators a pattern of anticipated action, as in Richard III's numerous declamations of the bloody steps which will constitute his journey to the throne and to infamy, or as in Iago's descriptions of the increasingly complex trap in which he intends to ensnare his commander. At the same time, it becomes increasingly significant as a philosophic device; from the brief glimpses of the

21. "To Know Himself: An Aspect of Tragic Structure," *REL*, V (1964), 40–41.

agitation that leads to a commitment to passion in Richard III, Richard II, and more extensively in Brutus, to the agony of self-knowledge gained through error and its consequent suffering in Othello, Lear, and Macbeth, it sketches the inner struggles through which Shakespearean tragedy achieves its most powerful impact. In both instances, the soliloquy clarifies the developing personality of the protagonist, reflecting a consistent quality—whether of his ambition or of his moral torment—by which the spectators are made to share the struggle and to anticipate the future events of the plot occasioned to a large degree by the decisions of such moments.

These generalities will not hold for *Hamlet*, however. To be sure, the assertion is commonplace that the essential power of *Hamlet* results directly from the spectators' descent into the Dane's "war within himself."[22] But the significant feature is not the number of soliloquies; it is the structural arrangement by which they reflect diverse, even polarized, aspects of his total personality.[23] In effect, they function in this play as a device for complication, not for clarity. Here the soliloquy does not establish a vision of a consistent personality; since the decision of one moment is forgotten or ignored in the next, the soliloquy does not project a pattern of narrative anticipation; it is not used for any conscious articulation of commitment to passion; nor—following the precipitous actions which leave a trail of human carnage from Gertrude's bedchamber to the great hall of the castle—is it used to describe any moment of insight: indeed there is no soliloquy whatever after IV, iv—Hamlet's final words prior to his sea adventure.

22. Granville-Barker, I, 31.
23. Both Madeleine Doran ("The Language of *Hamlet*," *HLQ*, XXVII [1963–64], 259–78) and Maurice Charney (*Style in Hamlet* [Princeton: Princeton Univ. Press, 1969]) refer to Hamlet's various styles which reflect the complexity of his personality. E. E. Stoll correctly notes the impossibility of labeling a single weakness the "tragic fault" (*Hamlet: An Historical and Comparative Study* [Minneapolis: Univ. of Minneapolis Press, 1919], p. 24) in a character whose "first attribute . . . is mysteriousness" (Maynard Mack, "The World of *Hamlet*," *Yale Review*, XLI [1952], 504). His values cannot be reduced to a single principle (Norman Rabkin, *Shakespeare and the Common Understanding* [New York: Free Press, 1967], p. 7). Above all, according to Harold Skulsky, Hamlet is guilty of judging everything in terms of

The protagonist's eight soliloquies, to be more specific, are clustered within fourteen of the twenty scenes of the play as marked in modern editions, from I, ii, to IV, iv. During this section of the play Hamlet does not achieve vengeance—for himself or for God; he pierces neither Gertrude's soul nor Claudius' body. He does, however, face the moments that impel him to an irrevocable stand against his uncle-king and to an impulsive attack in Gertrude's bedchamber—moments which forever dispel his glimpses of stoic dislocation from the intrigues swirling around him. When the pirates release him on Danish soil, he is no longer the contemplative man; however much one might argue the point, there is not one shred of evidence in the play that Hamlet, having been previously bent on private and personal revenge, is concerned with finding the proper public moment for the king's execution.[24] He is now simply a man determined to act. And, quite frankly, he never worries further over the moral implications of such action—at least insofar as the spectators are permitted to see within him. Granted, he is now convinced that a providential God is in His heaven once again and that a part of His providential scheme is for murder to reap its proper rewards. Under the umbrella of this conviction, he is able to accommodate everything from the proxy execution of Rosencrantz and Guildenstern to the double slaughter of Claudius with the sword and the cup. On the other hand, to insist that Hamlet following his sea-change is a man totally purged

the "literary *notatio*" ("'I Know My Course': Hamlet's Confidence," *PMLA*, LXXXIX [1974], 477).

24. On the one hand, given the conventions of revenge tragedy, we cannot assume—as do Roy Walker (*The Time is Out of Joint* [London: Dakers, 1948]) and Paul N. Siegel (*Shakespearean Tragedy and the Elizabethan Compromise* [New York: New York Univ. Press, 1957])—that the average Elizabethan would have condemned blood revenge in dramatic context any more than we would morally judge James Bond for an act of political assassination. On the other, we have no reason to assume that Hamlet, like Hieronimo, attemps to distinguish between the morality of public and private revenge, as Fredson Bowers claims ("Hamlet as Minister and Scourge," *PMLA*, LXX [1955], 740–49; "Dramatic Structure and Criticism: Plot in *Hamlet*," *SQ*, XV [1964], 217). All we can say with assurance is that he, in V, stands ready to act in either capacity "as the instrument of justice rather than the dispenser of it" (H. S. Wilson, p. 39). For a similar view see Michael Taylor, "The Conflict in *Hamlet*," *SQ*, XXII (1971), 159; and Gerard Reedy,

of passion is to disregard his essential nature in the last four scenes. He is anything but dispassionate as he leaps impulsively into Ophelia's grave and grapples with Laertes in a dispute over whose love for the maiden was greater, as he is piqued to a more than passing interest in the possibility of besting Laertes at fencing, and as in high fury he forces the king, the "incestuous, murd'rous, damnèd Dane" (V, ii, 314), to drink off the last dregs of the potion.

At the risk of oversimplification, the difference between the Hamlet of the first four acts and the Hamlet of the final act is that in Act V Hamlet is a man prepared to face the fortunes of life with both consistency and conviction; his actions move almost predictably toward the final confrontation between uncle and nephew in which, already fatally wounded, he will find the provocation to accomplish a vengeance whose moral justification he now flatly takes for granted. It is true that he has achieved this conviction far too late to save himself either from moral stain or physical harm; his rash impetuosity which resulted in Polonius' death has long since marked him for destruction.[25] But the Hamlet of the end of the final act of the play is a man of undivided mind and philosophy; his actions and his thoughts —as expressed in dialogue with Horatio and others—are of a piece.

The earlier Hamlet sorely lacks this coherence of personality; his psychic complexity results from the various aspects of his spirit, each struggling for predominance and control.[26] At one moment he is

---

"'Alexander Died': *Hamlet*, V, i, 216–40," *SQ*, XXIV (1973), 129. He with honor comes to grips with his grief (Norman Council, *When Honour's at the Stake* [London: Allen and Unwin, 1973], p. 89).

25. Hamlet has not totally "capitulated to the side of violence" (H. C. Goddard, *The Meaning of Shakespeare* [Chicago: Univ. of Chicago Press, 1951], I, 338), a "Black Priest" who—his "natural conscience" drowned— is minister of the poisoned chalice (Roy W. Battenhouse, *Shakespearean Tragedy* [Bloomington: Indiana Univ. Press, 1969], pp. 222, 250, 257–60). Instead, "blinded by pride" (G. R. Elliott, *Scourge and Minister: A Study of Hamlet* [Durham: Duke Univ. Press, 1951], p. 108), he has become "contaminated by his world" (Helen Gardner, *The Business of Criticism* [Oxford: Clarendon Press, 1959], p. 47); escape without stain is impossible from such a dilemma which, "by definition, is an all but unresolvable choice between evils" (Harry Levin, *The Question of Hamlet* [New York: Oxford Univ. Press, 1959], p. 105).

26. Numerous contemporary issues have been raised in the analyses of the

profoundly concerned with the moral implications of murder despite the apparent justification; at another he is disturbed at the possibility that the ghost (and hence the justification) be false; at another he possesses a fire-eyed determination to strike down the tyrant king whatever the ramifications spiritual or political; at another he ponders turning the knife against himself rather than facing these cruelly enigmatic issues; at another his words reflect an awesome frenzy not far short of madness. Critics on occasion have seized upon one single aspect as the real Hamlet; similarly, in order to achieve a coherence of personality, an actor may emphasize the angry young man, or the melancholy Dane, or the moralist, or the incipient madman.

The sheer enigma of the character, however, is that he is all of these faces; the Hamlet of the first four acts cannot be reduced to a single complexion without distortion and oversimplification.[27] And the key structural feature is the soliloquy. By convention the spectator must accept the character's word in soliloquy as straightforward and sincere; at such moments pretensions and façades crumble, and the

---

hero's complexity. As Theodore Spencer has noted, "In the sixteenth century each one of the interrelated orders—cosmological, political, and natural . . . was being punctured by a doubt" ("Hamlet and the Nature of Reality," *ELH*, V [1938], 258). "The play's hero stands between a Christian, medieval world of fate, and one of skeptical uncertainty" (David Bevington, ed., *Twentieth-Century Interpretations of Hamlet* [Englewood Cliffs, N. J., 1968], p. 12). The play mirrors the full intrigues of the Renaissance court (John W. Draper, *The Hamlet of Shakespeare's Audience* [Durham: Duke Univ. Press, 1939], p. 13); it reflects allegorically the political destiny of Essex, Southampton, Bothwell, and James I (Lillian Winstanley, *Hamlet and the Scottish Succession* [Cambridge: Cambridge Univ. Press, 1921], p. 172); the hero's delay as an instrument of policy is analogous to Queen Elizabeth's vacillation (William Empson, "Hamlet When New," *Sewanee Review*, LXI [1953], 17).

27. Among the myriad claims, Hamlet is a victim of melancholy (A. C. Bradley, *Shakespearean Tragedy* [London: Macmillan, 1904], pp. 100 ff.), lacking courage and resolution (the romantic view of Goethe, Hazlitt, Schlegel, and Coleridge) as a result of his "over-cultivated imagination" (Chambers, p. 182); he is unable to kill the "man who [as Gertrude's lover] shows him the repressed wishes of his own childhood realized" (Sigmund Freud, *The Interpretation of Dreams*, 4th ed. [London: Allen and Unwin, 1915], IV, 266; Ernest Jones, *Hamlet and Oedipus* [New York: Norton, 1949], p. 100); he is a woman in disguise (E. P. Vining, *The Mystery of Hamlet* [Philadelphia, 1881]).

character stands before us—and before himself—for what he is. In the soliloquies of Shakespeare's other tragic protagonists, the character realizes to some degree the nature of his predicament. He senses the mounting tensions and attempts to describe either the decisions or the course of developing events which impel him to disaster. Hamlet's soliloquies, to the contrary, provide no such guidance for the spectators. They are emotional reactions to the thoughts or events of the moment, and consequently they lack the significant continuity that would reflect a genuine comprehension of himself or of his relationship to the events that surround him.

In effect, the gap between what the spectator knows and what the protagonist knows is wide indeed. Not only are the spectators aware of the external forces that gather against the Dane, culminating with the venom-tipped rapier and the poisoned wine; they also see him more fully than he sees himself. That is, they are forced into the position of comparing and evaluating the many faces of the protagonist—something of which he himself is incapable, despite his intensively introspective nature.

The Hamlet of the first soliloquy (I, ii, 129–59) is a victim of melancholy despair. His grief is not so much for his dead father as for his living mother who has wedded again with inordinate haste—and within the family. Nor is his chief concern embarrassment for what the people may say; as indicated by his comment that he must hold his tongue, though his heart break, he recognizes that the court has been fully satisfied by the apparent political wisdom in securing the throne against outside intervention. Here, though, is the son shocked to the core by a mother whose actions he can hardly force himself to admit. He indulges in thoughts of suicide, though he acknowledges a belief in a God who condemns self-slaughter. And God's decrees he does not dare to violate. Yet he is a man obsessed with the corruption and meaninglessness of creation—the sullied (F solid, Q_2 sallied) flesh, the "weary, stale, flat, and unprofitable uses of this world" (133–34), the rank and gross things that completely possess it, the incestuous mother driven by bestial lust. The face here, in short, is sensitive, frustrated, morose, and religious—though despairing of the nature and intent of the material creation.

The fifth Soliloquy (III, i, 56–90), with its emphasis on the morality of human action, bears a kinship of sorts with the first. While here are no thoughts of mother or a corrupted universe, there is undeniably a similar frustration arising from a conviction that life in some fashion exists beyond the limits of physical mortality and that man beyond the grave must account for his actions on this side of it.[28] These comments of an explicitly Christian Hamlet obviously form the philosophic center for those who focus on the conflict of two value systems—whether one argues that a Hamlet of finer intuitive sensibilities is being corrupted by the demands of Old Testament vengeance, or that a Hamlet of stubborn will and personal vindictiveness must learn to accommodate himself to Divine Providence. In any event, the emphasis of the soliloquy is again on the face turned inward to a frustrated concern for weighing his finite decisions and actions against some infinite metaphysical standard. Hence, when he considers the relative values of stoic passivity as opposed to those of positive action, his concern is how his decision will wear beyond this mortal coil. And through such conscience, or self-interrogation, the will is puzzled and resolutions turned awry.

The fourth (II, ii, 533–91) and eighth (IV, iv, 32–66) soliloquies, on the other hand, present a strange contrast to this Hamlet convinced of values beyond his own. True enough, he questions the honesty of the ghost as a spirit from purgatory (II, ii, 584–90), thus establishing a part of his justification for testing Claudius through the play within the play. But primarily in both soliloquies he verbally lacerates himself for failure to achieve vengeance, for not killing the "remorseless, treacherous, lecherous, kindless villain!" (566). Indignantly branding himself everything from a "dull and muddy-mettled rascal" (552), to a coward who is "pigeon-livered" and lacks "gall" (563), to a "whore" (571), a "drab" (572), a "stallion" (575),

28. L. E. Orange has recently argued to the contrary. Hamlet, realizing he is being overheard, feigns madness by appearing to contemplate suicide ("Hamlet's Mad Soliloquy," *SAQ*, LXIV [1965], 65). Alex Newell, while not denying the spiritual dimension, avers that the major thrust is the Dane's formulating a plan that will force Claudius to betray himself ("The Dramatic Context and Meaning of Hamlet's 'To Be or Not To Be' Soliloquy," *PMLA*, LXXX [1965], 48).

he berates the "bestial oblivion" (IV, iv, 40) and the precious
moralizing ("ever three parts coward") that has produced his "dull
revenge" (33). No longer is he concerned with God's view; instead
he is determined "to find quarrel in a straw" when honor is at stake.

However contradictory the logic, a significant common factor in
these four soliloquies is the protagonist's relative passivity. Despite
the varying degrees of agitation, Hamlet gives the impression of
contemplating from a distance his failure to act. In contrast, on two
further occasions in the privacy of his soliloquies he is anything but
a contemplative man delayed by thought. The brief second soliloquy
(I, ii, 255–58) describes his physical and emotional difficulties as he
anticipates the night, which will bring his encounter with the ghost.
Even more striking, the sixth soliloquy (III, ii, 373–84) finds him a
creature of verbal fury who could

> drink hot blood
> And do such bitter business as the day
> Would quake to look on.   (375–77)

If one is tempted to dismiss this moment as a mere flurry of words
occasioned by the prince's flair for rhetoric, he need only recall that
Polonius is dead very soon thereafter.

His subsequent soliloquy (the seventh, III, iii, 73–96) reflects
a Hamlet no less bloody of thought; yet, instead of concern for the
morality of his action or for the nature of the spirit's mandate, his
obsession is to destroy Claudius in both body and soul. Refusing to
kill his uncle while at prayer and presumably at the "physic" of repentance, he chooses to search for a "more horrid hent" (88), a time
which

> has no relish of salvation in't—
> Then trip him, that his heels may kick at heaven,
> And that his soul may be as damned and black
> As hell, whereto it goes.   (92–95)

No thoughts are wasted on heaven's attitude either now or later.
Perhaps the most startling insight into the protagonist—all the
more so since it occurs early and thus inevitably colors the spectators'

response to his other actions—is provided in the third soliloquy (I, v, 92–112). Amazed by the words of the spirit of the elder Hamlet, the prince reacts with a wild distraction as his fragmented thoughts flash frantically from his own pounding heart, to the ghost's mandate, to the pernicious woman who bore him, to the "smiling, damnèd villain" (106) who occupies the throne. Certainly, in this soliloquy, the young Dane is not feigning madness; yet, in writing on his tablets —whether in pretense or in actuality—that "one may smile, and smile, and be a villain" (108), his grotesque antics are not unlike those later moments when (so he informs Horatio) the audience is to assume he has but feigned an antic disposition. Similarly, nineteen lines following Horatio's charge that Hamlet's words are wild and whirling, the prince hardly gives assurance of equanimity as, hearing the ghost below the stage, he chases it from point to point in bizarre fashion with labels such as "truepenny," "old mole," and "a worthy pioner."[29] Obviously from this point forward, the spectators are never sure when, or if, Hamlet is feigning madness; these moments have forced them to confront first hand the tenuous balance of his sanity.[30]

29. Neville Coghill (*Shakespeare's Professional Skills* [Cambridge: Cambridge Univ. Press, 1964], pp. 6–19) and Eleanor Prosser (*Hamlet and Revenge* [Stanford: Stanford Univ. Press, 1967], pp. 140–41) find in the action proof of the evil nature of the ghost. According to J. Dover Wilson (*What Happens in Hamlet* [Cambridge: Cambridge Univ. Press, 1935], p. 48), the ambiguity of the nature of the ghost is built into the action. See also Philip Edwards, *Shakespeare and the Confines of Art* (London: Methuen, 1968), p. 92. The ghost, as described recently by Harold Fisch, provides Hamlet a "covenantal encounter" (*Hamlet and the Word* [New York: Ungar, 1971], p. 101).

30. The question of Hamlet's sanity has raged since the eighteenth century. It was the *cause célèbre* of nineteenth-century German criticism (see *Hamlet: A New Variorum Edition of Shakespeare*, ed. H. H. Furness [Philadelphia: Lippincott, 1877], II, 195–235). Recent critics have asserted him to be "perfectly sane" (Bernard Grabanier, *The Heart of Hamlet* [New York: Crowell, 1960], p. 80), subject to madness cured by the conversion of grief to anger (Paul Jorgensen, "Hamlet's Therapy," *HLQ*, XXVII [1963–64], 252), to madness synonymous with sin (Roger L. Cox, "Hamlet's Hamartia: Aristotle or St. Paul?" *Yale Review*, LV [1965-66], 353), to madness in the form of a death wish (Burton R. Pollin, "Hamlet: A Successful Suicide," *Shakespeare Studies*, I [1965], 253).

Hamlet, then, a man of varied—even contradictory—emotions, but slenderly knows himself. In moving from soliloquy to soliloquy, his convictions and dispositions appear to change drastically, as if they were a kaleidoscope of new faces rather than emotional projections of the same fundamental personality. Moreover, the comments of the surrounding characters tend to underscore this fragmentation. Several are convinced that they comprehend the mystery of Hamlet: to Polonius it is madness caused by his unreciprocated passion for Ophelia; to Rosencrantz and Guildenstern it is a frenzy not devoid of political ambition; to Gertrude it is melancholia arising from his father's death and her hasty marriage.

In effect, through the diverse comments of the surrounding characters and through the eight soliloquies, which reveal fragmented glimpses of Hamlet's personality, the spectators alone are in a position fully to see the protagonist. If to see is not totally to comprehend, these spectators nonetheless are compelled to become a vital part of the dramatic process as the pattern of Hamlet's actions in the first four acts assumes form and meaning essentially in the mind of the beholder. In a very real sense, then, the critics speak of *Hamlet* as the most universal of plays; the initial stages of the tragic experience are determined by the manner in which the spectators put together the pieces of the puzzle to provide the answers or assumptions which the play itself refuses to yield; the "experience of the audience on the stage (which includes all the *dramatis personae*) is shared by that in the theatre."[31] The spectators, for example, must ultimately decide for themselves the question of Hamlet's sanity at any given point in the eleven of fifteen scenes in which he appears through IV, iv. They must determine the extent of Gertrude's guilt and the son's precise attitude toward both her and that guilt; they must draw their own conclusions concerning the nature of Hamlet's relationship with Ophelia; in the early scenes at least they must determine whether

31. T. McAlindon, "Indecorum in Hamlet," *Shakespeare Studies*, V (1969), 78. See also McAlindon's *Shakespeare and Decorum* (New York: Barnes and Noble, 1973). Hamlet's personality takes shape in terms of its confrontations with the other inhabitants of the *Hamlet*-world (Bernard McElroy, *Shakespeare's Mature Tragedies* [Princeton: Princeton Univ. Press, 1973], p. 67).

Hamlet's hesitation to move against the king is occasioned by moral fortitude, physical or psychological incapacity, personal vindictiveness, sincere doubt, or arrant cowardice—whether, for example, Hamlet's moral impasse is the accidental by-product of Shakespeare's placing the pagan concept of revenge within the frame of Christian morality, or whether Shakespeare deliberately juxtaposes the two systems to produce just such an enigma. There obviously is no single face which the pieces of these first four acts must or can be made to depict, and the actors or critics who force the protagonist into a rigid mold make a mockery of his essential complexity. The impact of the drama emerges from the continuing mystery of Hamlet prior to his sea-change, a mystery created fundamentally through the soliloquies and through the comments of the surrounding characters whose diverse explanations for the Dane's personality only underscore the enigma.

Additionally, two features contribute significantly in the early scenes to the pervasive ambiguity which casts such a powerful emphasis upon Hamlet's indecisions. For one thing, Shakespeare makes the nature of the ghost an open question indeed.[32] During the first appearance of the dreaded sight, Horatio's crossing it without consequence (whether simply by confronting it or by forming the sign of the cross in front of it) suggests a spirit in God's alliance; yet, with the crowing of the cock it starts, "like a guilty thing" (I, i, 148). At its next appearance Hamlet greets it as either a "spirit of health" bringing "airs from heaven" or a "goblin damn'd" bringing "blasts from hell" (iv, 40–41). The Dane is determined to speak

---

32. Rigid views on the ghost include claims that he is a liar (L. Kemp, "Understanding Hamlet," *CE*, XIII [1951], 9–13), a hallucination (W. W. Greg, "Hamlet's Hallucination," *MLR*, XII [1917], 393–421), a devil (Prosser, pp. 140–41), a pagan spirit (Battenhouse, *Tragedy*, p. 239; see also his "The Ghost in *Hamlet*: A Catholic 'Linchpin'?" *SP*, XLVII [1951], 161–92), and an honest spirit from Purgatory (I. J. Semper, *Hamlet Without Tears* [Dubuque, Iowa: Loras College Press, 1946], pp. 14–40; Sister Miriam Joseph, "Discerning the Ghost in *Hamlet*," *PMLA*, LXXVI [1961], 493–502; Richard Flatter, *Hamlet's Father* [New Haven: Yale Univ. Press, 1949], p. vii). More plausible is the assumption that the playwright achieves "ambiguity" (C. S. Lewis, "*Hamlet*: The Prince or the Poem?" in *Proceedings of the British Academy*, XXXVIII [1942], 11) by "knowingly mix[ing] the evidence" (Robert West, p. 63).

with it whether its intentions are wicked or not. And while at one moment he swears the apparition to be "an honest ghost" without question (v, 138), at another he admits it may be a devil since the devil has power to assume a pleasing shape. "The whole picture," as Lily Bess Campbell has aptly observed, "is skillfully wrought to show the reality viewed so contradictorily from many angles. . . . If a Papist and King James and Timothy Bright had seen the play, as they all probably did, each would have gone home confirmed in his own opinion about ghosts."[33]

For another thing, Claudius' guilt is skillfully kept a matter of conjecture for virtually half the play.[34] As long as the integrity of the ghost of the elder Hamlet is in question, so also are his implacable charges against his brother. Obviously, too, Claudius in the early scenes acts with kingly dispatch in matters of both foreign and domestic policy. His alacrity in posting Voltimand and Cornelius to Old Norway prevents a direct altercation with Fortinbras. At the same time he is wise enough to argue from a position of strength; Marcellus informs the audience of the "strict and most observant watch," the "daily cast of brazen cannon," the "foreign mart for implements of war," and the "impress of shipwrights" (I, i, 71, 73–75). The seemingly forthright explanation for his hasty marriage to Queen Gertrude, the "sometime sister, now . . . / Th'imperial jointress to this warlike state" (I, ii, 8–9), reflects a similar prudence concerning his affairs at home.

Throughout Acts I and II, in other words, the spectators are no more certain than is Hamlet of Claudius' exact role in the action. Only as Hamlet's suspicions and frustrations reach the crucial stage is the spectators' perspective raised to the double vision by which they are compelled to share his emotional dilemma and at the same time

33. *Shakespeare's Tragic Heroes* (Cambridge: Cambridge Univ. Press, 1930), p. 128.
34. One simply cannot agree, with H. D. F. Kitto, that the spectator should detest Claudius from the outset (*Form and Meaning in Drama* [London: Methuen, 1956], pp. 256–57). Only later does one perceive that the "entire court, with the exception of Hamlet, becomes the tool of this [king's] corruption" (Stanley Cooperman, "Shakespeare's Anti-Hero," *Shakespeare Studies*, I [1965], 45).

to sit in judgment on it from the vantage of superior knowledge. More specifically, through four soliloquies in the course of seven scenes in the play's midsection Claudius' guilt is revealed to the audience and his emergence as a calculating Machiavel is complete. The first passage occurs mere seconds prior to the moral dilemma voiced in Hamlet's fifth soliloquy. Claudius admits, in an aside, to a conscience troubled by the "heavy burthen" of an ugly deed buried beneath the "plast'ring art" of his "painted word" (III, i, 51–54). The moment is brief, but the impact of the information it provides for the spectators at this particular juncture is powerful; the apparent honesty of the ghost (established for the audience well before the king's reaction to *The Murder of Gonzago*) adds a new and disturbing dimension to the question of Hamlet's responsibility to avenge the murder at the very point he raises his most profound moral objections. Claudius' fullest confession of guilt occurs two scenes later as in his longest soliloquy (III, iii, 36–72) he seeks for repentance on stubborn but bowed knees, crying out that his rank offense "smells to heaven" and describing his soul as "struggling to be free" from a "bosom black as death." The two remaining soliloquies reveal that repentance for Claudius is not possible. He admits, in rising from prayer, that his "words fly up" but his "thoughts remain below" never to ascend to heaven. In his final soliloquy his villainy no longer disturbs his conscience; under the guise of transporting the prince to a temporary exile in England, he sends secret letters commanding the death of Hamlet. The "hectic" (IV, iii, 65) now raging in his blood is not the impulse to repent but rather the same thirst for political power that previously led him to strike down his brother under equally furtive circumstances.

The devices of internalization, then, as is to be the case with Iago and Othello in Shakespeare's next tragedy, provide vital development for both protagonist and antagonist. More importantly, the relationship of the two patterns of soliloquies creates a sharply defined emphasis on the protagonist and at the same time conditions the spectators' response to him at critical moments in his tragic experience. As the period of Claudius' spiritual torment is important to the spectators' critical reaction to Hamlet's most passionate and vengeful moments, so the king's hardening into villainy and the undeniable erosion of his brave and dispassionate façade behind which he conceals a growing fear and alarm are essential to their openly sympathetic relationship with Hamlet in the final act. More precisely, the development of Claudius' personality is a consistent downward path to degradation and destruction, a development paralleling in a sense Hamlet's downward path to wisdom and destruction. At the outset, as previously noted, Claudius' posture is indeed kingly, and the spectators—uncertain of the full extent of his political intrigues—cannot avoid at least a degree of respect for his position and for his apparent equanimity. With the full revelation of his guilt comes also, at least initially, the spiritual torment that again evokes a reaction not entirely devoid of sympathy. In the final acts, however, this sympathy turns to disgust and eventually to repulsion.

The passages critical to this evolving degeneration of character are the last three scenes in Act IV depicting Laertes' return to Elsinore. One notes primarily that Claudius, withal a determined antagonist, is weakening under the constant pressure of external danger. Also, and ultimately more important, the spectator is prepared for the otherwise enigmatic manner in which Laertes and Claudius react to the news of Hamlet's return, Laertes with anticipation, Claudius with amazement and anger. In these scenes Laertes, bent on immediate revenge for his murdered father, storms into the castle and threatens the very life of the reigning monarch; Claudius subsequently diverts the wrath of the young courtier; together they receive the sudden news that Hamlet has returned to Danish soil and shortly will confront the king in person.

The critics' dilemma regarding these scenes is obvious. Harley Granville-Barker (p. 47) writes, for instance, "I have always felt that Laertes' appearance was a little too surprising, that the king's excuse only made the matter worse, that Shakespeare has, for once, been too slapdash." Similarly, it is asserted that Laertes has not had time to incite a rebellion between his return from France and his entrance, and J. Dover Wilson points out that scene vi does not allow enough time for Claudius to convince Laertes of his innocence, especially since Laertes had first to "make choice" among his "wisest friends."[35] On

35. Ed., *Hamlet* (Cambridge: Cambridge Univ. Press, 1957), p. 227.

only two matters is there general agreement. Laertes' aggressiveness acts as a foil to Hamlet's lethargy; his "Let come what comes, only I'll be revenged / Most thoroughly for my father" (IV, v, 135–36) is in direct contrast with Hamlet's "How all occasions do inform against me / And spur my dull revenge" (IV, iv, 32–33). And the king, through his mental dexterity, again asserts himself as a "worthy antagonist"; just as earlier in his prudent dispatching of Voltemand and Cornelius to Old Norway in order to prevent an open conflict with Fortinbras, Claudius with remarkable swiftness is able to persuade Laertes and the "wisest friends" of his innocence of Polonius' murder, thereby averting Laertes' intended wrath and directing this anger upon Hamlet.

However, the full dramatic validity of the scenes is found in what they reveal about Claudius. First, this action displays much more than Claudius' Machiavellian adroitness; it also reveals the initial cracks in his public face. The spectator has listened to Claudius, in asides, describe the soul in anguish within him. He has also seen the king rush distractedly from the play scene, to Hamlet at least, an obvious indication of guilt. Here, it simply makes good stage sense for the actor interpreting the role of Claudius to display a frenzied fear, a temporary loss of courage, in his call to his guards at the first sign of noise and confusion (IV, v, 97). Surely Shakespeare is consciously portraying the corrosive effects of murder and usurpation with the fear and distrust that inevitably accompany such sins. Quite probably the troubled thoughts of the king, soul-sick in his inability to repent, fly first to Hamlet, and his reaction is almost a reflex. For, as soon as the messenger informs Claudius to save himself from young Laertes who overbears his officers, the king regains his presence of mind and, as noted above, is able to cope with and master Laertes' passion. Clearly, however, guilt is undermining the strong front—this is no longer the composed ruler of Act I who could describe his wedding in dispassionate terms and issue orders for personal and general security with such royal aplomb. Moreover, Claudius' momentary anxiety that Hamlet might have returned prepares the spectator for that very event in the following scene.

Second, the spectators for the first time perceive clearly Claudius'

attempts to manipulate another to his own devious ends. That is, Laertes' reaction to the news of Hamlet's return is the result of the half-
truths he has received from the king. Claudius, after asserting that he
is innocent of Polonius' death and is most sensibly grieved, craves a
patient ear from Laertes and promises to "labor with his soul / To
give it due content." And, after the explanation, Laertes is invited to
"let the great axe fall . . . where the offence is." When they next appear, two scenes later, Laertes, satisfied of the king's innocence and of
Hamlet's guilt, grimly proclaims that his revenge will come. In other
words, Laertes has not been told that Hamlet is far from Elsinore,
sailing toward England and presumably his execution; the king is
actually encouraging Laertes to anticipate gaining personal revenge
upon Hamlet. Such manipulation of Laertes would be impossible if
he were cognizant of Hamlet's being shipped to England. In short,
Claudius, his wits fully regained, has told Laertes only so much as he
deems prudent. Then, convinced of Laertes' wrath toward the young
prince, he plans to divulge the further information ("You shortly
shall hear more") that Hamlet has already been disposed of. It is
at this critical moment, ironically, that the messenger enters with
Hamlet's letters to the king revealing his return to the kingdom.
Now, certainly, it is obvious why Claudius reacts with a moment of
terror and startled disbelief, and Laertes with "Let him come. / It
warms the very sickness in my heart." Laertes, unaware of Hamlet's
voyage, has no reason for consternation; he merely sees his opportunity for personal revenge approaching. Claudius, however, sees another of his probes against Hamlet foiled; and in his hasty scheming
with Laertes to destroy Hamlet by any method, he is constrained
openly to reveal his villainous nature.

These scenes, in short, are far from "slapdash," "irrelevancies to the
plot," or mere evidence, by analogy with Laertes' action, that Hamlet
could have raised the people in his support had he been so disposed.
Through Claudius' momentary horror followed by his clever manipulation of Laertes (actions more easily communicated on stage than on
the printed page), the spectators perceive the degeneration of character that will be complete in the climactic dueling scene of Act V.
Here, in a desperate and cowardly attempt to cover his treachery, the

king will cry out that Gertrude merely swoons to see the combatants bleed.

This manipulation of Claudius' development to achieve maximum impact upon the spectators' interest in and attitude toward Hamlet is only one example of the structural skill that is responsible for the power of the tragedy. Also significant, as various critics have noted, are the numerous other character foils and thematic parallels.[36] Hamlet, for example, is surrounded by characters who, though they perform individual roles important in themselves, function also to cast emphasis upon particular aspects of his total personality. Like the various simplistic explanations for Hamlet's distraction given by Polonius, Rosencrantz and Guildenstern, and the queen, in the final analysis these foil relationships—by reflecting the impossibility of accommodating the prince's problem and his condition within the limitations of any single posture—underscore the essential complexity of his nature. That is, the spectators time and again cannot avoid noting how divergently Hamlet and another character react to a generally similar situation; at the same time, however, they cannot avoid observing how fundamentally more complex is his problem than that of the character with whom the analogy is drawn. Fortinbras, for instance, invites comparison with Hamlet. He too has lost a father and passionately desires to retaliate for his death; but he successfully curbs his temper, diverts his attention to an action (the Polish expedition) which presumably will gain him honor, and is in the comfortable and profitable position to claim the Danish throne at the end of the play. How tempting, then, to draw a direct analogy between the man whom reason saves and the man whom passion destroys; but how misleading! Fortinbras has lost his father by a public and contracted duel, not by furtive design; he has received not a ghostly admonition to avenge his father's murder, but an uncle's rejoinder to quell his rebellious actions.

In similar fashion, Hamlet himself invites comparison between his

36. See, for example, Bevington, p. 8; Francis Fergusson, *The Idea of a Theater* (Princeton: Princeton Univ. Press, 1949), p. 119; John Vyvyan, *The Shakespearean Ethic* (London: Chatto and Windus, 1959), pp. 50 ff.; Wilson, *What Happens*, pp. 137 ff.; Granville-Barker, p. 223.

own passionate nature and the stoic fortitude of Horatio, a man who has taken Fortune's buffets and rewards with equal thanks and in whom blood and judgment are so well "commeddled" that they "are not a pipe for Fortune's finger / To sound what stop she please" (III, ii, 66–68), a man, in short, who is not "passion's slave" (69). Admittedly, in the scene in which Hamlet confronts the ghost, Horatio is far more a creature of self-control than his friend; so also, his behavior in the play scene is calm and dispassionate in comparison with Hamlet's frenzied excitement. Yet, insofar as the spectators are permitted to know Horatio, he has no real reason for loss of self-control: his father has neither been murdered nor assumed the shape of a spirit; nor does his uncle sit on a throne which he had every reason to anticipate. All that Horatio's equanimity proves is that he has not faced the issues and challenges that confront Hamlet.

Laertes provides a similar comparison. Certainly his storming of Elsinore after he has rallied a group of supporters in order to obtain immediate revenge for his father (an analogy of sorts with Fortinbras' original intentions) contrasts sharply with Hamlet's failure to act. Again, however, the foil underscores the greater complexity of the protagonist, whose intellectual and moral fiber Laertes does not possess. More specifically, Laertes can strike out wildly, mounting an open attack without knowledge of who his enemy is. Whether it involves something so innocuous as his presumptuous judgment on the nature of Hamlet's love for Ophelia, or something so pernicious as a life in retaliation for a life, his judgments—like his actions—are impetuous and precipitous. Hence, it is not really surprising either that Claudius should be able to manipulate the young crusader to serve his own devious ends or that Laertes should accept without question the king's assurances that Hamlet's madness is the source of all evil within the court. Laertes' lack of conscience is perhaps not unrelated to Polonius' earlier concern for the son's conduct in France. In any case, his son brazenly asserts that he would cut the prince's throat in the church and hesitates not a moment in agreeing to the king's treacherous scheme to strike down Hamlet in a friendly duel with an unbated sword.

In effect, then, the characters of Fortinbras, Horatio, and Laertes—

by reflecting certain aspects of Hamlet's situation—compel the spectators more knowledgeably to confront the total complexity of his dilemma. Various thematic parallels, in addition, indirectly guide the attention of the viewers to a more intense concentration on Hamlet's private hell. For instance, in light of Hamlet's morbid response to the appearance in state of Claudius and Gertrude and his suspicions of foul play when informed by Horatio of the visitation of his father's spirit, much of Polonius' advice to his son assumes an unmistakable relevance. "Give thy thoughts no tongue. . . . Beware / Of entrance to a quarrel; but being in, / Bear't that th'opposed may beware of thee. . . . Reserve thy judgment. . . . This above all, to thine own self be true" (I, iii, 59, 65–67, 69, 78)—these observations the spectators can relate far more directly to Hamlet than to Laertes, of whom at this point they know nothing save that he is a young man returning to his studies in Paris.

Additional parallels are scattered throughout the action. The plot of *The Murder of Gonzago*, with Hamlet's some dozen or sixteen lines inserted, constitutes an obvious and exact reiteration of the ghost's description of the elder Hamlet's murder as well as of a queen who, after swearing she will never wed again, immediately takes to bed the murderer of her first mate. And the actors provide additional parallels. In one, as Rosencrantz and Hamlet discuss the economic difficulties encountered by the adult actors as a consequence of the sudden emergence of the eyrie of children, "little eyases, that cry out on the top of question, and are most tyrannically clapped for't" (II, ii, 332–34), the prince draws a direct analogy to the fickle people of the kingdom who now rush to obtain a "picture in little" of a new king at whom they "would make mows . . . while my father lived" (356–58). A second parallel arises from the player's recitation of Pyrrhus' slaying of Priam. Not only does the scene involve a son (of Achilles) gaining a measure of revenge by slaying the opposing king; it includes also a queen whose mourning is so intense that the "burst of clamor . . . / Would have made milch the burning eyes of heaven / And passion in the gods" (II, ii, 490, 503, 505–6).[37] A more general parallel involves the juxtaposition of Polonius' family, character-

37. Levin (pp. 24 ff.) examines the parallels in detail. See also, Clifford

ized by happiness and true affection, with the king's family, characterized by suspicion, distrust, and hatred; ironically, of course, both units are totally destroyed by the evil unleashed by Claudius' murder and usurpation. Then, too, Polonius' senility and Ophelia's insanity provide sobering reminders of the dangers of Hamlet's incipient madness.

Certainly the most extensive thematic parallels concern Hamlet's attempts—through conversations with Ophelia and with his mother and through the play calculated to test the integrity of both Claudius and the ghost—to discover the truth before he acts. His antagonist is no less active, spying on him both directly and indirectly in order to determine the extent of his suspicions. To this end Claudius invites Rosencrantz and Guildenstern to visit Elsinore in the hope that, under the guise of friendly conversation, they will learn from Hamlet the concerns nearest his heart. So also, Polonius—who assures the king that he can find where the truth lies, wherever it is hidden—is on three occasions set upon by the young prince. At one point he "boards him" in conversation (II, ii, 170–219); at another he stands with Claudius behind the arras while the unwitting Ophelia—used as a decoy—is subjected to vicious and repulsive contumely; at another he meets his death while eavesdropping on the conversation between mother and son in the queen's bedchamber. Polonius provides still another parallel early in the play by sending Reynaldo to Paris to spy upon his son and make inquiry of his behavior.[38] He urges his servant to scatter insinuations and lies as necessary to provoke the reactions which carry the truth:

> Your bait of falsehood take this carp of truth,
> And thus do we of wisdom and of reach,

Leech, "The Hesitation of Pyrrhus," in *The Morality of Art*, ed. D. W. Jefferson (New York: Barnes and Noble, 1969), p. 48.

38. Thomas N. Kettle flatly accuses Polonius of "complicity in the murder of the elder Hamlet" (*The Day's Burden* [New York: Scribner's, 1918], p. 66). Similarly, Myron Taylor asserts that Polonius, as well as his children, deserves his fate ("Tragic Justice and the House of Polonius," *SEL*, VIII [1968], 279). Barry B. Jackson has recently analyzed the critical timing involved in Polonius' murder ("Shakespeare's 'Deceptive Cadence,'" *SQ*, XXIV [1973], 117).

With windlasses and with assays of bias,
By indirections find directions out. (63–66)

Shakespeare, then, in *Hamlet* has created an intricate plot in which character and thematic associations consistently converge upon the central figure to underscore for the spectators the complexity of his situation and his enigmatic responses to it. Through the first two acts, with Claudius' guilt by no means certain and with the protagonist's reactions in soliloquy ranging from total despondency to anxious anticipation to distraction to frustrated self-chastisement for his failure to act, there is no single explanation for Hamlet's actions and no simplistic attitude toward the ghost or toward the morality or the justification of revenge. As the lines of guilt become clear in the third act, the abrupt juxtaposition of Hamlet's moral introspection with his passionate lust for revenge combined with Claudius' apparent desire for repentance continues to render impossible complete empathy for the prince. Certainly the play scene, the cruel logic by which he refuses to kill the king at prayer, and the impetuous thrust which takes Polonius' life signal his descent into passion even as the villainy of the king also becomes indelibly clear. Throughout the first four acts, in other words, the spectators catch penetrating insights into Hamlet's personality but never are they permitted fully to share his emotions, both because they never totally comprehend his values, which would provide the key to consistency of character, and also because the play is carefully structured to maintain a pervasive ambivalence toward protagonist and antagonist.

The ambiguities of the play are essentially resolved in the final act. Following his sea adventure, Hamlet no longer is frenetically inconsistent in his approach to the destruction of Claudius.[39] No longer

39. E. M. W. Tillyard denies "any powerful spiritual growth" (*Shakespeare's Problem Plays* [London: Chatto and Windus, 1950], p. 17), and Robert Stevenson (*Shakespeare's Religious Frontier* [The Hague: Nijhoff, 1958], p. 30), H. B. Charlton (*Shakespearian Tragedy* [Cambridge: Cambridge Univ. Press, 1952], p. 11), and George Seibel (*The Religion of Shakespeare* [London: Watts, 1924], pp. 29 ff.) focus on Hamlet's denial of Christianity and immortality. But, as R. M. Frye observes, "The words spoken by the dying Hamlet were interpreted in sixteenth-century theology as . . . words of faith" (*Shakespeare and Christian Doctrine* [Princeton: Princeton Univ. Press, 1963],

does he question the moral justification of the act; now he flatly considers it to be perfect conscience to strike him down. No longer is he a man whose obsession with the corruption and depravity of the world and its inhabitants is exceeded only by his desire to escape from it. Now he asserts that there is "a divinity that shapes our ends, / Rough–hew them how we will" (V, ii, 10–11). Heaven ordained his escape from death in England through the manipulations that send Rosencrantz and Guildenstern to their destruction (deaths which are not "near" his conscience). Hamlet is now "constant" to his purposes, prepared for every alternative. Nothing, he now proclaims, happens by accident: "There is a special providence in the fall of a sparrow. If it be now, 'tis not to come; if it be not to come, it will be now; if it be not now, yet it will come. The readiness is all" (209–11). He acknowledges a divine purpose within him, something dangerous which Laertes would do well to fear. Hamlet is now a man who, albeit too late, is able to articulate his love for Ophelia, able to exchange forgiveness freely with Laertes. Instead of his earlier callous attitude toward death and the human corpse, now the prince is incensed that the gravedigger has no feeling of his business, that he can play at loggets with a man's bones. His remarks concerning Yorick reveal a sympathy and affection foreign to the earlier Hamlet. Here, too, is a man concerned that his story be told fully and accurately, lest a "wounded name" shall survive him (ii, 333). And, in giving his voice to the election of Fortinbras, he now is capable of looking beyond his death to the stability of the country. The final words of both Horatio and Fortinbras underscore the nature of Hamlet's tragic growth.

Spectators may not all be happy with a God who condones blood revenge and utilizes human agents to expedite His divine wrath, but

---

p. 53). He has been forced to wield the "poisoned sword" (Allan C. Dessen, "Hamlet's Poisoned Sword," *Shakespeare Studies*, V [1969], 67), but in the final analysis he transcends the values of those around him (Ruth M. Levitsky, "Rightly To Be Great," *Shakespeare Studies*, I [1965], 161) and achieves his "final understanding" (S. F. Johnson, "The Regeneration of Hamlet," *SQ*, III [1952], 207).

the thrust of the play—which "emphasizes the mystery of existence by illuminating the nature of human responsibility"[40]—is clear. The protagonist finds a peace of soul and mind only after he accommodates himself to a will and purpose greater than his own. This peace of soul, which the play proclaims, is of this world and not of the next, to be sure; nonetheless, it comes only with the purgation of an ego that at the outset prompts him to judge all else in terms of his own frustration and despair and that later hardens into the cynical assumption that decisions of death and life (the slaying of Polonius, the sparing of Claudius) rest only with his own distorted logic.

Probably because the soliloquy is used extensively in the first four acts to reflect the fragmented nature of Hamlet's character, it is not used to signal the whole character of the final act. Instead, Hamlet's transformation is articulated through his dialogue with Horatio. As a result of his new posture and of Claudius' further degeneration into villainy, the spectators' identification with Hamlet, for the first time in the tragedy, is complete—all the more strongly because they realize that his own destruction will be the inevitable consequence of his earlier acts of passion.

Shakespeare, then, has created his first delineation of the full tragic experience. Before Hamlet falls, he recognizes himself as both sinned against and sinning, and he reflects in dialogue the wisdom and self-knowledge that error and suffering have produced. But the essential power of the tragedy lies in the ambiguities of the first four acts created through the soliloquies, some of which provide flickering insights into a complex and profoundly human personality and some of which reveal the development of the antagonist, and through the numerous character foils and thematic parallels which guide and underscore the intensity of the spectators' concern. In provoking the spectators to judgment on the ambivalent tensions and conflicts between the flesh and the spirit which Hamlet is heir to, Shakespeare has created a situation in which powerful and disturbing ramifications linger far beyond the particular resolution of the final act.

40. Thomas McFarland, *Tragic Meanings in Shakespeare* (New York: Random House, 1966), p. 17.

In adapting to the stage Cinthio's "Tale of the Moor of Venice" Shakespeare developed his principal roles along familiar lines. Like Richard III, Shakespeare's ensign is possessed of a bold audacity and devilish wit; predisposed to evil, he delights in sharing his machinations with the audience. The Moor, like Brutus, is heroic and noble, but naively idealistic; his own magnanimous forthrightness and his assumption that others are equally genuine make him susceptible to the schemes of clear-sighted men of evil intent and blind him to the bestial side of his own nature, which pride bides its time to reveal. Both characters are more powerful delineations than their earlier dramatic counterparts. Although Iago is more totally a single-dimensional creature of calculated self-control than Richard, Shakespeare manipulates him to give the appearance in the early acts of credible and intriguing character development. And Othello, far more so than Brutus, is provoked to the cruel and vicious consequences of pride and is forced more completely—and, to most spectators and critics, more satisfactorily—to experience the full cycle of tragedy.

By its very nature drama is inseparable from the reaction of the audience. Indeed a major purpose of this study is to underscore the concern for control of the spectators' reactions which Shakespeare progressively brings to bear upon the narratives he adapts for the stage. *Othello* is an excellent case in point. Conceded to be among his best plays, though not perhaps his greatest work,[41] *Othello* has a "grip upon the emotions of the audience," writes the Arden editor, that "is more relentless and sustained than that of the others."[42] The success is in large measure the result of Shakespeare's structural skill in creating, through the two principals, two perspectives by which to accommodate a plot of mounting tension and of progressively restricted focus. On the one hand, the spectators are forced credibly and sympathetically to experience the protagonist's dilemma while, on the other, their more expansive perception of the values that control the stage

41. The occasional charges epitomized in Thomas Rymer's view of the play as a "Bloody farce, without salt or savour" (*A Short View of Tragedy*, in *The Works of Thomas Rymer*, ed. Curt Zimansky [New Haven: Yale Univ. Press, 1956], p. 150; see also T. S. Eliot, *Selected Essays* [New York, Harcourt, 1932], p. 141) attract attention largely because they are so anomalous.

42. M. R. Ridley, ed., *Othello* (London: Methuen, 1958), p. xli.

world forces them to sit in judgment on his decisions and anticipate the consequences. Specifically, Iago, fully integrated within the narrative, functions as a tragic pointer through whom the spectators observe the forces that create Othello's situation and the values against which he must contend; and Othello is a protagonist with whom, through the devices of internalization, the spectators share fully the private agony of passion and also the insight to which he is led.

Iago, though deprived of even the momentary flash of a live conscience which to a degree humanizes Richard III, gives the impression of being far more alive. Like the Yorkist king, he is not merely the cold, calculating abstraction which critics delight in tracing from medieval drama; his soft underside is the agony of envy and unsatisfied ambition.[43] He experiences, for instance, the same fear of cuckoldry he implants in Othello: he suspects that the Moor has done his office between his sheets,

> the thought whereof
> Doth, like a poisonous mineral, gnaw my inwards;
> And nothing can or shall content my soul. . . .
>
> (II, i, 290–92)

He also fears with his "night–cap" (301) Cassio, who has a "daily beauty in his life" which makes him ugly (V, i, 19–20). Such fears arise largely from his own twisted personality. As his own comments reveal, he has no conception of love beyond its basest connotations.[44] Othello, married, dwells "in a fertile climate" (I, i, 70);"an old

43. At least one critic seriously assumes that Iago believes Othello has cuckolded him (J. W. Draper, "Honest Iago," *PMLA*, XLVI [1931], 736). "Behind the mask, Iago is as restless as a cage of those cruel and lustful monkeys that he mentions so often" (Fergusson, *The Pattern*, p. 222). His revenge demands that Othello feel the "same gnawing jealousy which is destroying him" (Campbell, p. 160).

44. Iago is "the champion of the absolute autonomy of the will" (Daniel Stempel, "The Silence of Iago," *PMLA*, LXXXIV [1969], 258). Both Wolfgang Clemen (*The Development of Shakespeare's Imagery* [Cambridge, Mass.: Harvard, 1951], pp. 121–22) and Caroline Spurgeon (*Shakespeare's Imagery* [Cambridge: Cambridge Univ. Press, 1935], p. 335) comment on his fondness for images of animals engaged in obscene activity. As Carroll Camden has pointed out, he makes extensive use of the "traditional anti-feminist literature" of the period ("Iago on Women," *JEGP*, XLVIII [1959], 57). Ralph

black ram" is "tupping" Brabantio's "white ewe" (88–89); the daughter is "covered with a Barbary horse" (111); Othello, Cassio is informed, has "boarded a land carack" (I, ii, 50); it is a "common thing," he tells Emilia, to have a "foolish" wife (III, iii, 302, 304); a woman who has beauty but refuses to use it freely for self-advantage is fit only to "suckle fools and chronicle small beer" (II, i, 159). On occasions when he feels rebuffed, his animosity burns suddenly brighter. At the outset, for example, he painfully asserts that he knows his price in the face of Cassio's promotion, proclaiming that he must serve Othello outwardly though he hates him as he does hell-pains. Later the perceptive actor should not miss a similar cue when Cassio refuses to listen to Iago's song a second time, informing him that he holds a person unworthy of his office who engages in such activities. So also, Iago could hardly fail to be momentarily furious a few lines later when Cassio in his cups pulls rank on him, mumbling that he hopes his soul will be saved—to which Iago perfunctorily responds that he does too; Cassio, in turn, blurts "Ay, but . . . not before me. The lieutenant is to be saved before the ancient" (II, iii, 104–5).

Along with this gnawing frustration, Iago possesses the cruelly fascinating wit that also characterizes Richard III; he takes a similar unholy delight in the machinations that contort in agony those who trust him unquestioningly. He gloats, for example, over his counsel to Cassio that Desdemona be persuaded to intercede in the lieutenant's behalf, noting that devils cover the "blackest sins" with "heavenly shows" (II, iii, 334–35). So also he delights that the Moor, in the temptation scene, changes with his poison; two scenes later he stands over the collapsed general exclaiming ecstatically that his medicine is working to catch a credulous fool. In the final act he relishes the fact that, whether Cassio kill Roderigo or Roderigo, Cassio, he stands to profit. Some perverted sense of superiority prevails even in his assertion that Othello has not dealt him a mortal wound and that from this time forth he will never speak a word. In a sense the success of his scheming is more amazing than Richard's, since he operates, not from

Berry calls the Iago-Emilia relationship a key to understanding the major struggle of the play ("Pattern in *Othello*," *SQ*, XXIII [1972], 17).

the base of a royal position which in itself commands obeisance, but from a relatively insignificant position of third in command in a Venetian military force. As a matter of fact, every character whom Iago manipulates into destruction or physical harm is his social or professional superior—Brabantio, Montano, Cassio, Desdemona, Othello. Even Roderigo, a fool whom the ensign rightly claims to be his purse, possesses far more wealth, if not common sense.

Most significant in contrast with the characterization of Richard III, Iago becomes progressively more sophisticated in his ability to practice upon virtually everyone else in the stage world.[45] To be sure, he is firmly committed at the outset to his own interest and to the destruction of all who oppose it, and never once does he swerve from dedication to this end. Consequently, in ethical terms he is totally static. There is no abortive attempt to reveal a conscience alive to moral principles, as in the character of Richard in his final soliloquy, and certainly there is no effort to make him sympathetic at any point. Nonetheless, he does become simultaneously more appalling and more fascinating as his audacity and subtlety increase. At the outset he operates from the shadows, goading Roderigo to incense Brabantio against Othello. As the distraught father descends to the main stage and calls for a taper, Iago quickly exits in order to avoid identification, informing Roderigo that he must leave since it is not in his best interest to be recognized in this situation. Throughout the first act Iago's double face quite literally must be concealed in darkness for its effectiveness. In the second act, after exhibiting his mental dexterity by bandying words with Desdemona and Emilia, Iago moves into the physical light in order to practice upon minds confused by alcohol: Roderigo, having caroused at length, is persuaded to attack Cassio; Cassio, drunk and "full of quarrel and offense" (II, iii, 46), as Captain of the Guard allows himself to become involved in a brawling squabble which disrupts the peace;[46] Montano, having done justice in

45. His plot and his "gambler's *sang-froid*" grow with his opportunities (A. P. Rossiter, *Angel With Horns*, ed. Graham Storey [New York: Theatre Arts Books, 1961], p. 205). Joseph T. McCullen, Jr., observes that Iago's use of proverbs lends an air of increasing complexity to his machinations ("Iago's Use of Proverbs for Persuasion," *SEL*, IV [1964], 261).

46. This scene revealing Iago's destructive manipulation of others may

pledging the health of his general, gullibly swallows Iago's insinuations that Cassio is an alcoholic and bluntly charges that the captain is drunk.

Iago's practices in Act I are obviously intended as total retaliation for his supposed injury. Had he succeeded in goading Brabantio and Duke to annul the marriage, Othello presumably would have experienced both personal grief and public ignominy. Had he provoked Brabantio's party to open attack (which he personally strives to initiate by drawing his sword and mocking an assault upon Roderigo), Othello would have lost at least his reputation and his military command, perhaps even his life. In Act II the ensign moves against the Moor through his practice upon Cassio. While he makes two brief references to the possibility that Cyprus may rise to immediate mutiny as a result of the affray between Roderigo and Cassio, his new design will require additional time and circumstance. If Othello, then, is still untouched at the conclusion of Act II, Cassio is displaced; more important, Shakespeare, through the progressive sophistication and complexity of Iago's methods, has both made the antagonist dramatically interesting and also prepared the spectators for the moment of his greater success.

The third act is the ensign's most glorious moment as the fires of insinuation and implication raze his most precious adversaries. In the great temptation scene, as before, the playwright achieves maximum interest through a successive delineation of the villainy. More specifically, Iago's manipulation of Othello in this scene involves three distinct phases. In the first (35–192), carefully avoiding any reference whatever to Desdemona, he subtly and unobtrusively plants the seeds of suspicion against Cassio which, as they take root in the general's mind, will suggest the possibility of his wife's infidelity. Iago does not like Cassio's stealing away "so guilty-like" from Desdemona, or his knowledge of Othello's love during the courtship; perchance Cassio is honest, but the ensign is not bound to utter his deepest thoughts; Othello must beware of jealousy—not (as one might expect to hear) because jealousy preys destructively upon the mind but be-

---

provoke a few apprehensive chuckles, but it hardly "borders on slapstick" (Robert A. Watts, "The Comic Scenes in *Othello*," *SQ*, XIX [1968], 349).

cause the cuckold (how carefully the implication is inserted) "lives in bliss" who knows not his condition. In the second phase (193–369), with the poison in Othello's mind taking hold, Iago's comments are marked by increasing insolence as he slants his attacks indirectly against Desdemona: she must be observed with Cassio; she deceived her father; her refusal to accept a match of "her own clime, complexion, and degree" betokens a "most rank" will. In the third phase Iago confronts the passion-ridden Moor with direct charges of his cuckoldry: he speaks blatantly of Desdemona's being "topped," of her giving Cassio the handkerchief that had been Othello's wedding gift, and of Cassio's protestations of love in a dream.

Physical darkness, inebriation, spiritual darkness—each in turn serves as a basis for the increasing audacity of Iago's schemes; so also, from insinuations against Cassio to indirect and direct charges against Desdemona, the spectator witnesses a carefully modulated delineation of the antagonist in action. And his fortunes have indeed reached remarkable heights. To be sure, he will continue to goad the Moor; he —with both Cassio and Othello disposed of—will even entertain thoughts of a command in Cyprus. His control of others for his own benefit, however, will never transcend this moment when in III, iii Othello commissions his ensign to destroy Cassio and commits himself to the destruction of Desdemona.[47] Nor is there any further progression in the complexity and perverse artistry of his villainy which to this point has given the impression of steadily developing characterization.

In this key scene, on which the play literally turns, Shakespeare shifts the major focus from Iago to Othello—and he does so primarily through the devices of internalization. To this point Iago has spoken five soliloquies and two asides (a total of 111 lines); Othello has had *not one* such line. In this central scene Iago has one soliloquy (nine lines) and Othello delivers his first two soliloquies (twenty-two

47. In 1937, following the lead of Dr. Ernest Jones, Laurence Olivier as a homosexual Iago and Ralph Richardson as Othello played the exchanging of vows in III, iii, as virtually a love scene (Marvin Rosenberg, *The Masks of Othello* [Berkeley: Univ. of California Press, 1961], pp. 175–84); see further, N. N. Holland, *Psychoanalysis in Shakespeare* (New York: McGraw Hill, 1964), pp. 246–58.

lines). For the remainder of the play Iago speaks only four brief soliloquies (twenty-six lines) whereas Othello has six soliloquies and thirteen asides (sixty-eight lines). Through the first half of the play, then, the spectators' attention is drawn sharply to Iago; the issues and events of the action they see in large part through the ensign's eyes. All is colored by his hatred and envy. Admittedly the soliloquies provide no real explanation for Iago's malignity; as a foil to the unsuspicious Othello, he does, however, establish with unrelenting intensity the egocentric values that destroy man's judgment and will convert the Moor to a passionate monster of destruction. On the other hand, he does not in the final analysis force the protagonist to commit murder any more so than does the ghost in *Hamlet* or than do the witches in *Macbeth*. Like these forces the ensign is only a single and dreadful aspect of the environment which triggers the Moor's passion. Any assumption that the play is a "pure melodrama" (as George Bernard Shaw would have it)[48] disregards the fact that the evil culminating in Othello's destruction wells up from within him, from the same reservoir of pride that previously has generated the self-esteem that makes him a leader among men. Through Iago the spectators recognize how stupidly—yet how understandably—Othello has acted (or is going to act); through him they confront the brutal necessity in such a world of the self-knowledge which ultimately the Moor so painfully achieves.

As an arrant villain, the ensign is, of course, a figure about whom the spectators have no delusions and with whom—though they may sit in awe—they can develop no trace of a sympathetic rapport.[49] Quite candidly he proclaims himself a creature of absolute self-interest: he always makes his "fool" his "purse," spending time

48. *Shaw on Shakespeare*, ed. Edwin Wilson (New York: Dutton, 1961), p. 159.

49. Maud Bodkin labeled him the devil archetype (*Archetypal Patterns in Poetry* [London: Oxford Univ. Press, 1934], pp. 211–18), and Bernard Spivack is one of the most recent to trace his descent from the Vice of the medieval moralities (*Shakespeare and the Allegory of Evil* [New York: Columbia Univ. Press, 1958]). Like Othello and Cassio he has an inordinate concern for what others think about him (David L. Jeffrey and J. Patrick Grant, "Reputation in *Othello*," *Shakespeare Studies*, VI [1970], 205).

"with such a spine / But for [his] sport and profit" (I, iii, 377, 379–80); he is a devil deceiving with "heavenly shows" (II, iii, 335). His conversations with Roderigo underscore this egocentricity: he knows his price; "trimmed in forms and visages of duty," he keeps his heart in attendance on himself (I, i, 50). One has only himself to blame for failure to thrive at another's expense:

> Virtue? a fig! 'Tis in ourselves that we are thus or thus. Our
> bodies are our gardens, to the which our wills are gardeners;
> . . . The power and corrigible authority of this lies in our
> wills.   (I, iii, 319–21, 325–26)

In his singular dedication to self lies his chief importance as a tragic pointer; so clear is his obsessive self-interest and so obvious is his hatred for Othello that his very detestation points the spectators to admiration for the Moor. Since, from the moment he appears on stage, there is no doubt whatever about his villainous nature, the playwright through him develops our sympathy for the protagonist and at the same time, through dramatic irony, can involve the audience in a sense of impending disaster.[50] Iago resents not receiving the promotion; he suspects Othello of cuckolding him; he detests Othello's military hauteur and greatly resents the high regard of the community for the commander. That time and again his remarks should underscore his leader's abilities reflects doubly to Othello's credit. Of the Cyprus expedition, for instance, Iago admits to Roderigo that the Venetians have not another of Othello's "fathom" (I, i, 151) to lead them. Even as in soliloquy his machinations take form, he observes that the Moor is of a free, open, constant, loving, and noble nature.

Various minor characters, in conjunction with Iago, firmly guide our response to the protagonist. In the first scene, for example, the emphasis is sharply against Othello, to whom the spectators are introduced through the observations of Iago, Roderigo, and Brabantio as a prideful general who has foolishly selected an inexperienced lieu-

---

50. John Robert Moore, "Othello, Iago, and Cassio as Soldiers," *PQ*, XXXI (1952), 190. See also Rabkin, p. 60; Walter Raleigh, *Shakespeare* (London: Macmillan, 1907), p. 141.

tenant and who with gross disrespect and possibly even with the practice of black magic has eloped with a daughter of a Venetian senator. This initial impression the two subsequent scenes totally reverse—in scene ii by Othello's first appearance on the stage and in scene iii by the additional minor pointers and by Iago's first soliloquy.[51] The Duke and the senators welcome valiant Othello, to whom they will entrust their national defense; Desdemona lovingly acknowledges her husband in the face of her furiously irate father, and the Duke's reactions to Brabantio's charge is that the "son-in-law is far more fair than black" (I, iii, 290); such a tale could win his daughter too. Additional pointers reinforce this perspective in Act II. Montano, the governor of Cyprus, describes "brave Othello" as a "worthy governor" who commands like a "full soldier" (i, 38, 30, 36). Cassio, whose toast is to the health of his general and whose "hopes do shape" Othello for the governor (i, 56), prays that the heavens will defend him against the sea so that he "may bless this bay with his tall ship" (79). The herald proclaims the orders of his "noble and valiant general" (ii, 1–2) and invokes a blessing on him. Desdemona greets her dear Othello with a love that increases even as the "days do grow" (i, 193).

In the first half of the play, Othello's personality (which we see only from the outside) affirms these opinions. He is a man, all things considered, who acts with understandable assurance and confidence. In Act I, he is a veritable paragon of reason in his ability to maintain self-control. He refuses to be ruffled by Iago's inflammatory remarks about Brabantio; to the contrary, he calmly asserts that his services to the state will "out–tongue" (I, ii, 19) any of Brabantio's complaints to the duke. Moreover, if the time comes when boasting is an honor, he can proclaim that he fetches his "life and being / From men of royal siege." He personally prevents an open battle between his party and his father-in-law's; he unhesitatingly offers to face Bra-

---

51. Such action "serve[s] only to set in relief the magnificence of Othello" (Moody E. Prior, "Character in Relation to Action in *Othello*," *MP*, XLIV [1946], 226); it defines "the supreme importance of the hero" (G. R. Hibbard, "*Othello* and the Pattern of Shakespearean Tragedy," *Shakespeare Survey*, XXI [1968], 41).

bantio's charge before the duke and at the council table maintains his dignity in the face of pointedly insulting comments; he himself suggests that his wife be allowed to speak before the senators. Above all, his love for the gentle Desdemona is a relationship of mutual respect and devotion. Desdemona would "seriously incline" (iii, 146) to Othello's tales of "battles, sieges, fortunes" (130), his "disastrous chances" (134) and his "hairbreadth scapes" (136). With a "greedy ear" (149), frequent tears, and "a world of sighs" (Q; kisses, F) (159), she in time came to love him "for the dangers [he] had passed" (167) and he "loved her that she did pity them" (168). There is no witchcraft, then, except the emotion that compels Desdemona to acknowledge the Moor her lord. That the Duke allows Desdemona to accompany him to battle powerfully attests to the general assumption both that their love is indeed genuine and that Othello is a man whom passion can not shake. And the assumption appears to be confirmed in Act II as Othello quickly asserts control in the rush of events that threatens widespread disruption. At the same time, with dispatch and with rigorous impartiality he dismisses the officer against whom all evidence and testimony point—an officer he personally had chosen: "Cassio, I love thee; / But never more be officer of mine" (II, iii, 238–39).

Two moments, on the other hand, do ominously suggest the tragedy that is shortly to come. Cassio's remorse—although never developed beyond a mere lamentation that he has lost the "immortal part" of himself (his reputation) and that what is left is "bestial"—foreshadows the experience to which Othello's passion is shortly to lead him.[52] And this passion—all the more dangerous in combination with

52. Othello is "magnanimous" but "egotistic" (F. R. Leavis, "Diabolic Intellect and the Noble Hero," *Scrutiny*, V [1937], 265). In Iago Othello hears a voice that he would "fain hear and fain deny" (J. I. M. Stewart, *Character and Motive in Shakespeare* [London: Longmans, Green, 1949], p. 103). "He is inexpert in simple intellectual judgement. . . . The intellectual confusion . . . gives . . . opportunity for his passion to break through" (Charlton, p. 123); see also Paul A. Jorgensen, "Perplex'd in the Extreme: The Role of Thought in *Othello*," *SQ*, XV (1964), 275; and Katherine Stockholder, "Egregiously an Ass: Chance and Accident," *SEL*, XIII (1973), 257–72. Like

supreme self-confidence—does emerge significantly, if briefly, as he demands a full report of the strife between Cassio and Montano:

> My blood begins my safer guides to rule,
> . . . If I once stir
> Or do but lift this arm, the best of you
> Shall sink in my rebuke. (iii, 195, 197–99)

The fatal ingredients blend in III, iii to make Othello susceptible to Iago's machinations. His willingness to listen to insinuations about Cassio, couched subtly in terms of the ensign's love and regard for the Moor, soon lead him to demand a fuller version; and as Iago turns his remarks against Desdemona, the spectators through soliloquy move directly within the distraught protagonist. The remainder of the play they will experience, not through the eyes of one who with burning joy intrigues to trap another, but through the eyes and soul of the victim who must bring himself to admit both the crime of passion against the fair Desdemona and also the stupidity and naivete that render him susceptible to jealousy. Questioning the prudence of marriage, Othello considers his age and his color, concluding that marriage is the plague of great ones; "Prerogatived are they less than the base" (274). At this point the general is visibly disturbed, as Iago notes on three occasions within the scope of ten lines (214–24). By the end of the scene Othello has himself seized the initiative, agonizing that his occupation is gone. His

> name, that was as fresh
> As Dian's visage, is now begrimed and black
> As mine own face.   (368–88)

It is the supreme irony of the play for Othello to kneel ritualistically and in the due reverence of a sacred vow to lift his voice to heaven. Iago's most precious moment must surely be the Moor's response to his request to let Desdemona live:

> Damn her, lewd minx! O, damn her! damn her!
> . . . I will withdraw

---

the Pelegians, he understands justice but not mercy (Ruth Levitsky, "All in All Sufficiency in *Othello*," *Shakespeare Studies*, VI [1970], 219).

To furnish me with some swift means of death
For the fair devil. Now art thou my lieutenant.

(476–79)

Once the spectators' vision has moved within Othello, comments
on his nobility become painfully ironic, as in Desdemona's greeting
her "good love" (III, iii, 54), her submissive obedience, her insistence that her "noble Moor" is "true of mind," possessing none of
the baseness of jealous creatures, and that his momentary rancor is
provoked by some matter of state:

> We must think men are not gods,
> Nor of them look for such observancy
> As fits the bridal.   (148–50)

The reference to Othello's being no god is especially ironic, of course,
in that it is precisely such a role that he deludes himself into assuming in his wife's execution. Desdemona later asserts to Emilia that
her love is so strong that "even his stubbornness, his checks, his
frowns" have "grace and favor" (IV, iii, 19–20). Most painful of
all, although it is to have a profound influence in convincing him of
her innocence, is her dying remark to Emilia that she dies a guiltless
death provoked by herself alone, a remark which carries not a word
of reproach or recrimination for her husband's hideous cruelty:
"Farewell. / Commend me to my kind lord. O, farewell!" (V, ii,
125–26). Lodovico, who warmly greets the worthy General moments
before Desdemona is slapped, best captures the amazement of all
save Iago at the bestial change that has transformed Othello into the
green-eyed monster:

> Is this the noble Moor whom our full Senate
> Call all in all sufficient? Is this the nature
> Whom passion could not shake? whose solid virtue
> The shot of accident nor dart of chance
> Could neither graze nor pierce? (257–61)

The structure of the last half of the play is remarkably firm as,
following III, iii, the spectators' attention is drawn toward Othello's

private struggles with increasing intensity. More specifically, in four successive waves Shakespeare repeats and intensifies Othello's commitment to passion, thus building the tension to a peak just prior to the murder in Act V. Othello's fateful decisions are made, to be sure, at the end of III, iii, without the benefit of one shred of evidence, and nothing essentially changes between this scene and V, ii. What the spectators do see, however, is the progressive deterioration of Othello's mentality as he grows more determined to commit the action to which a moment of hot passion has already forced him to agree.[53] The first such wave (III, iv, 32–98) occurs immediately after his decision, as he confronts Desdemona before the castle, addressing her as "chuck" and demanding the handkerchief which he believes she has given to Cassio and which he asserts has "magic in the web" (69).[54] As his anger waxes hotter, he for the first time becomes overtly disrespectful to his shocked and bewildered wife, stubbornly demanding the napkin in threatening grunts that become almost bestial: "Ha! Wherefore? . . . Is't lost? Is't gone? Speak, is't out o' th' way? . . . Say you? . . . How? . . . Fetch't, let me see't. . . . Fetch me the handkerchief! My mind misgives. . . . The handkerchief. . . . The handkerchief! . . . 'Zounds!" (78 ff.).

In the second wave (IV, i, 1–209), Iago is at further work upon the Moor's diseased mind. Far bolder now, he graphically describes Desdemona's liaison with Cassio, their kissing in private, their being naked in bed together, the handkerchief she has given him as a love token, Cassio's blabbing of lying with her. Othello's white-hot pas-

---

53. Recently Othello has been described as a composite character: "normal," "romantic," "psychotic" (Robert Rogers, "Endopsychic Drama in *Othello*," *SQ*, XX [1969], 213); he is transformed "from a tender trusting lover into an insanely jealous murderer" (K. P. Wentersdorf, "Structure and Characterization in *Othello* and *King Lear*," *CE*, XXVI [1965], 647).

54. The obsession with the handkerchief is a symptom of "the delusion which grips the hero in the middle phase of the tragic action" (David Kaula, "Othello Possessed: Shakespeare's Use of Magic and Witchcraft," *Shakespeare Studies*, II [1966], 127). See also Michael C. Andrews, "Honest Othello: The Handkerchief Once More," *SEL*, XIII (1973), 273–84. In an unusual reading, Julian C. Rice brands Desdemona as psychologically dishonest ("Desdemona Unpinned: Universal Guilt in *Othello*," *Shakespeare Studies*, VII [1974], 219).

sion (42–43) renders him literally incoherent ("Pish! Noses, ears, and lips? Isn't possible—Confess?—Handkerchief?—O devil!") moments before, in physical collapse, he reveals to the spectators and to the immensely pleased Iago the extent of the inner corrosion. Following the ensign's clever staging of the scene-within-the-scene in which Cassio appears to brag anew of his amorous conquest and in which the fateful handkerchief passes from Bianca's hand to Cassio's, Othello's spiritual perturbations are graphically reflected in his whirling dialogue:

> Let her rot, and perish, and be damned to-night; for she
> shall not live. . . . O, the world hath not a sweeter creature!
> . . . Hang her! . . . O, she will sing the savageness out of
> a bear! . . . The pity of it, Iago! O Iago, the pity of it, Iago!
> (178–79, 180–81, 184, 185–86, 192–93)

Within moments, however, Othello recommits himself to destroying Desdemona, responding to the suggestion of strangulation with the comments that the "justice of it pleases" (205).

The third wave (IV, i, 210–56) provokes Othello to strike his wife in public. Lodovico arrives with orders for Othello to return to Venice and for Cassio to replace him in command (an order which, assuming sufficient time has elapsed, sharply points up how ineffective the Moor's command and his communication with his home base have become). Again, when the orders remind him of Cassio, his speech (227 ff.) becomes fragmented ("Fire and brimstone! . . . Are you wise? . . . Indeed? . . . I am glad to see you mad. . . . Devil! . . . O devil, devil!"); and, when he overhears Desdemona indicate pleasure that Cassio is to assume command, he strikes her impulsively in what amounts to a painful foreshadowing of the deed he will shortly enact in the privacy of his bedchamber. Above all, this scene intensifies Othello's passion by forcing him to realize that his time and opportunity are limited and that, if he is indeed to move against the sinful lovers, it must be posthaste.

In the brothel scene (IV, ii, 1–94), the fourth wave, both Othello's misguided sense of honor and his language are at their most extravagant. Openly confronting Desdemona with charges of infidelity, he brands her "chuck" (24), "strumpet" (81), "weed" (67), and "cunning whore of Venice" (89), guilty of deeds at which "Heaven stops the nose" (77), the "moon winks" (77), and the "bawdy wind" is hushed (78–79); her honesty equates with "summer flies . . . in the shambles / That quicken even with blowing" (66–67). Claiming that she has transformed his heart into a "cistern for foul toads" to "knot and gender in" (61–62), he is furious that she has made him a figure for the age to scorn and mock.

In his soliloquy in Act V, the spectators see Othello as a man whose mind has been virtually paralyzed by the monstrous obsession with his own sense of justice. Torn between revulsion for his wife's degradation and affection for the woman he earlier loved beyond measure, he nonetheless moves with awesome resolution to the fulfillment of his role as both judge and executioner:

> It is the cause, it is the cause, my soul.
>
> . . . .
>
> She must die, else she'll betray more men.
> Put out the light, and then put out the light.
>
> . . . .
>
> O balmy breath, that dost almost persuade
> Justice to break her sword!
>
> . . . .
>
> This sorrow's heavenly;
> It strikes where it doth love.
>
> (ii, 1, 6–7, 16–17, 21–22)

His final conversation with his wife is replete with Christian terms: "repent," "prayed," "unreconciled," "heaven," "grace," "spirit," "soul," "amen," "confess," "sin," "oath" (10–54 passim). Beneath this verbal façade of piety, however, is the bloody passion which causes his eyes to roll, which prompts him to gnaw his lip, and which bursts forth in the cruelty of his yelling "strumpet" in defiance of her request for time to say but one prayer. The impact of the scene results in part from Desdemona's total innocence. Indeed, in her appearance immediately prior to her death (a scene that serves a purpose far more significant than one of comic relief) Desdemona has re-affirmed her determination to be faithful to her husband at all cost. Emilia, developed at this point as a foil to her mistress, coyly asserts that she would not abuse her husband for a small price, but for the world—well, "who would not make her husband a cuckold to make him a monarch?" (IV, iii, 74–75). After all, if one gained the world, would she not also gain the privilege of redefining wrong and right? Even in this unguarded moment of levity and in the wake of having received from Othello a gross repudiation both public and private, Desdemona is unable to comprehend such an action, observing that she really does not believe there is a woman in the world who would do such a wrong.

His tragic insight begins within seconds, as the shock of Emilia's call rings from him, "My wife! My wife! What wife? I have no wife. / O, insupportable! O heavy hour!" (V, ii, 98–99). And while in life she could not persuade him of her innocence, her dying words to Emilia (which, in returning love for hatred, makes no mention of his brutal act) apparently does. Confronted on every side with evidence of the stupidity and cruelty of his deed, his momentary reactions range from the painful "O! O! O!" (199) to his "why should honor outlive honesty?" (246). A conscious self-debasement (not unlike Lear's "I am a very foolish fond old man") is involved in his admission that it is only a "vain boast" that one "can control his fate" (265–66), an assumption that had been at the very center of his earlier proclamations concerning the cause and heavenly justice.[55]

55. At one extreme critics call this moment a "sacrament of penance" (R. N. Hallstead, "Idolatrous Love: A New Approach to Othello," *SQ*, XIX [1968], 122), "salvation" (K. O. Myrick, "The Theme of Damnation in Shakespearean Tragedy," *SP*, XXXVIII [1941], 244). At the other extreme, it is a final prideful act of "self-justification" (Whitaker, *The Mirror*, p. 253) in which "everybody loses" (Jan Kott, *Shakespeare Our Contemporary*, trans. Boleslaw Taborski [Garden City, New York: Doubleday, 1966], p. 125). Whatever moral judgments one may draw (at his own risk), the spectators are made to feel that Othello in his final moments is restored to a kind of dignity (Granville-Barker, IV, 116); if the Moor "has not the self-knowledge" of the other Shakespearean heroes, "he at least has a super abundance of vitality" (Clifford Leech, *Shakespeare's Tragedies* [New York: Oxford Univ. Press, 1950], p. 39); in "ask[ing] only that the truth be told about him" he achieves a kind of purgation, a "swearing of the truth" (Madeleine Doran,

So also it is deliberate humiliation that provokes him to assert that one look from Desdemona will "hurl" his "soul from heaven" (275) and to call for the devils to "whip" him from her "heavenly sight" (278–79), to "roast" him in "sulphur" (280), and to wash him in "steep-down gulfs of liquid fire" (281). In his most telling comment, he requests that the report of his deeds omit nothing, that he be set down as one who, perplexed in the extreme, "threw a pearl away / Richer than all his tribe" (346–48), as one whose "subdued eyes" drop tears (348), as a "circumcised dog" (355) whose only remaining honor was to destroy himself.

Christian apologists have argued at length that Othello's suicide is the act of pride and despair, that on the one hand his soul is saved and on the other hand that it is damned.[56] It may well be either; without a sixth act in which Shakespeare might conceivably be interested in the protagonist's eternal state, the most one can say with assurance is that such a matter is not a concern of the play. The essential thrust is the self-knowledge concerning *this* life which the protagonist gains (though the acquisition may well cost his life) and the implications of such an experience for the spectators. And, for Othello, the spectators are made to feel that his death, whatever the church might say about it, is somehow ennobling, that it is an act of expiation which he is capable of only after he achieves humility and self-knowledge through agony and heart-rending suffering. At the very least he recognizes his fundamental lack of wisdom, and in his final rhetorical efforts to rise above the muddle and death the audience is "released from antipathy and made able to react to the hero's demand for what is essentially sympathy . . . without the distorting necessity for moral judgment."[57]

"Good Name in *Othello*," *SEL*, VII [1967], 216); see also R. B. Heilman, *Magic in the Web* (Lexington: Univ. of Kentucky Press, 1959), p. 234.

56. Ribner (p. 112) claims, for example that "it is essential to the dramatic design that Othello think of himself as destined for hell." To the contrary, Marion Hope Parker (*The Slave of Life* [London: Chatto and Windus, 1955], p. 126) asserts that the "audience knows that in his renunciation of evil . . . Othello has merited salvation."

57. Peter Mercer, "*Othello* and the Form of Heroic Tragedy," *CQ*, XI (1969), 48–61. By emphasizing the "heroic intensity of the struggle, against

All things considered, *Othello* is probably the least complicated of Shakespeare's tragic plots. Once past the rush of events in Act I—which motivate the journey to Cyprus and also develop the spectators' perspective for the protagonist—very little actually happens. The action is simple, yet just such economy of design permits the playwright to focus the audience's attention intensely on the lack of self-knowledge which renders Othello woefully susceptible to jealousy concerning his new wife; the important thing is not what in fact happens, but what Othello thinks happens—not what he is told, but the monstrous fabrications that he allows to result from it.

Shakespeare's essential purpose, in short, is to force the viewers inside the mind of a man, noble and talented but incipiently wrathful and jealous, and (even as they observe the total sweep of the action) to confront them with the emotional impact of his destruction. If the dramatist is to succeed, the interest must arise, as in Hamlet and—less successfully—in Brutus, from the ever-intensifying pressures mounting in Othello's spirit rather than from the external events of the plot itself. To this end he creates an antagonist whose soliloquies and asides in the early acts provide a rich perspective of dramatic irony and whose comments guide the spectators' attention to both Othello's present nobility and his potential weakness. These same structural devices of internalization are transmitted to Othello in the last half of the play; and, in successive scenes which reiterate the situation of the protagonist's decision and intensify his spiritual agony, the spectators' interest increases progressively to the climactic moments of the murder and the subsequent heartsick despair of tragic waste coupled with the self-knowledge that results from his suffering. One may continue to speak of the cosmological implications—the storm which provides a macrocosmic "foretaste . . . of what is to

---

the conventional background of the *ars* [*moriendi*], Shakespeare evokes great sympathy for the human Othello" (Bettie Anne Doebler, "Othello's Angels: The *Ars Moriendi*," *ELH*, XXXIV [1967], 158). See also Albert Gerard, " 'Egregiously an Ass': The Dark Side of the Moor," *Shakespeare Survey*, X (1957), 105. On the complex connotations of color in the play, see Doris Adler, "The Rhetoric of *Black* and *White* in *Othello*," *SQ*, XXV (1974), 248–57.

happen to Othello's soul,"[58] the symbolic movement "from *the city* to barbarism, . . . from order to riot, from justice to wild revenge and murder, from truth to falsehood,"[59] the universal nature of the struggle between the higher and lower faculties of the human spirit. But, for all practical purposes, the dramatic focus is sharply limited: the time is condensed, too sensationally for many; and the action is single, permitting no diversion of interest. Othello's agony—involving the actual murder and the recognition of his error—is more isolated than that of any other Shakespearean tragic hero. The structure of the drama, which forces the spectators' focus to become progressively more personal and progressively more intense, is the key to its power.

58. Theodore Spencer, *Shakespeare and the Nature of Man* (New York: Macmillan, 1942), p. 125.

59. Alvin Kernan, ed., *Othello* (New York: New American Library, 1963), p. xxix.

IV

THE COSMIC DIMENSIONS OF TRAGEDY:
KING LEAR, MACBETH

In *Othello* Shakespeare sets forth his least complicated structure to concentrate the spectators' attention on the inner hell of a man blinded by pride and circumstance. The villain as an external pointer who establishes multiple layers of dramatic irony and the successive waves of action which reflect Othello's mounting passion combine to achieve an intense focus on the isolated figure who agonizes over a deed committed in the privacy of his bedchamber. In *King Lear,* most likely Shakespeare's next tragedy chronologically, the movement is reversed —outward and all-encompassing rather than inward and restricting. The disastrous errors of passion, the immediate and eventual consequences, and the painful joy of self-knowledge are enacted in the public arena, and the effects and ramifications are registered on several macrocosmic levels.

The difference is primarily in the structure—the devices by which the spectators' interest is engaged and controlled, by which the audience is made an emotional part of the experience. Most obvious is Shakespeare's use of the fully realized double plot, among the tragedies a feature unique to this work. Lear and Gloucester face similar dilemmas, are guilty of similar misjudgments, and must pay similar consequences. Their full tragic cycle—involving the commitment to passion and in turn a clearly perceptible anagnorisis—is delineated, not (as with Hamlet, Othello, and Macbeth) through the usual devices of internalization, but through the Fool (for Lear) and Edgar in disguise as Tom o' Bedlam (for Gloucester)—characters whose most significant dramatic function is to provide the principals an effective means by which to express their innermost thoughts. Finally, through soliloquies and asides the playwright establishes three major tragic pointers to guide the audience's response to this experience— Edmund as spokesman for the self-interest which ever stands ready to profit from the prideful naivete of others and Kent and Edgar (apart from his disguise) as spokesmen for the disinterested self-knowledge vital to man's successful completion of his journey through this tainted society, knowledge which enables one both to have a clear vision of reality by removing self from the center of one's universe and also to realize human love in its profoundest sense. These characters, unlike the Fool and Poor Tom, perform roles important to the narrative itself, but they also sporadically function as spokesmen for the polarized values that both destroy and regenerate Lear and Gloucester.

The single most important structural element is the double action, the extension of "a reinforcing sub-plot . . . to every situation and motive."[1] Elsewhere Shakespeare occasionally utilizes parallel strands of plot, as in the successive and mounting waves of action in *Richard III* that depict the fall from high to low degree of illustrious individuals and set the stage for Richard's final moments, or as in Laertes' and Fortinbras' desire to gain revenge for the death of their fathers, action that both contrasts with and reinforces Hamlet's central problem. He frequently utilizes a foil to sharpen characterization, as with Mercutio, whose attitude toward love contrasts with Romeo's, or Virgilia, whose love for Coriolanus contrasts with Volumnia's. But in no other play does he rely so extensively on the parallel relationship of character and action.

While there are numerous foils (for example, Albany and Corn-

1. Ashley H. Thorndike, *Tragedy* (Boston: Houghton Mifflin, 1908), p 169. The Gloucester plot "helps us to understand, and feel, the enduring agony of Lear" (G. Wilson Knight, *The Wheel of Fire* [Oxford: Oxford Univ. Press, 1930], p. 169). "Lear's tragedy is progressive or incremental, . . . Gloster's . . . catastrophic" (J. I. M. Stewart, "The Blinding of Gloster," *RES*, XXI [1945], 266). Gloucester's fall, partly as a result of Lear's, follows it in the play, but events in the last two acts precede the related actions of the main plot and become a specific commentary on them (Virgil Whitaker, *The Mirror Up to Nature* [San Marino, Calif.: Huntington Library, 1965], p. 218). Maynard Mack has recently described this structure as homiletic (*King Lear in Our Time* [Berkeley: Univ. of California Press, 1965], p. 71. See also John Ellis, "The Gulling of Gloucester: Credibility in the Subplot of *King Lear*," *SEL*, XII (1972) 289. Both Sigurd Burckhardt (*Shakespearean Meanings* [Princeton: Princeton Univ. Press, 1968], p. 238) and Bridget G. Lyons ("The Sublot as Simplification in *King Lear*," in *Some Facets of King Lear: Essays in Prismatic Criticism*, ed. Rosalie L. Colie and F. T. Flahiff [Toronto: Univ. of Toronto Press, 1974], p. 36) stress the "related but contrasted ways of structuring experience."

wall as the king's sons-in-law, Burgundy and France as suitors for Cordelia, Oswald and Caius as messengers to Regan), the central dramatic reiteration is the parallel experiences of Lear and Gloucester, both of whom are "old men who learn . . . too much too late"[2]— men of social authority who have grown old in vanity and who have with smug self-confidence long since ceased to question either the intelligence or the justice of their decisions. At the outset they exemplify the unexamined life; by the conclusion personal and public tragedy has forced each of them to gaze directly at the emotional void that results from egomania and to reaffirm the supreme value of selfless love, even though beyond the point of being able to live to enjoy it.

The opening scenes establish several fundamental similarities and thus, as Norman Rabkin has recently noted, force the spectators to "make sense of the play" by questioning "the principles underlying the . . . analogies."[3] Without seeming to realize the possible consequences, both Gloucester and Lear admit publicly to a deed of dubious propriety—for Lear, one of the immediate moment; for Gloucester, one of the past. Gloucester acknowledges the "good sport" in "making" his "whoreson" (I, i, 22), whose mother grew "round-wombed" and had a "son for her cradle" before she had a "husband for her bed" (13–15). Meanwhile Lear peremptorily announces his "darker purpose" (36) of dividing his kingdom into three portions. From these deeds, which are the center of attention as each principal first appears on stage, stem the mutual disasters. Both men have acted whimsically toward their children. However loudly Gloucester may affirm that his legitimate son is "no dearer" (19) in his account than his "knave," Edmund has grown up under the stigma of bastardy. In-

2. Mark Van Doren, *Shakespeare* (New York: Henry Holt, 1939), p. 215. Each at the outset is blinded by a kind of hubris (Lawrence Rosinger, "Gloucester and Lear: Men Who Act Like Gods," *ELH*, XXXV [1968], 491–504); and, as Russell A. Fraser has observed, "Evil, which is yoke fellow to ignorance, stems from a failure rightly to distinguish the good" (*Shakespeare's Poetics* [London: Routledge and Kegan Paul, 1962], p. 119).

3. *Shakespeare and the Common Understanding* (New York: Free Press, 1967), pp. 32–33. The subplot, according to W. F. Blissett ("Recognition in *King Lear*," in Colie and Flahiff, pp. 105, 108), gives coherence to the main plot, which is "directionless except in the direction of greater intensity."

deed, through specific reference to the fact that he has been away for the past nine years and that soon he shall again depart, Shakespeare underscores the extended period of time Edmund has been kept discreetly out of sight. No such time span is mentioned in *Arcadia*; his counterpart, Plexirtus, is simply called home by his father. Lear, at the other extreme, has openly catered to Cordelia, his joy; Goneril later affirms that he always loved Cordelia most. The ego of both men renders them susceptible to the hypocrisy of those they should know intimately—Goneril and Regan with their fulsome praise and Edmund with his obsequious determination to protect a father from a brother's dangerous avarice. And, in the alienation and banishment of the only child capable of true concern, each naively clears the cage for those who will stalk and destroy with unconscionable zeal.

In the initial stages of the turmoil neither proud man considers for a fleeting moment that the responsibility might lie with him. Lear assumes that the cruelty of his daughters is but a temporary anomaly in the "sweet sway" (II, iv, 185) of Nature, who maintains cosmic harmony through insistence on due reverence and obedience to elder, father, and king.[4] For Gloucester the fault is also a momentary deviation in an essentially benevolent nature: "These late eclipses in the sun and moon portend no good to us" (I, ii, 101–2); "Nature finds itself scourged" by disaster as "love cools, friendship falls off, brothers divide" (103–4). As the schemes of malicious ambition take firmer root, both Lear and Gloucester are deprived of the warmth, protection, and sovereignty of the home. The doors are literally shut on the old king, who, forced to "taste his folly" (II, iv, 286), must contend with the "fretful elements" and the "impetuous blasts" (III, i, 4, 8) of the approaching storm. Gloucester's dilemma is similar. Control of his own home is usurped by Cornwall, and shortly thereafter he is bound and tortured—even as he protests the monstrous horror of guests' committing foul play upon the host.

4. Emrys Jones, who sees Lear as "James's 'anti-type' " in seeking to divide England ("Correspondence on *King Lear*," *CQ*, III [1961], 74), and R. H. Darby, who believes that Shakespeare here becomes critical (like James) of astrology ("Astrology in Shakespeare's *Lear*," *English Studies*, XX [1938], 256), assert that Shakespeare may be providing courtly compliments for the new king. E. K. Chambers, on the other hand, asserts that "such a play could

In a broad sense Lear's mad scenes (III, ii, iv, vi) are the emotional equivalent of Gloucester's blinding; the mental anguish of the one and the physical anguish of the other compel each sufferer to recognize the truth and to confess the stupidity of his earlier judgment. At this point they are, however, far indeed from a reassertion of right reason: both swing wildly from the position of disregarding the significance of human responsibility in a teleological universe controlled by benevolent deities to the position of disclaiming the possibility of such responsibility in a nihilistic one. Gloucester now thinks man a worm: "As flies to wanton boys, are we to th' gods; / They kill us for their sport" (IV, i, 36–37). In despair he renounces the world as no longer bearable and collapses in what he assumes to be a fall to death and to release from a meaningless life. So also Lear—beyond the delirium of his madness—proclaims the world a place fit only for copulation and justice merely a system by which one man exploits another; man is but a "natural fool of fortune" on "this great stage of fools" (IV, vi, 188, 180).

Both Gloucester and Lear emerge from this despair in Act IV. Gloucester in scene vi, amazed to be alive, swears that never again will he permit his "worser" spirit to tempt him to doubt the purpose of life. Lear in scene vii awakens in Cordelia's arms, admitting that the tears of contrition "scald like molten lead" (48) and acknowledging that he is "a very foolish fond old man" (60). Even in prison he and Cordelia—reunited in love—will profess to read the riddle of existence, to take upon themselves "the mystery of things" as if they were "God's spies" (V, iii, 16–17). Finally, both men face a brutal test of their convictions in Act V, and both suffer a momentary regression—Gloucester when he hears that Cordelia's forces have been defeated and Lear when he carries his dead daughter on stage. The despair is but momentary, however; caught between the beauty of selfless love which they have discovered and the cruel forces of nature which demand full payment for earlier destructive forces set in motion by pride's misjudgment, each dies of a broken heart. Gloucester's

---

never have been performed at court at all" (*William Shakespeare* [Oxford: Clarendon Press, 1930], I, 470).

"flawed heart," held in tension between the extremes of joy and grief, bursts "smilingly" (iii, 197, 200), and Lear breathes his last while gazing on Cordelia: "Do you see this? Look on her! Look, her lips, / Look there, look there" (V, iii, 311–12). While one can never be absolutely certain whether Lear does or does not assume his daughter to be alive as he holds her in his arms, the fundamental significance of the drama does not rest on this particular point. Belief that she is alive can certainly increase his joy, just as belief that she is dead can add to his profound despair. But the impact of his final moments results from the combination of both emotions held in heart-rending tension. He is ecstatic over his love, newly found and experienced through Cordelia, which directly gives the lie to a meaningless and nihilistic universe, while at the same time he is tormented by her tragedy for which ultimately he is responsible.

Since Shakespeare himself chose to interlace the story of the king with the story of the earl, he was obviously aware of the similarities, and to assert that he develops a careful relationship between the two would be an understatement. Lear and Gloucester for the spectators are separate-but-related reflections of the same tragic dilemma. The experience of the one clarifies and intensifies the experience of the other. And the spectators' attitude toward the one reinforces the attitude toward the other. In these characters, in effect, Shakespeare depicts a composite portrait of a noble man led by pride to disastrous misjudgment, who through torturous agony must lose physical comfort—indeed eventually life—before he is able to gain a true vision of himself and of those around him. Each must revolve a complete cycle on the wheel of fire—from the wrath and fury provoked by vain self-complacency, to the self-pity and despair resulting both from the physical pain and the emotional agony of wounded pride, to the humility that comes after the purgation of selfishness and relegates physical fortune or misfortune to secondary importance.

By common consensus this is the most profoundly absorbing experience in Shakespeare's tragedies, yet surprisingly neither Lear nor Gloucester speaks a single line of soliloquy or aside. Instead the playwright creates for each a stylized character whose dialogue with the principal has the effect of soliloquy and prompts the spectators to share emotionally his spiritual struggle. The Fool, perhaps Shakespeare's most important addition to the legend, serves such a purpose for the old king. In the early scenes Lear acts without thinking: his pompous indignation is almost instinctive, the result of years of autocratic rule in which his word has been an unchallenged command. Without a moment's hesitation, for instance, he slaps Oswald for bandying looks with him. Later, during his suffering, his confused thoughts will underscore just how blindly presumptuous he has become:

> They flattered me like a dog, and told me I had the white
> hairs in my beard ere the black ones were there. To say "ay"
> and "no" to everything that I said! "Ay" and "no" too was
> no good divinity. . . . They told me I was everything. 'Tis
> a lie—I am not ague-proof.   (IV, vi, 96–100, 103–4)

When a retainer observes that the king is not entertained with that ceremonious affection of the past, the spectators note his first glimmer of reflection: "I have perceived a most faint neglect of late, which I have . . . blamed as mine own jealous curiosity" (I, iv, 65–66). Significantly, at this very moment—well over six hundred lines into the play—Lear calls for "my Fool." From this point through III, vi, the Fool will appear on six occasions; he will speak a total of two hundred and forty lines, almost exclusively to Lear (with the exception of two lines to Goneril and scattered lines to Kent, all of which relate directly to his master); and he will disappear as abruptly as he comes. On several occasions (I, iv, 226 ff.; II, iv, 122 ff.; III, iv, 108 ff.; III, vi, 84 ff.) he will fall suddenly silent when other characters appear on stage; while one can assume that such silence is natural and proper to a fool during the conversation of his social superiors, it is hardly consistent with the blunt and forthright liberties he takes with the king. A character totally without individual personality and totally without narrative purpose, he in effect is a stage device for Lear's articulation of his emotional condition.[5]

5. The Fool has been branded everything from "reason itself" (Robert Speaight, *Nature in Shakespearian Tragedy* [New York: Collier Books, 1962], p. 108) to the "indiscretions" of an "immature boy" (J. W. Bennett, "The

Like Feste in *Twelfth Night*, the Fool defines his role carefully for the spectators. He sees himself neither as buffoon nor sycophant, but as one who entertains with the facts of reality. He is not, for example, like the "bitter fool" who has counseled Lear to give away his lands (I, iv, 129); nor is he "altogether fool" (144) since "lords and great men" will give him no "monopoly" (145–46). He is incapable of lying though he is frequently in danger of being "whipped for speaking true" (174). And he is also incapable of infidelity when his master's fortunes are marred:

> ... the Fool will stay,
> And let the wise man fly.
> The knave turns Fool that runs away;
> The Fool no knave, perdy. (II, iv, 78-81)

In fulfilling his role, the fool's only weapon is the barbed phrase, a "new form of . . . dialogue . . . which is no longer based upon rational communication . . . but which is a finer and more subtle interplay of shifting meanings and hints."[6] Initially he quite bluntly speaks the truth the king cannot bring himself to admit. Lear has done Cordelia "a blessing against his will" (I, iv, 97–98) since by giving all his titles away he now is no better than a fool. Time and again this fact is reiterated. "When thou clovest thy crown i' th' middle and gav'st away both parts, thou bor'st thine ass on thy back o'er the dirt" (I, iv, 152–54). He has given his daughters the rod and put down his

---

Storm Within: The Madness of *Lear*," *SQ*, XIII [1962], 144–45), from "one aspect of Lear's own nature" (Paul A. Jorgensen, *Lear's Self-Discovery* [Berkeley: Univ. of California Press, 1967], p. 111), "Lear's alter ego" (R. H. Goldsmith, *Wise Fools in Shakespeare* [Liverpool: Liverpool Univ. Press, 1958], p. 66), to the "consciousness of a split society" (J. F. Danby, *Shakespeare's Doctrine of Nature* [London: Faber and Faber, 1949], p. 113). In any case, it is naive to call what he does "irrelevant" (Harriett Dye, "The Appearance Reality Theme in *King Lear*," *CE*, XXV [1964] 516). His antics are like a "screen on which Shakespeare flashes . . . readings from the psychic life of the protagonist" (Maynard Mack, "The Jacobean Shakespeare," in *Jacobean Theatre* [London: Arnold, 1960], p. 24).

6. W. H. Clemen, *The Development of Shakespeare's Imagery* (Cambridge, Mass.: Harvard Univ. Press, 1951), p. 142. See also Kenneth Muir, ed., *King Lear* (London: Methuen, 1952), p. lv.

own breeches (164–65). Now he is "an O without a figure, . . . nothing, . . . Lear's shadow" (183–84, 185, 221). As Lear makes ready to travel to Regan's home, the Fool ominously predicts that the second daughter will act no differently from the first and that the ultimate result can only be tragedy. Lear, he quips, should not have been old until he was wise.

In the second stage the Fool, just as methodically as he earlier insists on the bitter truth, pushes the king to the brink of insanity—and beyond. Lear has admitted the truth; now shut out of the house, he rails at the approaching storm. While he calls down the world's destruction on ingratitude, the Fool provokes him with one thrust after another: "Good nuncle, in; ask thy daughter's blessing" (III, ii, 11–12); anyone with any sense would have a house to put his head in during such a night; the "realm of Albion" has "come to great confusion" (91–92). As Lear's mind snaps—first, as he believes Tom o' Bedlam to be a projection of his wronged condition and, second, as he tries his imaginary daughters before his macabre magistrates—the Fool harps on madness, even as he reiterates the stupidity of one's giving all to avaricious children: "This cold night will turn us all to fools and madmen" (III, iv, 75); is a madman "a gentleman or a yeoman?" (vi, 10); "he's a mad yeoman that sees his son a gentleman before him" (13–14); "he's mad that trusts in the tameness of a wolf, a horse's health, a boy's love, or a whore's oath" (18–19).

Through Lear's responses to the Fool, Shakespeare builds the spectators' sympathy for the king. Certainly at the outset Lear is an exasperating character whose alienation from the spectators is complete, vainly and stupidly banishing Kent and his daughter (whose two asides exist solely to signal the sincerity of her love and the agony of her inability to mouth it in artificial terms). Using the love of others to gratify his selfishness, he is hardly less detestable at Goneril's home as he demands constant attention and arrogantly asserts that he will "not stay a jot for dinner" (I, iv, 8).

Whereas the old Leir play depicts only a character of extremes, a wrathful king in Act I and a humble penitent in the remaining action, Shakespeare emphasizes the growth of self-knowledge which in turn permits the audience sympathetically to share Lear's dilemma. And on each occasion the statement that signals such introspection is a direct result of the Fool's barbs and is uttered in his presence.[7] In I, iv, for instance, as Goneril proves an inhospitable hostess, Lear responds to the Fool's insinuation that the cart is drawing the horse with a query that reveals he is beginning to perceive the horrible truth, at least dimly: "Does any here know me? This is not Lear. . . . Who is it that can tell me who I am" (216, 220). A few lines later he bewails the miseries of repenting too late, and for a fleeting moment he considers what a small fault was Cordelia's by comparison with her sister's: "O Lear, Lear, Lear! / Beat at this gate that let thy folly in" (261–62). In I, v he for the first time asserts Cordelia's innocence, and his comments reflect his spiritual agitation: "O, let me not be mad, not mad, sweet heaven! / Keep me in temper; I would not be mad!" (40–41). In II, iv his response to the Fool's song again indicates his mounting passion: "Hysterica passio, down, thou climbing sorrow" (55); and he specifically calls for the Fool to be his companion as he stalks into the storm-ridden heath. His words in III, ii are filled with self-pity as he calls for the elements to do their worst since they owe him no obedience; again, when the thought of madness occurs, he calls for the Fool: "My wits begin to turn. / Come on, my boy. How dost, my boy?" (67–68). He realizes by III, iv that pomp must "take physic" (33) from the misery around it; and, as he tears off his clothes a few lines later, he acknowledges that he is no better

7. William Frost describes Lear's humility as possible only after the proud king outgrows the ritual of the opening scenes ("Shakespeare's Rituals and the Opening of *King Lear*," *Hudson Review*, X [1958], 584–85); the king in a sense must be invested with motley (Enid Welsford, *The Fool* [New York: Farrar and Rinehart, 1935], p. 253). As Harold Skulsky observes "The finest intelligence that Lear learns . . . is to resolve his abortive attempts at formulating a causal problem of evil" ("*King Lear* and the Meaning of Chaos, *SQ*, XVII [1966], 14). Initially guilty of what J. Leeds Barroll calls "ontological self-sufficiency" (*Artificial Persons: The Formation of Character in the Tragedies of Shakespeare* [Columbia: Univ. of South Carolina Press], p. 194), Lear in his final words, while ambivalent (Phyllis Rakin, "Delusion as Resolution in *King Lear*," *SQ*, XXI [1970], 30), does establish a sense of humility and integrity (Emily W. Leider, "Plainness of Style in *King Lear*," *SQ*, XXI [1970], 45). See also F. D. Hoeniger, "The Artist Exploring the Primitive: *King Lear*," in Colie and Flahiff, pp. 89–102.

than other men, that he shares their common destiny.[8] In III, vi he is at his most pathetic in the trial scene in which he imagines that even the small dogs Tray, Blanch, and Sweetheart bark at him.

With Lear driven to insanity he is also purged of the selfishness to which long years of autocratic rule have accustomed him, and he is successfully transformed into a character who commands the spectators' full sympathy. The Fool, having served his function, is abruptly dropped from the action with the enigmatic quip that he will go to bed at noon.[9] As a character who through dialogue provokes Lear to voice his innermost thoughts, he is in effect replaced by Cordelia. Following the period of despair, when the king kneels in humility before the daughter he has previously wronged so grievously, Lear's finest moments are prompted by her graciousness and total lack of vindictiveness. She prays that her kiss will "repair those violent harms" (IV, vii, 28) that her two sisters have inflicted and begs him to hold his hand in benediction over her head. Shortly thereafter it is over her lifeless body that he agonizingly expresses, not his concern for self, but his outgoing love for another. The Fool, to be sure, has long since been out of the action, but he is chiefly responsible for the possibility of such a moment. Lear's outcry in his final lines, "And my poor fool is hanged" (V, iii, 306), in all probability is an acknowledgment in his delirium of the similarity in nature and function of the only characters to whom he has spoken from the heart.[10]

8. See Dean Frye, "The Context of Lear's Unbuttoning," *ELH*, XXXII [1965], 17–31. R. B. Heilman provides an excellent discussion of the paradoxical themes of "reason in madness" and "madness in reason" (*This Great Stage* [Baton Rouge: Louisiana State Univ. Press, 1948], pp. 225–53). Most recently, Maurice Charney has analyzed the significance of Lear's putting aside his royal garments in " 'We Put Fresh Garments on Him': Nakedness and Clothes in *King Lear*" (Colie and Flahiff, pp. 77–88).

9. Whether the sudden removal is "the one great and grave oversight or flaw" (A. C. Swinburne, *Shakespeare* [London: Oxford Univ. Press, 1909], p. 67) or "a stroke of dramatic economy" (G. I. Duthie, ed., *King Lear* [Cambridge: Cambridge Univ. Press, 1960], p. xxxiii), "his exit line has a melancholy prescience" (John Wain, *The Living World of Shakespeare* [New York: Macmillan, 1964], p. 193).

10. Arthur J. Stringer ("Was Cordelia the King's Fool?" *The Shakespeare Magazine*, III [1897] 1–11) has asserted that the Fool is Cordelia in disguise,

Essentially Edgar in his role of the Bedlamite occupies a similar position with Gloucester. To be sure, he is far more significant than the Fool to the plot itself, appearing in almost twice as many scenes, speaking almost twice as many lines, and being among those conspicuously present at the conclusion. Not only does he function passively as the wronged son who must endure the machinations of his half-brother and the misdirected fury of his father; he also functions actively in the last four scenes of the play—slaying Oswald, delivering to Albany Goneril's message which describes the conspiracy against her husband's life, and successfully challenging Edmund to a duel and charging him openly with treason. Indeed he apparently is to inherit at least half the kingdom, and to him—in the Folio text, at least —is given the signally important task in Shakespearean tragedy of pronouncing the final words of restitution.[11]

Despite these considerable differences, however, the function of Edgar as a stylized character through whom Gloucester is made to articulate his spiritual struggle is in large part similar to that of the Fool. Edgar's character is not significantly developed in the early acts; hence, when he assumes the role of Tom o' Bedlam, he is—like the

---

and T. B. Stroup, among others, that Shakespeare intended the part to be played by the same actor ("Cordelia and the Fool," *SQ*, XII [1961], 127–32). In any case, Lear's reference probably suggests, not a renewed fit of insanity (William Empson, *The Structure of Complex Words* [Norfolk, Conn.: New Directions, 1951], pp. 152), but a confused recognition of their similar qualities (see H. C. Goddard, *The Meaning of Shakespeare* [Chicago: Univ. of Chicago Press, 1951], II, 162).

11. The position of Albany is never made clear. It has been argued that Albany will pick up all the pieces (Leo Kirschbaum, "Albany," *Shakespeare Survey*, XIII [1960], 29; Peter Mortenson, "The Role of Albany," *SQ*, XVI [1965], 217; Warren Stevenson, "Albany as Archetype in *King Lear*," *MLQ*, XXVI [1965], 260, 262). Waldo F. McNeir, to the contrary, claims that Albany's "willingness to relinquish authority to Kent and Edgar" is indicative of his moral growth ("The Last Lines of *King Lear*," *ELN*, IV [1967], 184–85); and John Shaw, that the interruption in Albany's final speech reflects an absolute lack of restitution at the end ("*King Lear*: The Final Lines," *Essays in Criticism*, XVI [1966], 264–65). Concerning Edgar, F. T. Flahiff is convinced that he is Shakespeare's primary figure of reconciliation and the renewal of order, in whom the dramatist consciously is recalling the positive attributes of the tenth-century Saxon king ("Edgar: Once and Future King," in Colie and Flahiff, p. 226).

Fool—essentially a dramatic device without individual personality. Specifically he has appeared in two scenes, speaking a total of twelve lines, most of which are merely reactions to Edmund's queries and, in sharp contrast with his garrulous outbursts as the Bedlamite, are only four or five words in length. On the one hand, the narrative is well advanced: Gloucester, tricked by Edmund into believing his legitimate son desires his estate at any cost, furiously denounces Edgar and seeks his arrest, and Edgar for self-protection is forced to "grime" his face with filth and "outface" the "winds and persecutions" of the sky (II, iii, 9, 12). The spectators, on the other hand, know virtually nothing about Edgar. He has in no significant fashion revealed his attitude either to father or brother. He is indeed legitimate, but he has been provoked to no value judgments; to the spectator he for the moment stands dispassionately between Gloucester and Edmund.

In his disguise he does not prod Gloucester to wrath in order to break his spirit. The most critical moments for Lear occur between the realization and the admission of error; true insight for him can come only through breaking a will so stubborn that it takes the mind with it, and the Fool is significant in that phase of the action. Gloucester, by contrast, simultaneously confronts his error and the disastrous consequences—loss of sight, of land, and of true son. There is no question of his admitting his prideful stupidity; the critical question the play focuses on, through Tom o' Bedlam, is whether he can survive the despair that suddenly closes in from all sides.

Gloucester's experience, then, reiterates and complements Lear's. When Cornwall and Regan take complete command of Gloucester's house, he continues to place full trust in Edmund, confiding in him that a "part of a power" is "already footed" (III, iii, 11–12) to aid the king and that the king must be relieved, even if they die for it. In the following scene, as the old earl observes the effects of grief on Lear, the spectators receive their initial glimpse of Gloucester's internal agony in his remark that, like Lear's, his flesh and blood is so vile as to hate what has begotten it.

> I am almost mad myself. I had a son,
> Now outlawed from my blood; he sought my life

> But lately, very late. I loved him, friend,
> No father his son dearer. True to tell thee,
> The grief hath crazed my wits.   (157–61)

In the painful blinding scene he decries the fierce sisters who sink "boarish fangs" in Lear's "anointed flesh" (III, vii, 58), screaming to the gods as his eyes are destroyed and—when he learns the truth about Edmund—begging the kind gods to forgive him for abusing Edgar. All faith has suddenly vanished, though, at his next appearance: man is but a worm; the gods "kill us for their sport" (IV, i, 37); plagues of heaven strike down "the superfluous and lust-dieted man" (67). His realization of his earlier pride is clear indeed:

> I stumbled when I saw. Full oft 'tis seen
> Our means secure us, and our mere defects
> Prove our commodities.   (IV, i, 19–21)

In utter despair he renounces the world and attempts through suicide to shake off his great affliction.

Convinced at this point that his life is miraculously preserved, he proclaims that he henceforth will bear affliction "till it do cry out itself / 'Enough, enough,' and die" (IV, vi, 76–77). Ironically he now must give audience to Lear's darkest and most anguished outcries, but despite their direct implications he is able to speak of the "ever-gentle gods" (213) and the "bounty and the benison of Heaven" (221). Like Lear he will experience a momentary regression, but like his king he will die assured that human love at its most godlike transcends any theological system that either man or the gods may devise.

Edgar, unlike the Fool, remains with his companion throughout the total experience, concealing his identity until the final moment. Whereas the Fool's major function is to agitate, Tom's is to provide compassion and, in due time, counsel. For such compassion he is schooled on the heath—by observing both the insane Lear and Gloucester, from whom he for the first time hears the reports of his supposed attempts on his father's life. With his disguise creating rich dramatic irony, Edgar strikes several significant chords as he babbles about the "foul fiend" leading him "through fire and through flame" making him "proud of heart" (III, iv, 50–51, 54), and of the necessity of proper obedience to parents. Through remarks concerning "the act of darkness" (83), "contriving of lust" (85–86), and the act of adultery with another man's "sworn spouse" (78), Shakespeare again subtly suggests Gloucester's guilt just prior to the earl's entry.

Edgar's capacity for sympathy is sorely tested in the subsequent scenes. As Tom, a magistrate in the trial of the king's daughters, he admits in an aside that he begins to take Lear's part so much that his counterfeiting is marred, and in a soliloquy he describes the horror of suffering in isolation and the comfort that companionship should provide in such moments. Significantly he also reveals his intention to seek from his father reconciliation, not revenge. Still in a soliloquy two scenes later, while musing over the double sharpness of a lamentable change in fortune for one in great prosperity, he confronts the awesome sight of his once-proud father, now blind and led by a poverty-stricken old man. The intensity of his reaction is registered in his soliloquy and in his five asides throughout the next forty lines. His first concern is not to know how the disaster occurred or who is responsible but to comfort and console, to "play fool to sorrow" (38). With difficulty he conceals the piercing sorrow beneath his disguise as he takes his father's arm and informs him that Poor Tom will lead the way.

In short, Edgar as Tom o' Bedlam serves, on the one hand, like the Fool, as a dramatic vehicle for his companion's emotional release, although through his various asides and soliloquies he constantly emphasizes his double role for the spectators. On the other hand, unlike the Fool, he also provides specific counsel for Gloucester's despair (again in conjunction with a clear statement to the audience): "Why I do trifle thus with his despair / Is done to cure it" (IV, vi, 33–34). Gloucester's survival of his supposed suicide leap provides the basis for Edgar to rebuild his father's shattered faith in life; this miracle is the will of "the clearest gods" (73). Similarly, in the final moments Gloucester's despondent remark that "a man may rot even here" (V,

ii, 8) is countered by Edgar's assertion that man is an individually responsible agent who has no choice but to assert his full energy and his
best capacity in a world over which he has no ultimate control:

> What, in ill thoughts again? Men must endure
> Their going hence, even as their coming hither;
> Ripeness is all.   (V, ii, 9–11)

Gloucester's death is kept offstage so that Lear's final moments will
achieve a maximum impact. The experiences of the two, however,
have been carefully interlaced throughout; and it is inconceivable that
Shakespeare does not intend Edgar's report of Gloucester's death to
be a leading comment on the nature of the king's death and on the
successful completion of Tom o' Bedlam's central function in the
play. The "flawed heart" which, caught between the extremes of joy
and grief, bursts "smilingly" (V, iii, 197) belongs both to Gloucester
and Lear. As Shakespeare envisioned the old men as diverse reflections
of a single human condition, so he conceived of the roles of the Fool
and the madman as similar structural devices through which to articulate that condition.

Although Lear and Gloucester themselves at no time in the play
speak in a soliloquy or an aside, Shakespeare does in other characters
utilize these devices of internalization to provide the moral and
philosophic context for their spiritual trauma and to provide a vision
of the system of values within which the principals must make their
choices. The spectators see directly into three characters—Edgar, Kent,
and Edmund—whose attitudes range from absolute selflessness to
total selfishness. Edgar and Kent reflect, both in their private moments
and in their public actions, an essential concern for others. Edgar, as
we have noted, delivers three soliloquies while guiding Gloucester
during his despair. In two of them, as well as in each of his six asides,
he expresses his compassion for those around him who are suffering,
despite the fact that he too is miserably deprived of family and social
position and forced to live the life of a hunted criminal. To be sure,
he has not sacrificed his position and his safety in order to give aid to
another; neither has he personally sought out the afflicted. But, con-

fronted with the tortured human condition, his immediate response is to provide succor and companionship.

More overtly selfless is Kent, who insofar as the spectators see him is the "embodiment of fidelity" and "selfless loyalty."[12] His love for Lear as king, father, master, and patron prompts him to denounce the banishment of Cordelia as madness and "hideous rashness" (I, i, 151). Interested primarily in Lear's safety, he insists that power is bowing to flattery and majesty falling to folly. This same insistence on the necessity of clear and rational perception is later behind his denunciation of Oswald as a sycophantic courtier: "A knave, a rascal, an eater of broken meats; a base, proud, shallow, beggarly, three-suited, hundred-pound, filthy worsted-stocking knave" (II, ii, 13–15). Such dishonest rogues, concerned only for self, will

> Renege, affirm, and turn their halycon beaks
> With every gale and vary of their masters,
> Knowing nought, like dogs, but following.
>
> (73–75)

For his good offices with Lear he receives banishment from the court and the country, thereby sacrificing everything one materially could hold dear. Nevertheless in his next appearance (his first soliloquy) he states his good intent, even though he stands condemned, to serve the master whom he loves; and he presents himself to Lear as Caius, a very honest-hearted fellow who will serve him truly and can keep honest counsel. Later, placed in the stocks by Regan and Cornwall, he reflects in a soliloquy on Lear's declining fortunes and asserts that only misery can perceive miracles; true perception can come only to the wretched. In his third soliloquy, which closes Act IV, he observes that within the day the aim and end of his life will be completed. Following Lear's death, his own "strings of life" beginning to "crack" (V, iii, 217–18), he admonishes anyone who would stretch the king out

12. Harold S. Wilson, *On the Design of Shakespearian Tragedy* (Toronto: Univ. of Toronto Press, 1957), p. 184; William Ringler, "Exit Kent," *SQ*, XI (1960), 316. Hugh Maclean's argument that Kent in disguise is "a clumsy novice" ("Disguises in *King Lear*," *SQ*, XI [1960], 54) is a strange distortion.

longer on the rack of this tough world. In brief, from first to last Kent—unconcerned for his own fortune, safety, and well-being—devotes himself to caring for Lear; serving another without identity and with no anticipation of reward, he exemplifies the selfless devotion that enables Lear and Cordelia (as well as Gloucester) to rise above the world even at the moment it destroys them.

Kent and Edgar, then, with a combined total of six soliloquies and six asides (eighty-three lines), point the spectators throughout the play to the higher potential of human love. Edmund, on the other hand, with seven soliloquies and one aside (sixty-seven lines) is an avid adherent of self-devotion, an "ego fascinated by its own powers [and] . . . untrammeled by real relation to others."[13] His every move is calculated in terms, not so much of hatred, but of ambition and self-aggrandizement. And only incidentally is his conscience active as he leaps at the most horrifying opportunities. Three soliloquies in the second scene establish his fundamental values as he decries the bastardy that deprives him of inheritance and social acceptance. Setting his sights directly on the legitimate Edgar's land, he produces the forged letter, which Gloucester unquestioningly takes to be genuine. Moments later he scoffs at his father's naive assumption that man is not himself totally responsible for his actions:

> This is the excellent foppery of the world, that when we are sick in fortune, often the surfeits of our own behavior, we make guilty of our disasters the sun, the moon, and stars; as if we were villains on necessity. . . . I should have been that I am, had the maidenliest star in the firmament twinkled on my bastardizing.   (I, ii, 115–18, 127–29)

13. Robert J. Brauer, "Despite of Mine Own Nature: Edmund and the Orders, Cosmic and Moral," *TSLL*, X (1968), 359. See also Theodore Spencer, *Shakespeare and the Nature of Man* (New York: Macmillan, 1942), pp. 135 ff.; Danby, pp. 20 ff.; R. C. Bald, " 'Thou, Nature, Art My Goddess': Edmund and Renaissance Free Thought," in *J. Q. Adams Memorial Studies* (Washington: Folger Library, 1948), pp. 337–49; and Harry Rusche, "Edmund's Conception and Nativity in *King Lear*," SQ, XX (1969), 161–64. For a provocative discussion of the poetic justice operative in Edmund's destruction, see G. T. Buckley, "Was Edmund Guilty of Capital Treason?" *SQ*, XXIII (1972), 94. On the credibility and genuineness of his conversion in the final

He delights in such naivete, however, assured that he will "have lands by wit" from a "credulous father" on whose "foolish honesty" his "practices ride easy" (176, 172, 173–74).

His schemes rapidly achieve success. Cornwall's visit in Gloucester's home, Edmund informs the spectators, "weaves itself" into his business (II, i, 15). Inflicting a wound upon himself to strengthen his claim for loving his father, he constructs a tale of Edgar's villainy which prompts both father and duke to proclaim the illegitimate son a "loyal and natural boy" (84). Predictably, the taste of victory only whets ambition's appetite. Soon he manipulates his father's trust to his own advantage, informing Cornwall that Gloucester is guilty of treason by virtue of knowledge concerning the landing of French troops in support of the king against his daughters; Edmund obviously stands to receive all; "The younger rises when the old doth fall" (III, iii, 23). When Gloucester out of pity seeks to give Lear relief, Edmund in an aside reveals his delight since the suspicion will stick more firmly if his father is discovered comforting the king.

In the final act the spectators realize fully to what grotesque proportions his aspirations have grown. He reflects amusedly on Goneril's and Regan's dispute over him; to both he has sworn his love, but his only concern is his sure and speedy acquisition of total power in the kingdom. To this end Albany, once he serves his role in battle, will be disposed of, and neither Lear nor Cordelia shall ever see pardon once they come within his power. It is quite true that Edmund briefly acknowledges a "sore" conflict between his ambition and his blood (III, v, 21) and that at the conclusion he melodramatically admits that the wheel has come "full circle" (V, iii, 175). Otherwise, however, he is a pure and dispassionate disciple of self as he points the spectators to those values by which Lear and Gloucester in their own ways have both been blinded at the outset of the drama.

At least two minor characters—Cordelia's suitors in Act I—also demand brief notice as pointers. Neither figures in the play beyond the opening scene, but through them Shakespeare effectively is able

moments, see Richard Matthews, "Edmund's Redemption in *King Lear*," *SQ*, XXVI (1975), 25–29.

to establish the opposing values that Edgar, Kent, and Edmund are to reflect throughout the action. Both the Duke of Burgundy and the King of France have indicated marital interest in Cordelia antecedent to the play, assuming, of course, that with her hand will come a princess's title and a handsome dowry. The disinheritance obviously eliminates her desirability to one primarily concerned with bolstering his political and financial power. And Burgundy, confronted with Lear's declaration that her only wealth is to be her father's curse, bluntly proclaims that election can not be made on such conditions. France, on the contrary, perceives that only wrathful fury at her refusal to flaunt her love in response to her sisters provokes the king to disparage the daughter who has been his "best" and "dearest" (214–16). Attracted by person rather than purse and by spiritual affection rather than material expectation, he seizes upon Cordelia's virtues, proclaiming her "most rich being poor, / Most choice forsaken, and most loved despised" (I, i, 250–51). Indeed France voices the major theme of the play—the lesson that both Lear and Gloucester are so painfully to learn—in his assertion that true love is not measured by material concern: "Love's not love / When it is mingled with regards that stands / Aloof from th' entire point" (239–41).

With the parallel experiences of Lear and Gloucester, the two internal pointers who prompt the principals to soliloquize in dialogue, the three external pointers who establish the range of values within which the critical choices occur, as well as the minor pointers and the various foil relationships, Shakespeare has devised in *King Lear* a "complex polyphonic development of . . . themes."[14] Structure is, of course, largely determined by the playwright's thematic intentions and

14. E. W. Talbert, "Lear, the King," in *Medieval and Renaissance Studies* (Chapel Hill: Univ. of North Carolina Press, 1966), p. 98; see also George R. Kernodle, "The Symphonic Form of *King Lear*," in *Elizabethan Studies and Other Essays in Honor of George F. Reynolds* (Boulder: Univ. of Colorado Press, 1945), p. 188. Thomas McFarland (*Tragic Meanings in Shakespeare* [New York: Random House, 1966], pp. 129 ff.) and D. A. Traversi (*An Approach to Shakespeare* [New York: Doubleday, 1956], p. 192) provide perceptive discussions of the multiple perspectives. The play is a "successive stripping away of the layers of appearance" (Ivor Morris, *Shakespeare's God: The Role of Religion in the Tragedies* [New York: St. Martin's Press, 1972], p. 184).

the kind of character he depicts. Certainly in this play a primary concern is to reveal the spiritual struggle within both Lear and Gloucester and to compel the audience to identify emotionally with both the agony and the joy of their growth in tragic insight. But the soliloquy would hardly be a natural medium of expression for men hardened by pride to crass insensitivity and unaccustomed to introspection. Far more effective and credible is a second character, viewed by the audience as objective, who can through conversation force the central figures to react emotionally and reflectively. Moreover Lear's mental lapses on the one hand and the nihilistic despair coincident with Gloucester's savage blinding on the other assume a more awesome significance against the grotesque background of the Fool's riddles and the lunatic's whirling words. Both clothe profound truth in outlandish language: the seeming absence of logic in the Fool's phrases forces Lear to seek the meaning within himself; and poor Tom's companionship and guidance, despite his own misery and destitution, constrain Gloucester to search his own heart for the charity that prompts such compassion without judgment.

This structure, in addition, literally demands that the spectators develop an intimate familiarity with a larger number of characters than in any other Shakespearean tragedy. Such a circumstance supports Shakespeare's obvious intentions to make the ramifications of this tragedy vast, radiating outward from the level of the individual, to the family, to the kingdom, and to the order of nature itself. The theme of the play is also best served by such a structure. Lear and Gloucester must learn the fundamental reality of existence—that humanity encompasses both the animal and the spirit. The insight they must achieve does not involve an isolated decision concerning the ethics of ambition, or of vengeance, or of wasted opportunity: instead it is directly concerned with their spiritual relationships with others—and is meaningless outside that context.[15] Although Cordelia, Edgar, and Kent are essentially static and stylized, Shakespeare through the

---

15. "The form and meaning of the play as a whole" is to be found in the "relationships" between the characters (Francis Fergusson, *The Pattern in His Carpet* [New York: Delacorte, 1970], p. 230), in the "theme of charity in human relations" (Sears Jayne, "Charity in *King Lear*," *SQ*, XV [1964],

soliloquy and the aside is able to stress their selflessness and thus to achieve the maximum emotional impact from the reconciliation of Lear and Cordelia, and Gloucester and Edgar, at the end of Act IV.

The painful testing of the strength of this reconciling love is the subject of the final act. Shakespeare envisions neither a nihilistic "imbecile universe" that makes a "mockery of the absolute and its desecration"[16] nor a sentimental world of easy poetic justice that minimizes the earthly struggle by opting for a glorious heavenly reward.[17] Tragic error and evil, once active, will play out their in-

---

277), in the discovery of "the true and whole meaning of service" (Jonas A. Barish and Marshall Waingrow, "Service in *King Lear*," *SQ*, IX [1958], 348), in the various meanings of love (Terry Hawkes, "Love in *King Lear*," *RES*, X [1959], 178). See further Johannes Allgaier, "Is *King Lear* an Antiauthoritarian Play?" *PMLA*, LXXXVIII (1973), 1037-38.

16. Judah Stampfer, "The Catharsis of *King Lear*," *Shakespeare Survey*, XIII (1960), 10; Jan Kott, *Shakespeare Our Contemporary*, trans. Boleslaw Taborski (New York: Doubleday, 1964), p. 132. The play is an "absolute negation of all forms of hope" (Nicholas Brooke, "The Ending of *King Lear*," in *Shakespeare 1564-1964* [Providence: Brown Univ. Press, 1964], p. 86), a vision of "limitless chaos and evil" (John Holloway, *The Story of the Night* [Lincoln: Univ. of Nebraska Press, 1961], p. 92), of a "universe in which all laws appear to be temporarily suspended" (E. M. Jackson, "The Grammar of Tragedy," *SQ*, XVII [1966], 26). Lear's view of death is "by definition a skeptical-pagan, not a Christian attitude" (William Elton, *King Lear and the Gods* [San Marino, Calif.: Huntington Library, 1966], p. 262); the play is "without a crumb of Christian comfort" (D. G. James, *The Dream of Learning* [Oxford: Clarendon Press, 1951], p. 92). See also Barbara Everett, "The New Lear," *CQ*, II (1960), 325-39; and J. K. Walton, "Lear's Last Speech," *Shakespeare Survey*, XIII (1960), 17.

17. On Lear's earthly existence as "a prelude to life," see: A. C. Bradley, *Shakespearean Tragedy* (New York: Macmillan, 1904), p. 48; Roy W. Battenhouse, *Shakespearean Tragedy* (Bloomington: Indiana Univ. Press, 1969), pp. 285 ff.; Paul N. Siegel, *Shakespearean Tragedy and the Elizabethan Compromise* (New York: New York Univ. Press, 1957), p. 186; Whitaker, pp. 209 ff. On his agony as a test of Christian endurance, see: Geoffrey L. Bickersteth, *The Golden World of King Lear* (London: Proceedings of the British Academy, 1946), p. 92; Carolyn S. French, "Shakespeare's 'Folly': *King Lear*," in *Shakespeare 1564-1964*, p. 70; O. J. Campbell, "The Salvation of Lear," *ELH*, XV (1948), 93-109. The danger of such emphases, as Sylvan Barnet has observed, is that they tend to "shift the focus from this world to the next, muting the conflict of the tragic hero" ("Some Limitations of the Christian Approach to Shakespeare," *ELH*, XXII [1955], 92).

evitable destructive roles, despite one's growth in self-knowledge. Inevitably the most innocent will suffer and die with the most guilty. Cordelia's death may be touching and agonizing, but there is nothing either ultimately negative or incredible about it: she is killed by the forces of destruction unleashed earlier by Lear's and Gloucester's passion. The significant fact is the capacity for spiritual growth reflected in Lear and Gloucester. Both men in the final act are guilty of momentary regression—doubt, uncertainty, despair, but both (to reiterate the previous discussion) die with inward peace though wracked by grief and pain—comforted by love even as they are destroyed by the world and their own previous error. "The victory and the defeat are simultaneous and inseparable,"[18] an "affirmation in the face of the most appalling contradictions."[19]

King Lear is not about a supernatural heaven and hell but about the human condition. As one critic has recently noted, "Almost every possible point of view on the gods and cosmic justice is expressed, from a malevolent, wanton polytheism to an astrological determinism, from an amoral, personified Nature-goddess to 'high-judging Jove.' "[20] With every character invoking his own concept of a deity, the play does not proclaim that there is or is not a god, and it most assuredly does not deny the horror and reality of death. What it does proclaim is that man is a responsible agent and that in the short span of this life he can most nearly experience the godlike ecstasy and comfort of heart through a love of mutual humility and concern, through a human relationship purged of self-interest. Through the complex pointers which converge on Lear and Gloucester, Shakespeare creates an effective structural base for a tragedy both micro-

18. Mack, *King Lear in Our Time*, p. 117.

19. Richard S. Sewall, *The Vision of Tragedy* (New Haven: Yale Univ. Press, 1959), p. 79. See also John D. Rosenberg, "King Lear and His Comforters," *Essays in Criticism*, XVI (1966), 146; Betty K. Stuart, "Truth and Tragedy in *King Lear*," *SQ*, XVIII (1967), 179–80. Rosalie L. Colie argues that Shakespeare is dramatizing "the actual decline of paternal authority" in the society of his own day ("Reason and Need: *King Lear* and the 'Crisis' of the Aristocracy," in Colie and Flahiff, p. 210).

20. Stampfer, p. 153.

cosmic and macrocosmic, and creates a perspective of double vision—forcing the spectators to share fully the protagonist's spiritual struggle while at the same time providing a sufficiently detached view to compel them to sit in judgment on his decisions and anticipate the consequences.

In *Macbeth*, Shakespeare pursues further the concept of tragedy set within a universe whose principal inhabitants lack clear assurance of its teleology. The effects of the tragedy, as in *Lear*, are registered on the level of the individual, of the family, of the state, and of physical nature.[21] In the earlier play, the characters, as we have observed, invoke their various concepts of a deity—with the end result of negating any assumption that a god (benevolent or malevolent) either controls the universe or is remotely concerned with the plight of the individual. Similarly in *Macbeth*, with even the royal diadem appearing only one golden opportunity away from the protagonist, contradictory assumptions of metaphysical authority from God's bright heaven on the one hand and from the witches of the heath on the other converge upon the ambitious Thane of Glamis. Both Macbeth and the spectators are left uncertain about the macrocosmic order, and the various natural phenomena tend to underscore the fundamental ambiguity. On the one hand, for instance, the breath of Nature herself seems foul in the exhalations of the misty tarns from which the weird sisters issue. On the other hand, the same Nature seems convulsed with horror on the night of Duncan's murder. In the "feverous" and trembling earth

> Lamentings [are] heard i' th' air, strange screams of death,
> And prophesying, with accents terrible

21. This "cosmic tragedy" leads to a "contemplation of good and evil in the totality of things" (E. K. Chambers, *Shakespeare: A Survey* [London: Sidgwick and Jackson, 1925], p. 227). Nature, which both "preserves" and "impedes" (L. C. Knights, "On the Background of Shakespeare's Use of Nature in *Macbeth*," *Sewanee Review*, LXIV [1956], 214), is "seen as the mirror of psychic and metaphysical convulsions" (Speaight, p. 53). Ultimately, as Paul Jorgensen has observed, the most striking quality of the play is the "dark and painful power resulting from unparalleled sensational artistry" (*Our Naked Frailties* [Berkeley: Univ. of California Press, 1971], p. 4).

Of dire combustion and confused events
New hatched to th' woeful time.

(II, iii, 52–55)

With the discovery of the assassination the next morning, "the heavens, as troubled with man's act, / Threatens his bloody stage" (II, iv, 5–6); the sun is in eclipse, the mouse-eating owl hawks and kills a falcon, and Duncan's horses break from the stalls and attack each other.

Banquo and Lady Macbeth—like Edmund, Kent, and Edgar—function as choric characters who establish the frame of values within which Macbeth must make his decisions. Through the devices of internalization, the spectator is compelled to share their inner struggles as well as Macbeth's, thus widening the scope of the tragedy beyond the intense focus on a single individual. As with Lear, however, the major emphasis is once more upon the single tragic figure; to the spectators the surrounding characters remain secondary to Macbeth's increasingly awesome descent into villainy. There is no full tragic cycle, no Lear-like regeneration or recognition at the moment of destruction. But there is pathetic regret; and Shakespeare carefully modulates the death of Macbeth's conscience and the parallel growth of his despair through four increasingly intense waves to the point of his death. At the same time, the playwright in the final act attempts to retain the full experience of tragedy by transferring the anagnorisis, in part, away from the tyrant through significant emphasis upon the humanizing effects of suffering (in Lady Macbeth) and upon the restitution of national order (in Malcolm, Duncan's proclaimed heir to the throne).

The philosophic context of the play, more specifically, assumes the existence of neither a benign nor malign God. Certainly the witches suggest the presence of a cruel and inexorable fate that manipulates Macbeth to disaster and destruction.[22] Bearded hags, they are "so

---

22. On the one hand, they are Destinies or Norns (G. L. Kittredge, ed., *The Complete Works of Shakespeare* [Boston: Ginn, 1936], p. 1114), demons credible to the Jacobean audience (W. C. Curry, *Shakespeare's Philosophical Patterns* [Baton Rouge: Louisiana State Univ. Press, 1937], p. 60; Arthur R. McGee, "*Macbeth* and the Furies," *Shakespeare Survey*, XIX [1966], 65),

withered and so wild in their attire" that they do not look like inhabitants of the earth (I, iii, 40); though they seem "corporal," they
melt as "breath into the wind" (81, 82). Macbeth affirms the "more
. . . than mortal knowledge" (I, v, 2–3) of these weird sisters, and
his wife acknowledges their "metaphysical aid" (27); both on at least
one occasion regard the prophecies as fate. Indeed, it is the witches
who introduce the play, setting a macabre and ominous context with
their account of past malice, their incantations, and their more-than-
passing interest in Macbeth.

However, references to God are equally evident, if not equally
mysterious. No less than sixty-one allusions to Christianity (God,
Devil, Heaven, Hell, Grace, repentance, angel, holy, prayers, Golgo-
tha) dot the text.[23] Moreover, no character in the play overtly challenges God's hierarchy; Macbeth himself in his early moments of
introspection unquestioningly refers to God's universe, the life to
come, and the deep damnation consequential to vaulting ambition.
Shakespeare has also carefully arranged the material to juxtapose a
scene reflecting conventional Christian values with a scene in which
allusions to fate and witchcraft predominate. The witches, for
example, appear in two segments of the action. Following I, i and
iii, in which Macbeth receives the prophecy of his future kingship,
Cawdor's execution is described, at which time he

> confessed his treasons,
> Implored your Highness' pardon, and set forth
> A deep repentance. Nothing in his life
> Became him like the leaving it.
>
> (I, iv, 5–8)

"subhuman creatures that bestialize man's nature" (W. A. Main, ed., *The
Tragedy of Macbeth* [New York: Odyssey, 1962], p. 3). On the other, they
are "his own ambition" (Snider, I, 172), a "psychic" phenomenon (James
Kirsch, *Shakespeare's Royal Self* [New York: Putnam's, 1966], p. 337). According to R. H. West, Shakespeare forces each reader to "make his own
rationale of the supernatural in *Macbeth*, . . . just as he might for similar
phenomena in the real world" (*Shakespeare and the Outer Mystery* [Lexing-
ton: Univ. of Kentucky Press, 1968], p. 78).

23. F. C. Kolbe counts over four hundred words and phrases related to sin
and grace (*Shakespeare's Way* [London: Sheed and Ward, 1930], p. 21).

Similarly, in IV, i the witches with their masters present to Macbeth through apparitions an extension of their prophecy. In sharp contrast, Lennox and another lord in III, vi invoke a "holy angel" (45) in their "prayers" (49) that Macduff will succeed in his mission to seek aid from pious and holy King Edward. And in IV, iii Malcolm— describing Edward's willingness to lend support against Macbeth— relates in detail the English king's heaven-sent powers to cure the king's evil. While the passage may well constitute Shakespeare's compliment to the new Stuart monarch, in context the references to his soliciting Heaven, his "holy prayers," the "healing benediction" which he leaves to "the succeeding royalty," the "heavenly gift of prophecy," and the "sundry blessings" which "hang about his throne / That speak him full of grace" (158–59) provide effective counterpoint to the powers of darkness suggested by the withered hags. Significant also is the porter's soliloquy following the murder of Duncan. The drunken babble does indeed provide striking comic contrast with the intense horror of the preceding moment. More important, it serves to thrust Christian references before the spectators at a crucial moment.[24] It is hardly likely that the porter's eight such allusions within twenty-two lines (ranging from "hell" [II, iii, 2] to "heaven" [11], from "God's sake" [10–11] to "everlasting bonfire" [18]) are merely coincidental.

The conflicting value systems are given additional emphasis through Lady Macbeth and Banquo. The structure of the play guides the spectator to a strategic rapport with each of them; as he observes both the external events that shape the situation and their resultant internal struggles, he is simultaneously forced emotionally to participate in their crucial moments and to sit in judgment upon their decisions. On a more intense level, of course, this is precisely the relationship shared by the spectator and the protagonist. Thus, in this fashion also, Shakespeare is widening the scope of the tragic perspective; even as their

24. Both Kenneth Muir (ed., *Macbeth* [London: Methuen, 1951], p. xxviii) and Glynne Wickham ("Hell–Castle and Its Door–Keeper," *Shakespeare Survey*, XIX [1966], 68) relate the figure to the traditional "porter of hell–gate" in the "Harrowing of Hell" miracle playlet. Harry Morris sees an analogy to Dante's *Inferno* ("Macbeth, Dante, and the Greatest Evil," *Tennessee Studies in Literature*, XII [1967], 33).

intimate association with the protagonist intensifies for the spectator the nature of Macbeth's tragic experience, their development independent of him constrains the spectator to appraise the effects of the tragic situation on a broader plane.

Lady Macbeth, in particular, is a tragedy in miniature.[25] Appearing in only nine scenes, she is one of the most intensely conceived characters in Shakespeare. An incredibly high eighty percent of her lines (209 of 262) direct the spectators to her innermost thoughts. More specifically, she delivers four soliloquies for a total of sixty-five lines, twenty-one lines in her sleepwalking scene (a passage which clearly has the impact of soliloquy since she is oblivious to the presence of the doctor and the gentlewoman) and 123 lines either in private conversation with Macbeth or in asides to him. In the course of these lines she evolves from steely ambition, to concerned affection for her husband, and ultimately to despair and madness.

Certainly in the first three acts she is walking testimony to the existence, on a totally human level, of the amoral values suggested by the witches. Her initial appearance, reading in soliloquy Macbeth's account of the prophecy, signals her brutal determination to seize the initiative. Macbeth shall be what he is promised; in order to "catch the nearest way" (I, v, 16), he must rid himself of the "milk of human kindness" (15) and of his reluctance to "play false" (19); he must accept the illness proper to his ambition. To this end she will

> pour [her] spirits in [his] ear
> And chastise with the valour of [her] tongue
> All that impedes [him] from the golden round.
>
> (24–26)

Moments later, informed that Duncan comes to visit the castle, her words are even more startling. With her own form of human witch-

---

25. She commits her husband to the role of "what she imagines manhood should be" (D. W. Harding, "Women's Fantasy of Manhood: A Shakespearian Theme," *SQ*, XX [1969], 247). If she consciously "will[s] submission to demonic powers" (W. M. Merchant, "His Fiend-Like Queen," *Shakespeare Survey*, XIX [1966], 80), her nature "pays at last in remorseful days and sleepless nights the full penalty of violated law" (T. R. Lounsbury, *Shakespeare as a Dramatic Artist* [New York: Scribner's, 1901], p. 415).

craft, she invokes the "murd'ring ministers" (46) associated with deeds of death to "unsex" (39) her, to fill her from the crown to toe with "direst cruelty" (41). Her blood she would have "thick" and devoid of compassion (43); her milk she would convert to "gall" (46). At this point she apparently intends to murder Duncan herself: she calls for "thick night" (48) to hide the "wound" her "keen knife" will make (50), and later she instructs her perturbed husband to leave the "night's great business" to her (66). When his reservations begin to surface, she plies him with charges of cowardice; he is "green and pale" (vii, 37), "afeard" (39), a "coward" (43), a "poor cat" (45), less than a man. In this manner she obviously focuses on the physical dangers involved, thus drawing Macbeth away from consideration of the moral dangers; but, then, one must admit that neither in soliloquy nor in dialogue does she herself seem to regard it as a moral problem.

Precisely why Macbeth has undertaken the deed in Act II is never made clear. Lady Macbeth herself may well be responsible, for in the midsection of the play she displays an undeniable trace of humanity not visible in Act I. To be sure, she still has no moral qualms. And her raw courage continues to be remarkable; she bolsters her husband's spirit during the murder, arranging the evidence herself when he flatly refuses to return to the bedchamber. She further attempts to stay his fears during the banquet scene, and she has the presence of mind to dismiss the group before more is revealed. But the mold is broken. In her third soliloquy she admits that she could not murder Duncan because he resembled her father. More important, in her fourth soliloquy she acknowledges that political power has brought only agonizing frustration: "'Tis safer to be that which we destroy / Than by destruction dwell in doubtful joy" (III, ii, 6–7). At the same time she reveals that she is capable of genuine affection for her husband. His solitary brooding perturbs her, and again and again she counsels him to regain his wonted composure, not to consider so deeply; indeed, her final sane words reflect a concern for his lack of sleep, the "season of all natures" (III, iv, 141). As Sarah Kemble Siddons writes, "Affliction has subdued the insolence of her pride and the violence of her will, for she now comes to seek him out, that she may, at least, participate [in] his misery."[26] Whereas before she spoke to him in lengthy passages bristling with challenge, now her responses on several occasions are briefer (fifteen speeches of one line or less in Acts II and III), encouraging self-control rather than action.

When Lady Macbeth appears for the last time, her mind is a victim of the tension their deed has provoked. As she walks in her sleep, her rambling words recapitulate the crucial moments—Duncan's blood on her hand, the murder-signal of the tolling bell, Macbeth's fear, her assurance that the guards will be blamed, the murder of Macduff's wife. Again one would be hard-pressed to claim that her insanity is based on moral guilt; she makes only one Christian reference in the scene—"Hell is murky" (V, i, 33), this apparently more in connection with Macbeth's fear than her own. She is, however, pathetically human, far different in posture from the earlier calculating and callous opportunist. Obviously there is no recognition scene in the conventional sense, but her madness with its heartsickening torment does render her most sympathetic at the moment of destruction. Moreover, her illness and death provoke a significant response in Macbeth himself.

Banquo's development is minimal in comparison with that of Lady Macbeth, but he does experience temptations similar to Macbeth's.[27] Furthermore, he does so as a credible character, not as a rigid, bloodless foil whose morality comes easy and who, consequently, is everything Macbeth is not. For one thing, his ambitions are real. When the witches predict Macbeth's future, he immediately requests that they address themselves to his "seeds of time" (I, iii, 58) as well. Once he is involved in the prophecy, he seems almost eager for the opportunity to discuss it further with his companion. His ambition is most

26. "Remarks on the Character of Lady Macbeth," in T. Campbell, *Life of Mrs. Siddons* (London, 1834), II, 10. See also Carol Jones Carlisle, *Shakespeare From the Greenroom* (Chapel Hill: Univ. of North Carolina Press, 1969), pp. 399–400.

27. Views range from those of Leo Kirschbaum ("Banquo and Edgar: Character or Function?" *Essays in Criticism*, VII [1957], 7), who asserts that Banquo as merely a foil has no real character and thus no real temptation, to those of Richard J. Jaarsma ("The Tragedy of Banquo," *Literature and Psychology*, XVIII [1967], 87, 89), who claims that Banquo, a "parallel and complementary" character to Macbeth, "undergoes a radical change."

clearly in evidence in his soliloquy in III, i. He fears that Macbeth has played "most foully" (3) for the throne, but he takes obvious comfort in recalling that he "should be the root and father / Of many kings" (5–6). If Macbeth, by whatever means, has fulfilled the prophecy,

> Why, by the verities on thee made good,
> May they not be my oracles as well,
> And set me up in hope?   (8–10)

It is inconceivable that the spectators could miss the irony in Banquo's remark to the new king that his duties to him are knitted with an "indissoluble tie" (17). If the ambition is real, so obviously is the temptation. Almost afraid to sleep and admitting that he has dreamed of the weird sisters (20), he laments in II, i the "cursed thoughts" (8) that his mind gives rise to in repose. Additionally, he acknowledges at least the possibility of "seeking to augment" (27) their predictions.

Most important, though, Banquo does not succumb, and throughout the seven scenes in which he appears he makes numerous pronouncements concerning his belief in God's well-ordered universe. When Ross announces Macbeth's new title of Cawdor, Banquo says of the witches, "What, can the devil speak true?" (I, iii, 107); and, even as Macbeth's ambition begins to respond, his companion warns in an aside that

> oftentimes, to win us to our harm,
> The instruments of darkness tell us truths,
> Win us with honest trifles, to betray 's
> In deepest consequence.   (123–26)

To Duncan's comment a scene later that the noblemen shall be planted in royal favor, Banquo quickly responds that, if he grows, the "harvest" will be Duncan's own (I, iv, 33). He assures Fleance of the "husbandry in heaven" (II, i, 4) and invokes the "merciful powers" (7) to curb him from the horror of ungoverned ambition. So also, he agrees to counsel with Macbeth only so long as his honor permits; above all he will keep his "bosom franchised and allegiance clear" (28). When he later receives word of Duncan's murder, he observes that, in his opposition to such "treasonous malice" (II, iii, 128), he stands in the "great hand of God" (126). In brief, while he is an effectively drawn character subject to human and spiritual infirmities, he becomes an external pointer for the positive values of the stage world—in consistently withstanding temptation in the name of Christian morality—just as is Lady Macbeth for the negative values.

The playwright, in effect, establishes as a backdrop for Macbeth's individual tragedy a consistent conflict for supremacy between the forces of darkness and the forces of light. And he refuses to tilt the balance; in the cosmos of this stage world, a "humanly relevant quality only exists in relation to a particular human outlook and standpoint."[28] Certainly this is not unequivocally God's world in which Macbeth's sinful aberration occurs in total isolation. The weird sisters do exist, after all; they are seen by Banquo as well as Glamis, and their malicious obfuscations sorely try him as well, while to Lady Macbeth they are disastrous. If Malcolm as God's vicar is eventually established on the Scottish throne, Macbeth lies dead, in part a victim of the witches. Innocents also like Lady Macduff, her son, young Siward, and nameless victims of the final battle are sacrificed to the perverse ambition fed by the withered hags.

By the same token, the simplistic assertion that the play is fatalistic mocks the philosophic complexity of the tragedy. The mysterious creatures of the heath clearly do not hold ultimate authority to compel the mortals of this world to destruction. For one thing, Banquo is able to withstand the temptations inherent in their prediction that his descendants shall rule the kingdom. Admittedly the drama focuses only sporadically and briefly on his inner turmoil; moreover, since the prophecy refers only to those of future generations, the temptation for him presumably is far less immediate. He does, however, respond both to ambition and to conscience; and he is depicted as one free to choose his own path. Unlike his companion, Banquo does nothing at the price of principle or soul, and any argument that affirms his villainy simply must read into the text what the playwright does not provide. On several further occasions the witches themselves admit

28. Knights, *Some Shakespearean Themes* (Stanford: Stanford Univ. Press, 1959), p. 122.

their limited powers. In discussing their various activities in I, iii, for example, the first witch is enraged against a sailor whose wife has insulted her. With the aid of her fellow spirits, she will "drain him dry" (18); unable to sleep, he, like "a man forbid" (21), "shall dwindle, peak, and pine" (23). Significantly, however, she holds no power of life and death; "his bark cannot be lost" (24). Thus, immediately prior to Macbeth's entrance the witches would seem to indicate that, though they can hound and taunt through the manipulation of surrounding circumstances, they cannot in the final analysis either force decisions or destroy for failure to comply with their desires. When Macbeth seeks them out to demand further insight into his destiny, they—with their charms "firm and good" (IV, i, 38) —can answer only that they are creating a "deed without a name" (49). The illusory apparitions they will display have no reality and no name; only he, duped by such appearance and subject to "an interplay of relations or circumstances as important as the motives themselves,"[29] can subsequently make the decisions and commit the deeds that will give truth to their vision. For that matter, their divinatory powers in the first act are suspect. The spectators hear of Cawdor's treason and Macbeth's appointment to the title in scene ii; the witches of the heath, who prophetically announce the position to Macbeth in the following scene, obviously are in the vicinity of Duncan's camp and might well also have had quite logical access to the information.

With the powers of witchcraft, then, far more limited than the protagonist realizes, *Macbeth* clearly is a tragedy of free will. But this free will involves the constraints of the human condition, what J. I. M. Stewart has called the "infra-personal levels of [Macbeth's] own being."[30] The Christian God of Macbeth's universe takes the initiative neither to save nor to destroy; He exists as an idea, aloof, removed,

29. E. E. Stoll, *From Shakespeare to Joyce* (Garden City, N.Y.: Doubleday, 1944), p. 305.

30. *Character and Motive in Shakespeare* (London: Longmans, Green, 1949), p. 96. The witches' knowledge is "conjectural," his "Fate . . . contingent . . . upon the degree of actuation which, by acts of free choice, he succeeds in giving to the potentialities of his essence" (Curry, p. 134). "Macbeth's acts are his own, . . . the outcome of his pride" (W. H. Auden, "The Dyer's Hand," *Listener*, 16 June 1955).

even indifferent. At the other extreme are man's regressive and animalistic instincts. The mortal with his limited, finite view and his constant doubts must struggle to restrain himself within boundaries of justice and morality tacitly assumed to exist, whether for religious or societal convenience. It becomes clear to the spectators that the forces of darkness can only tempt, not coerce. They represent the particular circumstances surrounding man that entice him to regard himself as the measure of all things, appealing to his tendency to see himself at the center and thus forcing him to play his providentially appointed role as God's fool rather than as God's self-effacing minister. Set into this philosophic cauldron is the individual man whose tragedy, through the devices of internalization, the playwright will force the spectators simultaneously to share and to judge.

Macbeth, unlike Lear, knows himself well; he is keenly sensitive to the opportunities that impel him toward the throne. Hence, quite appropriately, Shakespeare through soliloquies and asides projects the spectators into the psychic recesses where the conscience is bartered for success. Like Faustus, the usurper discovers only too late that each step toward power comes only at the price of a firmer commitment to self-aggrandizement; the ultimate consequence is not the exhilaration anticipated from unique human achievement, but the frustration inevitable to spiritual and social isolation, the separation from man as well as God. This climax in despair Shakespeare achieves through a pattern of four thematic waves, with each succession of scenes reflecting the mounting desperation in Macbeth's commitment. In his nine asides and eight soliloquies (a total of 161 lines) the spectators are forced to trace the hardening of ambition into foolhardy defiance of God and of man as well as the deterioration of cautious introspection to a fearful, driveling nihilism blind to all save destruction and death.

The first act, for example—with the temptations to which Macbeth is increasingly responsive, the moral qualms which give him a momentary pause, and the rash and importunate commitment to violence— sets forth the tragedy in microcosm. Most significant is the subtle manner in which Macbeth succumbs to his obsession for power and by which the spectators' interest is focused on this inner struggle. Macbeth is, to be sure, an ambitious man antecedent to the play; otherwise he would never have achieved his position of eminence. Both his natural valor and his aspirations are at their peak—"stimulated by his remarkable success and by the consciousness of exceptional powers and merit."[31] But his ambition—given free reign only in the service of God, king, and country—has been duly disciplined. To his military colleagues he is "brave Macbeth" (I, ii, 16), justice armed with valor, "Bellona's bridegroom" (54); to the king he is a "valiant cousin," a "worthy gentleman" (24), a "peerless kinsman" (iv, 58). That the aspirations of his private moments have carried him far beyond this point is clear, however, in his physical reaction when the witches' prophecy suddenly thrusts his private moment into public day. He can offer no response to Banquo's query, "Why do you start and seem to fear / Things that do sound so fair?" (I, iii, 51–52). When he does regain his composure, the witches taunt him further by vanishing the instant he requests further information. Their action, in effect, is calculated to combine the shock of surprise with the refusal to resolve the enigma it creates, and his subsequent admission that he would have preferred them to stay reflects how thoroughly they have succeeded. Moreover, a few lines later, so rapt in thought that he is momentarily oblivious of his companions and must be roused by Banquo, he suggests in his hurried apology that the weird sisters have breathed new life into a temptation with which he previously has struggled: "Give me your favor. My dull brain was wrought / With things forgotten" (149–50). This assumption seems confirmed by Lady Macbeth's assertion—as she attempts to persuade her husband to dispatch Duncan while the king is a guest in their castle—that Macbeth earlier had considered such an act even when neither time nor place provided a reasonable opportunity.

In any case, the spectators observe the steady progression of Macbeth's ambition in the five asides of scene iii. Informed of his new title of Cawdor, he allows his thoughts to leap immediately to the

---

31. Bradley, p. 279; Ruth L. Anderson, "The Pattern of Behavior Culminating in *Macbeth*," *SEL*, III (1963), 166. For Macbeth the "boundary between plain ambition and divine or virtuous ambition was . . . hard to achieve" (Kristian Smidt, "Two Aspects of Ambition in Elizabethan Tragedy: *Dr. Faustus* and *Macbeth*," *English Studies*, L [1969], 236).

"greatest" title beyond that (117); the apparent "truths" of the witches are "happy prologues to the swelling act" (127, 128). Certainly he is not at this point without doubt. He is unable to adjudge their "supernatural soliciting" either ill (else why the "earnest of success / Commencing in a truth" [132–33]) or good (else why the "horrid image" which makes his hair stand on end and his heart pound with such agitation [135]). If at one moment he decides to leave all to chance, at another he acknowledges that time and opportunity wait for no man. His inclination, however, is clear; and the rich dramatic irony created through the three levels of discrepant awareness further strengthens the internal focus upon Macbeth. At times in conversation with the three lords present, at times in asides to Banquo, at times in private expression, Macbeth—primarily through what he does and does not tell Banquo—alerts the spectators to his determination to hold his innermost conflicts in strictest confidence.

The remaining scenes of Act I establish Macbeth's firm commitment to regicide. Driven to a decision by Duncan's proclamation of Malcolm as heir apparent,[32] he would have the stars dimmed that his eye might not see the deed that must be done. As W. C. Curry (p. 117) has aptly noted, Macbeth in his first soliloquy is not concerned with moral issues; "if he could perform the deed and escape its consequences here upon this bank and shoal of time, he [would] jump the life to come." His apprehension concerns the possible repercussions on this side of the grave:

> We still have judgment here, that we but teach
> Bloody instructions, which, being taught, return
> To plague th' inventor. This even-handed justice
> Commends th' ingredience of our poisoned chalice
> To our own lips.   (I, vii, 8–12)

Duncan is so "meek" (17) and "clear in his great office" (18) that

32. Peter Alexander notes that Duncan is "introducing the later right of primogeniture"; "according to the ancient Celtic mode of tenure called Tanistry the right of succession lay not with the individual but with the family in which it was hereditary" (*Introductions to Shakespeare* [New York: Norton, 1964], p. 158).

pity will "blow the horrid deed in every eye" (24). For an instant, at least, he shrinks in horror from the vaulting ambition that spurs him to such abominable action. Moments later, however, his thoughts are focused entirely on the masculinity and "undaunted mettle" (73) to be proved through his ascent to the throne.[33] Spiritual concern forgotten, he will "bend up / Each corporal agent to this terrible feat" (79–80).

The second wave, covering II, i through III, ii, is doubly critical. In these scenes Macbeth commits both physical and spiritual murder. The assassination of Duncan renders irrevocable his role of political villainy and his repudiation of conscience sets him equally firmly in the path of Faustian humanism. The devices of internalization signal, through intensification of both his agitation and the lust for power by which he attempts to allay it, how profoundly the shock has affected him. In the second soliloquy (II, i, 33–64), at the very instant he draws his weapon to perform the deed, he experiences the hallucination of a dagger, handle toward his hand, which beckons him towards Duncan's chamber even as it exudes "gouts of blood" (46). Admittedly, within a few moments he is sufficiently rational to distinguish between substance and appearance:

> . . . art thou but
> A dagger of the mind, . . .
> Proceeding from the heat–oppressèd brain?
>
> .   .   .   .
>
> It is the bloody business which informs
> Thus to mine eyes.   (37–38, 39, 48–49)

Clearly, though, the scorpions of the mind[34] have already set about their work. The fear of conscience is similarly registered in the third soliloquy (II, ii, 56–62) shortly after the murder, as, terror-struck

33. His struggle "grows out of the conflict between the narrow concept of man as the courageous male and the more inclusive concept of man as a being whose moral nature distinguishes him from the beasts" (Eugene M. Waith, "Manhood and Valor in Two Shakespearean Tragedies," *ELH*, XVII [1950], 266).

34. Dennis Biggins asserts that Macbeth might well speak of his mind filled with scorpions since "the scorpion is the emblem *par excellence* of flattering

at the sound of knocking on the gate below, he stares incredibly at the hands from which the stain of blood can never be washed.

The moral dimensions are much in evidence at this point. Macbeth brands his act a "sorry sight" (20); his attempt to respond to the mumbled prayers of the drunken guards sticks in his throat; in a second hallucinatory moment he imagines a voice crying to all the house:

> Sleep no more. . . .
> Glamis hath murder'd sleep, and therefore Cawdor
> Shall sleep no more; Macbeth shall sleep no more.
> (40–42)

But these are merely the last flickers of the dying light of reason. Within three scenes he is confirmed in his tyranny. External prompting from the witches no longer necessary and Lady Macbeth herself excluded from his machinations, he coldly calculates the destruction of Banquo and Fleance. For the first time the spectators observe him, in his conversation with the murderers, manipulating others to a fever pitch, even as he earlier was prompted by the weird sisters. For the first time he acknowledges, in the fourth soliloquy (III, i, 48–72), that he has given his soul "to the common enemy of man" (69). In his desperate efforts to consolidate his power he foolishly challenges to the death the same fate by which earlier he implicitly justified his attack upon Duncan. His monstrous passion has outgrown that of his wife, who listens in startled disbelief. Acknowledging the "terrible dreams" (III, ii, 18) and "restless ecstasy" (22) which afflict him nightly, he would tear asunder the universe and exterminate every vestige of human feeling to assuage "life's fitful fever" (23).

The third wave (III, iv–IV, i) focuses on Macbeth's mounting distraction. There is no longer a conscience to prod him to a sane rational balance, only the emotional frenzy that impels the desperate individual to ever more stupid and outrageous deeds. In these scenes the tyrant's separation from reality is complete. For one thing, he can no longer distinguish substance from appearance. At his first official banquet,

---

treachery" ("Scorpions, Serpents, and Treachery in *Macbeth*," *Shakespeare Studies*, I [1965], 30).

an event of crucial importance to a new head-of-state concerned with establishing the authority and tenor of his rule, Macbeth twice beholds the entrance of Banquo's ghost.[35] Earlier in the privacy of soliloquy he was able quickly to recover his balance when the dagger appeared; later, with somewhat greater difficulty, in conversation with Lady Macbeth he regained his composure concerning the voice in Duncan's bedchamber. Now, on full public display, there is no reprieve, and his wife is forced to disperse the group—filled now with the worst suspicions—with the unconvincing excuse that her husband has long been subject to such seizures.

Additional moments, perceptible to the spectators alone, underscore his weakening grasp on reality. For one thing, when he makes the decision to murder Banquo and Fleance, he is desperate for some sense of security, frantically seeking out the witches for additional information: "More shall they speak. . . . I am bent to know, / By the worst means the worst" (III, iv, 134–35). In a sense his delusion is at its height; he puts at least some desperate stock in their ability to prophesy—else he would never consult them further, yet he still fondly assumes that he can force "all causes" to "give way" for his "own good" (136, 135). There is no trace of conscience here, no desire for repentance, only the compulsive madness to precipitate a crisis. Moreover, his acts of cruelty have grown so atrocious that he dare not permit himself to reflect upon them:

> I am in blood
> Stepp'd in so far that, should I wade no more,
> Returning were as tedious as go o'er.
> Strange things I have in head, that will to hand,
> Which must be acted ere they may be scanned.
>   (136–40)

In making his most outrageously inhuman decision to murder Macduff's wife and young son, Macbeth in an aside reflects further his degeneration into a creature of animal instinct: "From this moment /

---

35. To J. P. Dyson the banquet scene is the "great dramatic symbol of order disrupted, . . . the moment of insight for Macbeth" ("The Structural Function of the Banquet Scene in *Macbeth*," SQ, XIV [1963], 378).

The very firstlings of my heart shall be / The firstlings of my hand"
(IV, i, 146–48); "This deed I'll do before this purpose cool" (154).
Again his actions are consistent only in passion. He has no real motive
for destroying the family since the witches' warning touches only
Macduff himself, beyond this moment of ecstatic authority to command life and death; he refuses to consider that Macduff, indeed Malcolm and his army, will use this savage act as a rallying cry for destroying the "fiend of Scotland" (IV, iii, 233) whose "name blisters
our tongues" (12).

The final wave (Act V) projects Macbeth as a failure both politically and personally, and no one realizes this fact more poignantly
than Macbeth himself. Obviously as monarch he has rewritten the
rules for tyranny, and his nation in the most ignominious fashion
conceivable casts him out like a foreign or poisonous substance. When
Macduff drags in the tyrant's head by the hair, there can be no regrets
on political counts either from those on stage or in the audience; and
Shakespeare was wise indeed to withhold in Macbeth's last words
even the slightest semblance of concern for the state of the nation, lest
the spectators' repulsion for his rule be mitigated and their sympathetic response to Malcolm and the restoration of right reason in the
body politic blurred.

In personal terms, however, this man humanized by his fears is not
without sympathy.[36] For despite his several earlier attempts to assert
his independence and his invulnerability, both emotional and material,
he does not succeed in alienating himself from all humanity. Indeed,

36. Our reaction is not simply to rejoice at the fall of "immoral man in a
moral universe" (Roy Walker, *The Time is Free* [London: Dakers, 1949], p.
218); we also "admire the Promethean quality of his courage [and] . . . share
his guilt" (H. Wilson, p. 78). "[W]e . . . assent to complicity . . . because we
also feel the strength of our resistance to murder" (R. B. Heilman, "The
Criminal and Tragic Hero: Dramatic Methods," *Shakespeare Survey,* XIX
[1966], 14) in his struggle of "callous desire with moral sensitivity" (Arnold
Stein, "Macbeth and Word-Magic," *Sewanee Review,* LIX [1951], 284).
"While we never for a moment condone or excuse his crimes" (J. D. Wilson,
ed., *Macbeth* [Cambridge: Cambridge Univ. Press, 1947], p. lxviii), we never
forget his "potentiality for goodness" (Wayne Booth, "Macbeth as Tragic
Hero," *JGE,* VI [1951–52], 20) and his "native candor" which he "does not
strive to cloak . . . with conventional religiosity" (G. R. Elliott, *Dramatic
Providence in Macbeth* [Princeton: Princeton Univ. Press, 1958], pp. 29–31).

in his recognition of sorrow and despair lies the ultimate and cruel response to the hubris which sets one apart from his fellow man.[37] The sentiment is real which he experiences in his conversation with the physician concerning his wife's diseased mind and in his response to news that she is dead: "She should have died hereafter: / There would have been a time for such a word" (v, 17–18). On several further occasions Macbeth laments what his life has become. Instead of the "honor, love, obedience, troops of friends" (iii, 25) one normally could expect in the "yellow leaf" of life, he finds only "mouth–honor" and deep curses (27). His life he can compare only to a "brief candle" (v, 23), a

> . . . walking shadow, a poor player
> That struts and frets his hour upon the stage
> And then is heard no more. (24–26)

To attempt to extrapolate from these lines the philosophy of the play or of the playwright is sadly to miss the point.[38] Macbeth, in effect, is characterizing the misery and meaninglessness to which his particular goals and values have led—and by implication the agonizing vision of a richer life forbidden by such commitments. The tyrant himself is the "idiot" whose life is "full of sound and fury, / Signifying nothing."

Macbeth's despair, which has mounted steadily through each wave

37. Certainly this is not a "noble, though unrepentant, creature of sublime and courageous self–knowledge" (G. Wilson Knight, *Christ and Nietzsche* [London: Staples Press, 1948], p. 85), relishing the "fearfulness" of an inconsequential life "to the utmost" (Lascelles Abercrombie, *The Idea of Great Poetry* [London: Secker, 1925], p. 177). Nor is Macbeth engaged in "mere poetical whining" (G. Fletcher, *Studies of Shakespeare* [London: 1847], p. 166). Instead, this is "his last moment of deep sentience" (V. Y. Kantak, "An Approach to Shakespearian Tragedy: The 'Actor' Image in *Macbeth*," *Shakespeare Survey*, XIX [1966], 51) in which he "count[s] up the awful losses of having loved for his own ends" (Dolora G. Cunningham, "Macbeth: The Tragedy of the Hardened Heart," *SQ*, XIV [1963], 43).

38. See, for example, George Santayana, *Essays in Literary Criticism*, ed. Irving Singer (New York: Scribner's, 1956), pp. 141–42; Kott, pp. 94–97. As Muir observes, Shakespeare "restores meaning to life by showing that Macbeth's nihilism results from his crimes" (ed., p. lx). "The reality revealed is that of the dreariness of a misspent life" (Battenhouse, p. 198).

of the action, reaches its climax in the final scenes; as John Russell Brown writes, he "embraces conflicting passions with rapidity and completeness as if seeking some response strong enough to satisfy his untamed and unnamable feelings."[39] More specifically, juxtaposed with the passages of human sentiment noted in the two preceding paragraphs are moments of wild resolution which, in his sixth soliloquy, he aptly compares to the blind instinct of a bear who, "tied . . . to a stake," must "fight the course" (vii, 1, 2). He "cannot taint with fear" (iii, 3); he insists on donning his armor well before it is necessary, vowing to fight until his flesh is hacked from his bones. With the boast that his castle's strength will "laugh a siege to scorn" (v, 2–3), he orders the banners hung on the outward walls; when informed that Birnam Wood moves toward Dunsinane, he cries for wind and wrack and orders full battle so that he can die with his harness on his back. In his seventh soliloquy he smiles at swords and laughs weapons to scorn; a few moments later, in his final soliloquy, he refuses to "play the Roman fool" by dying on his own sword (viii, 1–2). Rather than surrender to Macduff and be the "show and gaze" of the time (24), he—impelled by the bravery of desperation, not conviction—challenges Fife to lay on. "And damned be him that first cries 'Hold, enough!' " (33, 34).

While the waves of Macbeth's increasing passion do indeed maintain the spectators' dramatic interest to the moment of his defeat by Macduff, the conclusion does not focus on the protagonist in the manner one has come to expect in Shakespeare. To provoke the tyrant to a renewed moral awareness would be not only melodramatic but antithetical to the pattern of his intensification; moreover, such a dramatic turn would concentrate and reduce the implications of the tragedy, whereas as we have noted several features throughout the play have pointedly widened the perspective. Shakespeare, in short, was constrained to move outside the protagonist for the effective achievement of some form of an anagnorisis. In this play, and even more so in his subsequent works, the causes of tragedy and the pattern of interrelationships between their public and private dimensions are

39. *Shakespeare: The Tragedy of Macbeth* (London: Arnold, 1963), p. 37.

far too complex to be served by a moment of recognition, however profound, with implications for the protagonist alone.

The essence of the anagnorisis in Shakespearean tragedy is, of course, a sense of regeneration in the face of destruction, of crucial insight and self-knowledge coupled with tragic suffering and waste. In the middle plays the impact of this moment has been registered in the individual, his understanding honed by adversity largely of his own making. With the movement toward a broader vision of tragedy in *Lear* Shakespeare doubles the anagnorisis, presenting offstage in Gloucester and onstage in Lear the painful wisdom gained from their wheels of fire. Still, however, the essential focus is on the old king. In *Macbeth* Shakespeare spreads this experience over several characters. Certainly Macbeth himself, erstwhile leader of men who blends bravado and despair, attests to the tragedy of the destruction of human potential. This distressing waste is compounded by the madness and apparent suicide of Lady Macbeth, whose development in the final act is suggestive of nascent tragedy. There is no moral awakening, to be sure (something which would be quite out of character). But her perturbations do mirror a mounting horror and an inability to live rationally with her atrocities of the past and her husband's of the present. Obviously her destruction is assured. But the sparks of humanity stirred by her suffering in the waning moments signal again the cognitive effects of tragedy for her and thus for the spectators. Like Lear, she would appear to be sanest at the point the world would brand her mad.

The principal regeneration Shakespeare transfers to the body politic of Scotland, thus effectively reiterating the cosmic dimensions of the tragic perspective.[40] Macbeth himself early in Act I articulates the proper relationship between king and subject through his remarks that he owes total service and loyalty to Duncan and his family. The

40. "Shakespeare's encompassing framework is not heaven and hell, but the life of man within the kingdom of Scotland" (R. M. Frye, "Theological and Non–Theological Structures in Tragedy," *Shakespeare Studies*, IV [1968], 135): see also Spencer, p. 160. "It is his own life which is gibberish—not life itself," as Ruth Nevo observes (*Tragic Form in Shakespeare* [Princeton: Princeton Univ. Press, 1972], p. 255).

horror of violating this relationship in an age sympathetic to the principle of rule by divine right is evidenced in the disloyal traitor, the thane of Cawdor, who at the moment of execution confesses his treasons and implores his Highness' pardon. Duncan's murder in Act II is described by Macduff as the destruction of the "Lord's anointed temple" (iii, 64), a view reinforced by the turbulence in nature on this fateful night.

The image of disease in king and kingdom alike, a major motif of the final scenes, is obliquely suggested in Lennox's remark at the close of the banquet scene that he hopes better health will attend his majesty.[41] The results of such rule are more candidly discussed two scenes later; the lords, with God above to "ratify the work" (III, vi, 33), would expel this tyrant in order to give meat to their tables and sleep to their nights, and to free their feasts and banquets" of "bloody knives" (35). As Ross later warns Lady Macduff, the times are cruel; the people "float upon a wild and violent sea" (IV, i, 21). In IV, iii the image reaches full development; indeed the entire scene exists primarily to give emphasis to the view of Scotland as a body in the throes of disease and of Malcolm as the rightful heir apparent who will provide it relief. Scotland is a "downfall 'n birthdom" in which "widows howl, new orphans cry, new sorrows / Strike heaven on the face" (4, 5–6). The "poor country" bleeds under its "great tyranny" (31–32); "it weeps, it bleeds, and each new day a gash / Is added to her wounds" (40–41). It is a nation suffering an untitled bloody-sceptered tyrant and despairing of seeing "wholesome days again" (105). Forced to relate the slaughter of Macduff's wife and children, Ross brands the nation not "our mother but our grave" (166), so accustomed to misery that "sighs and groans and shrieks" (168) are

41. Claims for the dominant image patterns in the play have been made for sleep (Clemen, pp. 89–105), loose–fitting clothes (Caroline Spurgeon, *Shakespeare's Imagery* [Cambridge: Cambridge Univ. Press, 1935], p. 325), the babe or child (Cleanth Brooks, *The Well Wrought Urn* [New York: Reynal and Hitchcock, 1947], 21–46), phantasmagoria (M. M. Morozov, "The Individualization of Shakespeare's Characters Through Imagery," *Shakespeare Survey*, II [1949], 91), and the player king (Anne Righter, *Shakespeare and the Idea of the Play* [London: Chatto and Windus, 1962], p. 118). The best survey is Kenneth Muir, "Image and Symbol in *Macbeth*," *Shakespeare Survey*, XIX (1966), 45–54.

commonplace, and the "dead man's knell" (170) goes unnoticed. At another point Malcolm is directly termed "the med'cine of the sickly weal" (V, ii, 27) as the noblemen swear with him to pour every drop of blood into their country's purge.

In two scenes the presence of a doctor reinforces this image of disease. In IV, iii, an English physician describes heaven's power granted to Edward the Confessor, who by touch can cure his subjects' ills. In V, i, a Scottish doctor observes the queen's mental distress and comments on the psychic nature of her illness. When Malcolm finally marches on Macbeth to bring his nation relief, he aligns himself with "the pow'rs above," which "put on their instruments" (IV, iii, 238–39). And, once proclaimed king, he moves with dispatch in ordering Macbeth's cruel ministers to trial.

There is pathos in the final act, but no essential restoration in the man Macbeth, who in order to assure his authority would have had "Nature's germains tumble all together / Even till destruction sicken" (IV, i, 59–60).[42] Instead, the anagnorisis focuses beyond the personal action on the emergence through disaster of a kingdom in which cure is possible only by a drastic purge and health can be maintained only if the individual—like a single member of the human anatomy—acts in compliance with the needs of the total body politic.

In this respect, *Macbeth* looks forward to the last plays in which the social implications are equally as significant as the personal. The view of social harmony which results from individuals working for the sake of the commonwealth points to one of the central concerns of *Coriolanus*. As in *Hamlet* and *Othello* the soliloquies provoke the spectators to share with the protagonist the critical moments that create the tragedy; this is, in fact, Shakespeare's last such excursion into the recesses of the human personality. As in *Lear* Shakespeare attempts to reflect through the disruptions in nature the cosmic

---

42. An occasional critic has denied that even Malcolm and Macduff are intended to be entirely sympathetic. Macduff's killing of Macbeth "at close range . . . has the disturbing ambivalence of all acts of violence" (Wilbur Sanders, *The Dramatist and the Received Idea* [Cambridge: Cambridge Univ. Press, 1968], p. 305); and "it is not easy to forgive [Malcolm's] contemptuous reference to 'this dead butcher and his fiend–like queen' " (B. L. Reid, "*Macbeth* and the Play of Absolutes," *Sewanee Review*, LXIII [1965], 46).

harmony which individual passion upsets; further, in the external pointers of both plays he extends the devices of internalization in order to mirror significant aspects of the tragedy in these spokesmen for the polarized views which converge upon the protagonist. At the same time, as in *Timon of Athens, Coriolanus,* and *Antony and Cleopatra,* he moves toward wider involvement in the anagnorisis, transferring the tragic insights to those who can profit from the wisdom gained in destruction; in doing so, he directs the spectators' attention to the positive as well as the negative manner in which a human life can affect those around him. Admittedly this transfer will be more powerful with specific characters like Aufidius and Cleopatra than with the body politic of Scotland; such characters will share the responsibility for the protagonist's tragedy as well as its consequences. Coupled with the spectators' focus on Macbeth's inner struggles, however, this total innocence of the body politic (as implied at the outset by the gracious qualities of Duncan and by the absence of any internal political unrest) does produce a powerful and terrifying delineation of the self-destructive qualities of uncontrolled ambition.

V

THE SOCIAL DIMENSIONS OF TRAGEDY:
TIMON OF ATHENS, CORIOLANUS,
ANTONY AND CLEOPATRA

The chronology of the last tragedies is at best an educated guess. Of
the three, however, *Timon of Athens* is the least successful in the
opinion of most critics and would most clearly appear to reflect the
difficulties resulting from Shakespeare's shifting tragic perspective.[1]
For one thing, the characterization of Timon is too rigid in its movement from prodigality to misanthropy. Shakespeare does not attempt
to depict in the protagonist a full tragic experience; no insight gained
through suffering justifies the tragedy aesthetically for the spectators,
prompting them to perceive the best hope for mankind in his purgation of self from the center of all decisions and evaluations.[2] Moreover, despite the numerous devices of internalization, the spectators
do not share with Timon any crucial moments of decision in which
he weighs various value judgments and articulates his choice of mis-

1. Whether a preliminary study of *Lear* (Walter Raleigh, *Shakespeare*
[London: Macmillan, 1927], p. 115) or an "after vibration" (S. T. Coleridge,
Coleridge's Shakespeare Criticism, ed. T. M. Raysor [London: Dent, 1930],
I, 238), *Timon* both in theme and technique "has [its] place in a tragic world
that also includes Macbeth, Antony, and Coriolanus" (Willard Farnham,
Shakespeare's Tragic Frontier [Berkeley: Univ. of California Press, 1950], p.
44).
2. "The utmost he attains," as J. C. Maxwell writes, "is to *see through*
particular shams and injustices" (ed., *Timon of Athens* [Cambridge: Cambridge Univ. Press, 1957], p. xxxvii). Timon in his plight might "stir the
emotions of a susceptible millionaire" (Hazelton Spencer, *The Art and Life of
William Shakespeare* [New York: Harcourt, Brace, 1940], p. 351), but he is
"too naive to arouse sympathy" (D. A. Stauffer, *Shakespeare's World of
Images* [Bloomington: Indiana Univ. Press, 1949], p. 223); "the action does
not knit together his fate and that of the other people in the play" (Una
Ellis-Fermor, "*Timon of Athens*: An Unfinished Play," *RES*, XVIII [1942],
282). Dehumanized by grief (Harry Levin, "Shakespeare's Misanthrope,"
Shakespeare Survey, XXVI [1973], 94), he represents Everyman in Shakespeare's inverted morality play (Anne Lancashire, "*Timon of Athens:* Shakespeare's *Dr. Faustus*," *SQ*, XXI [1970], 41).

anthropy. On the other hand, Timon's character is not flat; Shakespeare attempts to give it dramatic interest through development from prodigality, to naively idealistic rationalization, to self-pity, to a hatred that grows by degrees from his desire for immediate vengeance in kind, to his denunciation of false friends, his repudiation of his homeland and his few faithful companions, and finally his awesome execrations upon the entire race and his attempts to utilize his new-found wealth to provoke its destruction by war, rapine, and disease.

This characterization culminating in total misanthropy some would explain as a result of Shakespeare's source, others as the playwright's abortive attempt to write the kind of tragedy of his previous years. The play also has been an object for much special pleading: possibly it is unfinished, "roughed out" and then "abandoned,"[3] possibly to be taken up by another playwright.[4] Or perhaps it represents a particularly dark period of Shakespeare's life, a period when he was "spiritually and intellectually rudderless";[5] on the other hand, perhaps it "confirms the foundation of his faith in the essential nature of the human genus."[6] Or, possibly, it represents a consciously different kind of play—a tragical satire in the spirit of Jonson's *Sejanus* or his "so-called comedy" *Volpone*,[7] a moral *exemplum*[8] or morality[9] or dramatic

3. Ellis-Fermor, p. 271; E. K. Chambers, *Shakespeare: A Survey* (London: Sidgwick and Jackson, 1925), p. 269. G. B. Harrison suggests that Shakespeare simply became bored with the play (*Shakespeare's Tragedies* [New York: Oxford Univ. Press, 1951], p. 270).

4. A. C. Bradley, *Shakespearean Tragedy* (London: Macmillan, 1904), p. 14.

5. Margaret Webster, *Shakespeare Without Tears* (New York: McGraw-Hill, 1947), p. 184; Chambers, *William Shakespeare: Facts and Problems* (Oxford: Clarendon Press, 1930), I, 483.

6. H. B. Charlton, *Shakespearian Tragedy* (Cambridge: Cambridge Univ. Press, 1948), p. 242.

7. O. J. Campbell, *Shakespeare's Satire* (New York: Oxford Univ. Press, 1943), p. 168. Alice L. Birney claims that his death "effects a catharsis of such emotions of social censure that would have rocked the real world of 1609" (*Satiric Catharsis in Shakespeare* [Berkeley: Univ. of California Press, 1973], p. 16).

8. Virgil K. Whitaker, *The Mirror Up To Nature* (San Marino, Calif.: Huntington Library, 1965), p. 87; L. C. Knights, "*Timon of Athens*," in *The Morality of Art*, ed. D. W. Jefferson (London: Routledge and Kegan Paul, 1969), pp. 4–5.

9. A. S. Collins, "*Timon of Athens*: A Reconsideration," *RES*, XXII

fable,[10] an Elizabethan pageant or "show" prepared for private stage performance and depending not on plot but on a series of contrasting scenes written on a central theme.[11] None of these views is patently impossible; Shakespeare, as one can demonstrate time and again, was a practical playwright sensitive to the demands of popular tastes and opportunities. And, with no contemporary reference to performance and no publication of the piece prior to 1623—when it was apparently inserted hastily into the First Folio, one simply cannot disprove those who claim the play to be fragmentary.

Most probably, however, a large part of the answer is to be found in Shakespeare's general artistic development. In his attempt to create a perspective in which the personal and public flaw receive equal emphasis—in which tragedy is provoked both by the culpability of the individual and the pervasive evil in the characters who surround him—Shakespeare seems purposefully to minimize Timon's sympathetic qualities; and he eliminates the anagnorisis altogether, probably intending to provide in Alcibiades the qualities that redeem humanity from Timon's general curse. This dislocation from Timon becomes virtually total, however, and—coupled with the effective depiction of the hypocritical friends who surround him—leaves the spectators strangely alienated and confused.

In his efforts to achieve this perspective, Shakespeare utilizes a character foil and multiple pointers to manipulate the spectators' attention. Many of these pointers speak on occasion in soliloquy or aside. Here, such devices of internalization are vitally important to

(1946), 96–108; David M. Bergeron, "*Timon of Athens* and Morality Drama," *CLAJ*, X (1967), 181–88; Mark Van Doren, *Shakespeare* (New York: Holt, 1939), p. 252.

10. Maurice Charney, ed., *Timon of Athens* (New York: New American Library, 1965), p. xxxiii.

11. The concept was first proposed by Theodore Spencer (*Shakespeare and the Nature of Man* [New York: Macmillan, 1942], p. 179). Expanded by E. A. J. Honigmann ("*Timon of Athens*," *SQ*, XII [1961], 14–16), it has been most fully developed by M. C. Bradbrook (*The Tragic Pageant of Timon of Athens* [Cambridge: Cambridge Univ. Press, 1966]), who also suggests that the anonymous Timon play was a law students' burlesque of Shakespeare's play ("*The Comedy of Timon:* A Revelling Play of the Inner Temple," *Renaissance Drama*, IX [1966], 83).

the spectator, not because they reveal any sort of divided mind, but because they function as a signal of the validity of the character's observations. Timon himself speaks three soliloquies and four asides (a total of 125 lines), but none prior to III, vi. By this point he has turned his back on the world and on the possibility of true friendship, and his statements amount only to powerful curses upon the human race and upon all forms of supposed honesty. They in no way reveal an anguished realization of the falsity of his friends or the stupidity of his own prodigality, and in no way do they provide an insight for the spectators into the rationalization that is ultimately to harden into misanthropy.

More specifically, in the early acts Shakespeare surrounds the central character with various commentators on the state of his wealth, effectively establishing both Timon's improvident nature and the avaricious duplicity of his friends and associates.[12] The poet and the painter, the first characters on stage, point to the dangers of Timon's great wealth —his assumption of invulnerability to the vicissitudes of life. Although the poet asserts that "it stains the glory" of verse to praise the "vile" for "recompense" (I, i, 15–16), they themselves are clearly not without self–interest since each proffers a work in return for Timon's patronage. Primarily, however, they call the spectators' attention to the "magic of bounty" (6), the power of wealth that draws a variety of hearts to Timon's "love and tendance" (57–58).[13] The poet in particular sets a general pattern of anticipation through his description of the prodigal victimized by whimsical Fortune. When she, from her throne "upon a high and pleasant hill' (63), "wafts" Timon to her

12. Both Ellis-Fermor (p. 282), who complains that the minor characters fail to focus our attention on the central figure, and Maxwell ("Timon of Athens," Scrutiny, XV [1948], 196), who remarks that the pointers are "less obtrusive" and thus subject to misinterpretation, assume that Shakespeare intended to place a dominant emphasis on Timon alone.

13. As Madeleine Doran observes, the image they paint is a clear expression of de casibus tragedy (Endeavors of Art [Madison: Univ. of Wisconsin Press, 1954], p. 119). W. M. Merchant suggests that the painter's theory of art—the revelation of truth in appearance—accords with the highest Renaissance values; Timon's subsequent rejection of the artist "corresponds to his profound disgust with all appearance" ("Timon and the Conceit of Art," SQ, VI [1955], 256).

(70) and beckons him from the "rest below" (74), friends and concerned acquaintances are everywhere to be found:

> All those which were his fellows but of late
> (Some better than his value) on the moment
> Follow his strides, his lobbies fill with tendance,
> Rain sacrificial whisperings in his ear,
> Make sacred even his stirrup, and through him
> Drink the free air.   (I, i, 78–83)

When Fortune "in her shift and change of mood" lets him "slip down" (84, 87), however, not one such friend accompanies "his declining foot" (88).

Immediately following the conversation between the artists, which asserts that the Wheel of Fortune grinds unceasingly and that "mean eyes have seen / The foot above the head" (93–94), Timon proceeds to squander his wealth with unconcerned abandon. Without question he provides five talents to rescue Ventidius from his creditors; because an old Athenian objects to his daughter's engagement to a mere servant, Timon unhesitatingly offers to provide Lucilius with matching funds to equal her not inconsiderable dowry; to the painter he readily offers a handsome reward; when Ventidius comes into his inheritance, Timon with undeniable grandiosity refuses to accept repayment:

> You mistake my love:
> I gave it freely ever; and there's none
> Can truly say he gives, if he receives.
>   (I, ii, 9–11)

He feasts his host of friends—and the ladies whose unexpected visit furnishes a masque for entertainment—delighting in their adulations even as he exclaims that service is the only justification for friendship: "O you gods, think I, what need we have any friends if we should ne'er have need of 'em? . . . Why, I have often wished myself poorer, that I might come nearer to you" (89–91, 94–95). A jewel to one lord, a bay courser to another—Timon could "deal kingdoms" to his friends and "ne'er be weary" (214–15).

Throughout the first act, then, Timon plays the role of lavish dispenser.[14] Susceptible to flattery, however, and taking an obvious pride in his ability to meet another's needs, he does so without regard for the merit of his gifts or the state of his own affairs. And it is to these shortcomings, rather than to any virtues of largess, that the spectators' attention is directed through the remarks of the various pointer characters.[15] In addition to the poet and the painter, a senator (also a creditor) underscores the imprudence of Timon's prodigality and the transient nature of friendship based purely on material self-gratification. Speaking in soliloquy—thus for the spectators slicing through any possibility of hypocritical affection and adulation—the senator condemns Timon's "raging waste" which prompts friends to proffer a gift, knowing it will bring a seven-fold return. This senator determines that he will demand payment since "no reason" can sound Timon's "state in safety" (II, i, 12–13). And, indeed, nowhere is there a clearer reflection of the selfish interest which charac-

14. Roy Walker writes that, in *Timon*, "selfish society drives out true generosity" ("Unto Caesar: A Review of Recent Productions," *Shakespeare Survey*, XI [1958], 131). The most extravagant praise comes from G. Wilson Knight: Timon is "a universal lover" who suffers in "Christ-like" form (*The Wheel of Fire* [London: Methuen, 1930], pp. 211, 236). So also, Paul N. Siegel (*Shakespearean Tragedy and the Elizabethan Compromise* [New York: New York Univ. Press, 1957], p. 81) compares "Timon's boundless generosity and Christ's overflowing love," and Roy W. Battenhouse speaks of the "Man-centered Greekish analogue which unwittingly apes Christian charity" (*Shakespearean Tragedy* [Bloomington: Indiana Univ. Press, 1969], p. 92). On the other hand, R. M. Frye asserts that Timon's later life was totally "antithetical to Christian ideals" (*Shakespeare and Christian Doctrine* [Princeton: Princeton Univ. Press, 1963], p. 179), and W. M. T. Nowottny brands Timon an "Anti-Christ" ("Acts IV and V of *Timon of Athens*," *SQ*, X [1959], 497). Jarold W. Ramsey has recently argued that Shakespeare intends Timon to be a "parody of Christ" ("Timon's Imitation of Christ," *Shakespeare Studies*, II [1966], 169). See further, Francelia Butler, *The Strange Critical Fortunes of Shakespeare's Timon of Athens* (Ames, Iowa: Iowa State Univ. Press, 1966).

15. "Flagrantly wrong-headed in both halves" (David Cook, "*Timon of Athens*," *Shakespeare Survey*, XVI [1963], 83), his "generosity resembles lust rather than love" (John Wain, *The Living World of Shakespeare* [New York: Macmillan, 1964], p. 217), and he fails both intellectually and morally "to achieve a proper response to his situation" (Andor Gomme, "*Timon of Athens*," *Essays in Criticism*, IX [1959], 115).

terizes Timon's associates than in the callous assertion that Timon must serve his turn now that the spendthrift's days are past.

> I love and honor him,
> But must not break my back to heal his finger.
>
> . . . .
>
> Lord Timon will be left a naked gull.
>
> (II, i, 23–24, 31)

The caustic objurgations of Apemantus, who observes the situation without involvement and of whom it is said that he loves "few things" better than to "abhor himself" (I, i, 59–60), provides the most extensive commentary on the evils both within and around Timon.[16] In isolation his misanthropic diatribes would be dismissed as the utterances of a diseased mind. But flanked by the remarks of those characters who focus our attention on just such moral erosion, Apemantus' chilling attacks seem not only credible but strangely appropriate. Timon's friends are dishonest knaves who know not "plain-dealing" (209) and honesty; they are "flatterers" (ii, 76); their servants are "poor rogues and usurers' men; bawds between gold and want" (II, ii, 59–60). The poet is "a filthy piece of work" (I, i, 198), the merchant a disciple of the god Traffic, the ladies who present the masque of Amazons "a sweep of vanity" (ii, 125) who play the fools and spend their flattery upon Timon in his present affluence although in his age they will "void it up again / With poisonous spite and envy" (131–32). With such "serving of becks and jutting-out of bums" (225), laying out of wealth on curtsies, friendship is "full of dregs":

> . . . there should be small love 'mongst these sweet
> knaves,
> And all this courtesy! The strain of man's bred out
> Into baboon and monkey.   (I, i, 247–49)

Timon himself, in Apemantus' words, "loves to be flattered" (I, i,

16. Geoffrey Bush describes Apemantus and Timon as "two aspects of a single self, the extremes between which the personality of the human being can

224); he takes great pleasure in spreading a sumptuous feast and is "too proud to give thanks to the gods" (ii, 59)—blinded by his own ego to the fact that his associates "dip their meat" in his "blood," that the fellow seated next to him, breaking bread with him and pledging his health in a "divided draft," is "the readiest man to kill him" (39, 46). He is, in brief, a fool; this charge Apemantus levels publicly through the character of the fool, who in a single brief appearance provides the cynic a convenient opportunity for wide-ranging calumny.

Timon's culpability is signaled also by the steward Flavius, whose asides and soliloquies in the opening acts clearly establish both that Timon's liberality is compulsive and flagrantly immoderate and also that he has been repeatedly warned of the consequences of such actions. Flavius' first startled aside occurs when Timon calls for more jewels to dispense to friends and associates (I, ii, 154), and it is followed quickly by the observation that he scarce knows how his master will provide further entertainment. Moments later in an extensive aside he berates Timon for commanding provision and gifts from an empty coffer and for refusing to "know his purse" or to see "what a beggar his heart is" (188, 189). In a soliloquy two scenes later he again condemns the prodigal for refusal to manage either himself or his estate judiciously:

> No care, no stop; so senseless of expense
> That he will neither know how to maintain it
> Nor cease his flow of riot. . . .
> > He will not hear, till feel.
> > (II, ii, 1–3, 7)

The first movement of the action, in effect, methodically alienates the spectators from both Timon and from those around him. That is, multiple pointers direct the spectators' attention to Timon's flaws; at the same time these comments underscore the hypocrisy and the self-centeredness of those who so anxiously profit from his prodigality. Thus, Shakespeare creates a situation that blocks the viewer from developing a serious emotional sympathy either for the central figure

alternate" (*Shakespeare and the Natural Condition* [Cambridge, Mass.: Harvard Univ. Press, 1956], p. 62).

or for anyone around him. Clearly, the situation that here invites tragedy results from the immoderate passion and the decadence of all concerned. The technique is the same with both *Coriolanus* and *Antony and Cleopatra*, but in neither instance is the dislocation from the protagonist complete; the emphasis on Antony's magnanimity and on Coriolanus' heroism and on their internal struggle and the movement toward regeneration are sufficient to maintain a concerned interest in the principal. In this play, to the contrary, Timon's liberality is depicted as opprobrious, and his movement is unfalteringly toward bitter and cynical introversion.

Indeed, Shakespeare pointedly does not portray Timon in those moments crucial to his decision to turn his back upon society and all his acquaintances. In II, ii he does admit that his steward has repeatedly warned him of the mounting difficulties and dangers of his excessive liberality, only to be rebuked for his efforts. Here, however, he is still convinced that his friends, as soon as they are informed of his plight, will quickly and graciously leap to his support; if he has acted "unwisely," he has not given "ignobly" (171); and now he expects to reap the benefits of having associates who will be anxious to return his kindness. Then, abruptly, on his next appearance Timon has become a raging demon whose fury and venom, broadcast upon all in earshot, are as immoderate and ill-advised as his earlier prodigality. From this moment his growth toward total misanthropy is awesomely consistent. Not insignificantly, as noted earlier, Timon's asides and soliloquies occur only following his commitment to hatred, thus reflecting a dramatic intensification of his passion rather than an internal conflict of values.

His initial reaction is one of self-pity. Appearing amidst the messengers of his friends who now demand payment, he cries out, "Knock me down with 'em [the bills]; cleave me to the girdle! . . . Cut my heart in sums. . . . Tell out my blood! . . . Tear me, take me" (III, iv, 89, 91, 93, 98). Within moments, though, he has determined to entertain his friends once more. His first aside (III, vi, 30–31) is a signal that he fully realizes the fawnish hypocrisy of the friends who rush back at such an invitation; thus the spectators are not surprised that this turns out to be a mock feast, staged in order that he may achieve a revenge of sorts. His prayer of thanksgiving to the gods is transformed into a plea that the Athenians be made "suitable for destruction" (80) and is followed by the condemnation of his guests as parasites, wolves, bears, flies: "Henceforth be no feast / Whereat a villain's not a welcome guest" (99–100).

Renouncing his homeland shortly thereafter, Timon delivers his first soliloquy as he looks back upon the walls of Athens. In a vicious malediction he calls for the destruction of the city and of all mankind through an inversion of values that would produce incontinent matrons, disobedient children, rebellious slaves, defiled virgins, murderous bankrupts and heirs, and universal impiety to the gods. He appeals further for plagues, infectious fevers, sciatica, and general leprosy to descend upon the race.

> Instruction, manners, mysteries and trades,
> Degrees, observances, customs and laws
> Decline to your confounding contraries,
> And yet confusion live!   (IV, i, 18–21)

Still in soliloquy two scenes later he invokes the sun to breed forth "rotten humidity" to "infect the air" (IV, iii, 2, 3). In his perverted rationalization he asserts that, if one man be a flatterer, so are they all; "all's obliquy; / There's nothing level in our cursed natures / But direct villainy" (18-20).

Discovering gold while digging for roots, he is convinced that the gods have provided him "this yellow slave" (34), this "common whore of mankind" (43), as a means of destroying the "damned earth" (41).[17] To this end he offers gold to Alcibiades and his army as they march on Athens, imploring him to paint the ground red with man's blood. "Let not thy sword skip one. / Pity no honored Age.

---

17. H. C. Goddard considers this a critical moment; Timon's refusal with new wealth to "revert to his former frame of mind" indicates that he has learned his bitter lesson of wisdom (*The Meaning of Shakespeare* [Chicago: Univ. of Chicago Press, 1951], II, 177). Both E. C. Pettet ("*Timon of Athens:* The Disruption of Feudal Morality," *RES*, XXIII [1947], 321–36) and J. W. Draper ("The Theme of *Timon of Athens*," *MLR*, XXIX [1934], 20–31) view the play as a straightforward attack upon usury and the decline of feudal magnanimity.

. . . Let not the virgin's cheek / Make soft thy trenchant sword. . . .
Spare not the babe. . . . Make large confusion" (IV, iii, 60, 111–12,
115–16, 119, 128). To the whores Phrynia and Timandra he dis-
penses coins and instructs them to continue long in their profession
in order to give man diseases:

> Consumption sow
> In hollow bones of man; strike their sharp shins,
> And mar men's spurring. . . .
> Plague all,
> That your activity may defeat and quell
> The source of all erection. There's more gold.
> Do you damn others and let this damn you.
> (151–53, 162–65)

To a band of robbers he proffers wealth provided that they continue
to "suck the subtle blood o' th' grape" (425). "Take wealth and lives
together. . . . / Rob one another. . . . Cut throats. / All that you meet
are thieves" (429, 441–42).

A total misanthrope by this point, Timon is no longer able to respond in kind to the offer of sincere affection. Thus, for example, he
brushes aside Alcibiades' friendship and returns only insults for the
soldier's offer of gold. So also he repudiates Flavius, who in soliloquy
proclaims his "honest grief" for the "dearest master" in his present
misery (IV, iii, 466, 467) and who earlier has bled inwardly for his
lord and frequently has shaken his head and wept. Timon appears
momentarily to relent to the steward's protestations of innocence,
admitting the possibility of "one honest man" (492). But, within
twelve lines he is again suspicious that the kindness has subtle and
covetous motivations; and the only blessing of which he is capable is
by any normal standard a curse: "Go, live rich and happy. . . . / Hate
all, curse all, show charity to none. / . . . Give to dogs / What thou
deniest to men" (521, 523, 525–26). His final and most emphatic
renunciation greets the senators who appear before him remorseful
of their earlier actions and fearful of Alcibiades' impending invasion
of the city. These emissaries repent their earlier disregard for Timon's
well-being both through their present penitence and through their

senate decree offering him abundant material recompense and a position of political authority. They are not without their selfish protective concerns, to be sure, but Timon himself clearly faces the call for selfless action on behalf of those with whom he previously has been closely associated. Unlike Coriolanus, he flatly refuses this commitment, again cursing the city and all who inhabit it; mockingly he offers to allow his erstwhile companions to hang themselves on a tree that grows near his cave in order to avoid the sword of Alcibiades' soldiers. Both his desire for isolation and his contempt for the world are reiterated at his death through his epitaph, which Alcibiades reads from the wax impression taken by a solitary soldier from the lonely grave by the sea and in which, after admitting the misery of his life, Timon asserts again his hatred of "all living men" and his conviction that a plague will consume the "wicked caitiffs" who are left alive (V, iv, 72, 71).

Apemantus, in his final confrontation with Timon, signals just what the prodigal has become. Long a madman and now a fool, Timon in his melancholy is merely the result of a sudden change of material fortune:

> If thou didst put this sour cold habit on
> To castigate thy pride, 'twere well; but thou
> Dost it enforcedly.   (IV, iii, 239–41)

Timon's assertion that he can sense the misery of deprivation all the more sharply as a result of his previous affluence provokes Apemantus to brand him still egocentric and proud, still the creature of immoderate passion who has never known the "middle of humanity," but only the "extremity of both ends" (299–300).

The churl's observations do indeed articulate the spectators' attitude toward Timon, in whose experiences they have found no point of identification. They have seen in him no growth in wisdom or compassion through suffering, no purgation of selfishness; instead, in the self-pity, the vengefulness, the repudiation of his city and of all mankind, the curses, and the attempts at destruction, there is only his steady descent into the privacy of selfishness and hatred, into the fearful isolation and meaninglessness of a life that fails to touch and affect the lives of others in a positive way.

As the extent of Timon's derangement becomes apparent, Shakespeare through additional pointer characters also intensifies the spectators' repugnance of those whose avarice and hypocrisy have helped to mold Timon's misanthropy. For example, in an aside Lucullus delights in the arrival of Flaminius because he anticipates a gift from Timon; yet, when he hears that his friend wishes to receive rather than give, he offers the servant a reward to say he was not to be found. Flaminius, in a soliloquy moments later, berates this "disease of a friend" with "such a faint and milky heart" (III, i, 50, 51). In another scene strangers discuss the "monstrousness of man" in which "policy sits above conscience" (ii, 71, 86) as they observe Lucius, Timon's friend, weaving an elaborate web of lies to avoid loaning him money. Later, another of Timon's servants, faced with Sempronius' haughty claim that he would have aided Timon with alacrity had not he been the last to receive such a request, asserts in soliloquy that such is the nature of "politic love": "The devil knew not what he did when he made man politic. . . . How fairly this lord strives to appear foul" (III, iii, 28–29, 30–31). Even the servants of Timon's creditors balk at their task, one maintaining that it is against his heart, that "the gods can witness" how he is "weary of this charge" (III, iv, 26), while another observes the irony of Timon's giving so many gifts and then being required to pay for them. Flavius, sharing equally with his fellow servants the meager portion of his remaining money, laments that his master lived but in a "dream of friendship" amidst "varnished" friends (IV, ii, 34, 36). Finally, the poet and painter—offstage since establishing at the beginning of the play the concept of Timon's struggling on Fortune's hill with false friends and with the uncertainties of life—rush to the misanthrope's cave when they hear of his new supply of gold. In their arrant hypocrisy each will promise him a new work since "promising is the very air o' th' time," "courtly and fashionable" (V, i, 22–23, 26).

In effect, so sharply has Shakespeare depicted the opprobrium both of Timon and of those around him that the alienation for the spectators is virtually total. Now, in the experience of Alcibiades and his development as a character foil to Timon, Shakespeare apparently attempts to provide something akin to the anagnorisis and the restitution of right reason in the individual and in the society at large which are characteristic of his earlier tragedies.[18] The Athenian soldier figures in only four scenes, speaking a total of 157 lines. His last three appearances, however, provide an experience that is woven into the final portion of the play as a parallel to that of Timon. Juxtaposed with the scene in which Timon, enraged at the greed and hypocrisy of his friends, plans his mock feast in revenge, is Alcibiades' appearance before the Senate to plead for the life of a battlefield companion accused of murder. Irritated by his persistent argument, the senators peremptorily banish him; like Timon, he reacts with the blind wrath and fury of injured pride:

> I hate not to be banished;
> It is a cause worthy my spleen and fury,
> That I may strike at Athens.
>
> (III, v, 111–13)

Alcibiades' banishment, like Timon's self-renunciation, results in total estrangement from his homeland. As in IV, iii, the misanthrope curses society and provides gold for those who will destroy it, the soldier readies his army for a devastating attack upon Athens. Here, however, the similarity ends. Timon repudiates the overtures of repentance from the senators, refuses to aid the besieged city, and dies in bitter isolation tossing a final curse against the human race from his grave. Alcibiades, on the other hand, entertains the emissaries from the city, agrees to withhold his attack in return for autocratic powers, and— though still tainted by a degree of self-interest—is resorbed into the

---

18. E. H. Wright (*The Authorship of Timon of Athens* [New York: Columbia Univ. Press, 1910], p. 44) asserts that the "Alcibiades material" has "not the slightest reference to Timon." On the other hand, J. E. Phillips argues that "Alcibiades' function in the drama is the achievement of reformation" in a situation in which Timon can only "rant" (*The State in Shakespeare's Greek and Roman Plays* [New York: Columbia Univ. Press, 1940], p. 145). The principle of connection, according to H. J. Oliver, is not a "plot-link" but "counterpoint" (ed., *Timon of Athens* [London: Methuen, 1959], pp. xlviii–xlix). As Irving Ribner notes, Shakespeare in the subplot "may have tried to effect for his audience the kind of tragic reconciliation which the fate of Timon alone could not effect" (*Patterns in Shakespearian Tragedy* [London: Methuen, 1960], p. 138).

society from which, like Timon's, his departure had been so violent.

Through this development of a secondary character in the final crucial scenes, a technique he is to utilize in Aufidius and, more effectively, in Cleopatra, Shakespeare attempts to project a catharsis arising from the tragic experience of the protagonist, at the same time avoiding the kind of emotional engagement that would be the consequence of the spectators' directly confronting this occurrence in the principal figure. Such direct confrontation with the protagonist's tragic experience would require the fuller dramatization of his divided mind and his crucial decisions and would destroy the delicate balance between the forces of tragedy that bore from within the character and that assail him from without.

The principal difficulty in the use of Alcibiades as a device for transferring the emotion of the tragic catharsis is Shakespeare's failure to provide a vital relationship between the two plot strands.[19] In both *Coriolanus* and *Antony and Cleopatra,* the fate of the character through whom the anagnorisis is achieved is bound up inextricably with that of the protagonist; the situation of the one character produces and controls the situation for the other; the secondary character is consciously reacting to the experiences of the principal figure. Aufidius, for example, in his final praise of Coriolanus, is perhaps in part responding to the single magnanimous moment when Marcius capitulates to the pleas of his mother and wife and thus spares the city at the expense of his martial reputation and of his own safety. While Shakespeare avoids a direct representation of the agony of Coriolanus' decision—emphasizing instead the subsequent regression into the petty fury of injured pride—he does, through the Volscian leader's reaction at the very moment of total victory over his arch political and martial foe, underscore the influence of the one moment of human compassion for which the protagonist has sacrificed his life. More significantly, Cleopatra—in response to a dying Antony on whose lips

19. Alcibiades' action against the city may signal that he is more discriminating than Timon (R. Swigg, *"Timon of Athens* and the Growth of Discrimination," *MLR,* LXII [1967], 393); but, as R. P. Draper observes, the "shift of emphasis from Timon to Alcibiades leaves the psychological evolution of Timon inadequately represented" (*"Timon of Athens,"* *SQ,* VIII [1957], 200).

there is not the least hint of reproach either for her cowardice or deceit—transcends the selfishness of her former life, choosing in death a union with her "husband" in preference to a continuation of the political game with her male conquerors to which so successfully, in material terms, she has previously dedicated her life. In other words, the full impact of any values achieved by Antony at his death is registered, not by any articulation on his part, but by the words and actions of Cleopatra in the following act. And, again, Shakespeare— by blocking a total emotional identification with Antony—forces the spectators to confront the evil both in the principal and in the situation and characters who surround him, while at the same time recognizing the power beyond death of a protagonist who through suffering and death has attained—like the earlier protagonist—knowledge of the wisdom of love and the virulence of egocentricity and hatred.

Primarily because there is only a tenuous relationship between the actions of Timon and those of Alcibiades, such an impact is absent from *Timon of Athens*. Not only is the subplot developed at an awkwardly late point in the action and the motivation which prompts Alcibiades' pleas for his friend's life and the Senate's drastic reaction dangerously superficial; the soldier's hatred that prompts him to lead an army upon the city is totally unrelated to Timon's repudiation of his homeland and his desire to destroy it. Nor is Alcibiades' decision to spare the city (beyond the fact that he refers to enemies of Timon's and his own) in any way based upon his association with Timon— either in some desperate hope that the misanthrope is still capable of reconciliation with society—or in horrified reaction to the nature of Timon's grotesque death. Indeed, news of Timon's death reaches Athens after the city has been spared, and its only discernible effect is Alcibiades' curt observation: "Dead / Is noble Timon, of whose memory / Hereafter more" (V, iv, 79–81)—following which he continues to stipulate the conditions of his mercy. Moreover, there is no suggestion of any kind of mental struggle leading to Alcibiades' decision. At one moment, standing before the walls with his troops, he condemns the citizens' "licentious measure" (4) and their "pursy Insolence" (12); "now the time is flush" (8) to put "breathless wrong" (10) to "fear and horrid flight" (13). In his very next words, he tosses his glove as a token of honor and a symbol of peace, accepting without question their protestations of innocence and their pledge to offer the guilty among them to the wrath of his sword. In short, Alcibiades' mercy seems to arise not from wisdom and compassion gained from adversity but from a position of total strength that can dictate its own terms;[20] and, lacking any intrinsic relationship with Timon's, his actions fail to lend meaning and impact to the experience and death of the protagonist.

In several important respects, then, the play lacks coherence and consequently fails to achieve either the power or the significance of Shakespeare's earlier works. Timon's character is too rigidly drawn, both in prodigality and misanthropy, the result of Shakespeare's determination to prevent the spectators' close emotional identification with the character. The protagonist's final moments, unrelieved by even the slightest suggestions of insight into the human condition, are increasingly aberrational; as his attitude grows progressively more extreme and illogical, the spectators' dislocation becomes complete. At the same time the subplot fails to function convincingly in the establishment of a secondary character whose illumination or compassion could provide the rationale for tragedy. Then too, many of the characters surrounding Timon are strangely impersonal, labeled only by profession or occupation.

Nevertheless, the structure of the piece—albeit applied to the action like a straitjacket—provides a signpost for charting the perspective of Shakespeare's final tragedies. Concerned with a vision of evil and its operation different from that of the middle tragedies, he utilizes the very devices by which heretofore he has depicted the private, inner struggle with passion and thus has provoked close emotional rapport

20. As L. C. Knights observes, he is not "an acceptable norm" (p. 16); his character "undergoes no change" (H. S. Wilson, *On the Design of Shakespearian Tragedy* [Toronto: Univ. of Toronto Press, 1957], p. 144). His "intention may be laudatory; but he will administer by military supremacy, playing war against peace at his pleasure" (Judah Stampfer, *The Tragic Engagement* [New York: Funk and Wagnalls, 1968], p. 200); his appearance "with a brace of whores undercuts his heroic pretensions" (Charney, p. xxix), and he engages in a "political compromise with the city that is hard to stomach" (Ramsey, p. 171).

between the spectators and the protagonist. Now, however, he demonstrably blocks such a relationship, at least in part, in order to place a greater emphasis on the forces of evil that operate on the protagonist from without. The soliloquies spoken by this principal, instead of depicting a moment of crucial decision, emphasize a particular state of mind. Or, spoken by a minor character, they signal the veracity of some observation about the protagonist and the situation he confronts. Instead of one or two such characters who rivet attention on the central figure, Shakespeare utilizes multiple pointers to direct the spectators' attention to the public dimensions of evil. Moreover, by developing a second figure to whom is transferred at least a part of the emotional impact of the tragic illumination arising from the protagonist's experience, he not only avoids the total emotional commitment to the protagonist that would block the spectators' realization that the judgment against evil must fall equally upon the individual and upon those around him; he also stresses a similar fact about the wisdom, heroism, compassion, or sacrifice which the protagonist achieves—that such a quality, in touching and influencing the life of another, also has its public dimension.

The assertion of Shakespeare's final plays, to reiterate, is that no tragedy occurs only in the isolation of the protagonist's soul, in terms of either the destructive forces that produce it or the fundamental insights achieved concomitantly with devastation and death. To a degree, such is obviously the case in all Shakespearean tragedy, but the emphasis in the earlier plays is on the individual and the anguish of his internal struggle. In the last plays, Shakespeare broadens the perspective in order to emphasize both the personal and societal nature of such tragedy. While *Timon*, then, is not among Shakespeare's great tragedies, the structural complexities, which here fall short of the mark, do provide the groundwork for more powerful and more successful efforts in both *Coriolanus* and *Antony and Cleopatra*.

More so than in Timon, sporadic moments of internalization provide the spectators glimpses of a psychic struggle within Coriolanus. Again, however, the central figure is seen in large part through the eyes of the other characters. And, unlike the external pointers of the early and middle tragedies, every eye is tainted; each perceives the attributes of the principal character through the filter of his own self-interest.

Such a structure, as we have noted, precludes the intensely personal vision that prompts full sympathy with the protagonist. In this respect it is significant that Shakespeare for these final dramas chooses narratives in which the central figure is not directly guilty either of abdication resulting in destruction of family and kingdom, or of murder—whether in the name of state, God, or self.[21] With the character thus innocent of a heinous act involving moral aberration that requires a profound cathartic experience based on virtues of good and evil upheld by the play, Shakespeare is able to draw the spectators back from an intensely personal commitment to the protagonist and to force them to evaluate his actions from several points of view and in constant relation to the motivations and value judgments of those around him. The result is a structure in which, more penetratingly than in the earlier tragedies, two or more concepts, philosophies, or ideologies make equally valid (or equally invalid) claims upon the viewer.

This pervasive ambivalence is a hallmark of Shakespeare's final tragic vision. Admittedly, a powerful ambiguity is at the center of Hamlet's commitment to passion, and that of the other major protagonists; each faces choices or alternate paths of action that at the moment defy clear moral judgment. Ultimately, however, the ambiguity is resolved as the protagonist in meeting his death acts in accordance with (Brutus, Hamlet, Othello, Lear) or in defiance of (Macbeth) certain positive social and metaphysical values. In the late plays, on the other hand, the ambiguity is never resolved. The protagonist becomes the central agent through whom the spectators

21. In this sense the heroes of the late tragedies are by no means "more deeply flawed" than the earlier (Farnham, p. 11). On the other hand, neither do they represent a form of goodness which cannot "make the necessary kinds of adjustment to hard reality" (H. J. Oliver, "Coriolanus as Tragic Hero," *SQ*, X [1959], 60). More to the point is the observation that "Shakespeare forces us . . . to see a crucial characterization according to opposing systems of value" (Norman Rabkin, *Shakespeare and the Common Understanding* [New York: Free Press, 1967], p. 127). See further J. L. Simmons, *Shakespeare's Pagan World: The Roman Tragedies* (Charlottesville: Univ. Press of Virginia, 1973), p. 49.

observe man's corrupt values at every turn. Not only does the play center on a protagonist who, though possessing the potential for martial or political leadership, is flawed by a passion which destroys his ability to guide his own destiny, the focus shifts on occasion to those characters around the protagonist who use and misuse him for their own material and emotional ends.

In *Coriolanus* the characterization and the tragic experience of the central character—in comparison with those of the earlier protagonists —are admittedly sketched somewhat superficially.[22] To a large degree the spectators' attention is fixed externally upon the martial valor and the insufferable arrogance that seem to make up his personality in equal parts. Certainly no one is his rival on the field of battle. At sixteen he bravely confronted Tarquin, and in seventeen battles since that time, "brow-bound with the oak," (II, ii, 96), he consistently has proved the best man in the struggle. At Corioli he personally prevents a Volscian victory, deriding the Roman soldiers for their retreat and single-handedly fighting within the walls of the city against incredible odds. Bloody but still alive, determined, and fearless, he issues forth from the gate to rouse the plebeians to a new and successful attack. Following the capitulation of the city, he is exhausted and literally covered with the cruel stains of war,[23] but he rushes without pause to the second battle area, breathlessly inquiring whether he has come too late. He demands that he be pitted singly against Aufidius and, once again, is the inspiration for an army that has retreated—or, as its leader insists, has fought at a disadvantage and has retired to win its purpose. Rallying to the thrill of his courage, the Romans carry the day—afterwards bestowing on him the "war's garland," the name of Coriolanus. Still later, when in Rome the citizens have

22. The spectators' "vision is aloof," their "gaze insufficiently comprehensive" (Theodore Spencer, *Nature of Man*, p. 179). "We are . . . detached observers" (Harley Granville-Barker, *Prefaces to Shakespeare* [Princeton: Princeton Univ. Press, 1946], III, 198); "we seem to see all there is of him from the outside" (Huntington Brown, "Enter the Shakespearean Tragic Hero," *Essays in Criticism*, III [1953], 287).

23. Leo Kirschbaum maintains that Shakespeare, in depicting the hero covered in gore, is emphasizing "the brutality of the military hero" ("Shakespeare's Stage Blood and its Critical Significance," *PMLA*, LXIV [1949], 527).

turned on him and attempt to arrest him (III, i), his powerful arm is instrumental in beating them back. Similarly, after he is banished, he "rages" upon the Roman territories; under his leadership the inspired Volscians cut down the Romans like "boys pursuing summer butterflies" or "butchers killing flies" (IV, vi, 95–96).

The pride of the man is equally furious;[24] the plebeians he considers beneath him in birth and pitifully subordinate in martial skill and courage. These common citizens are to him but "dissentious rogues" (I, i, 159), "scabs" (161), "curs" (163), "hares" (166), "geese" (167), "a sick man's appetite" (173), "fragments" (217), "rats" (157). Were he free to use his sword, he would "make a quarry / With thousands of these quartered slaves as high / As I could pick up my lance" (193–95); the news of impending war he welcomes as a "means to vent" Rome's "musty superfluity" (220–21). When the citizens fall back before Corioli, they are "shames of Rome" (iv, 31), "base slaves" (v, 7), a herd of "boils and plagues" that "infect" one another (iv, 31, 33). When they retract their approval for consul, they are "the mutable, rank-scented meiny" (III, i, 66), the "cockle of rebellion, insolence, sedition" (70), "Hydra" (93), a "bosom multiplied" (131), a "rabble" with "multitudinous tongue" (136, 156). "The beast / With many heads" (IV, i, 1–2), he later remarks, "butts" him from Rome. The tribunes who "prank" themselves in authority (III, i, 23) he despises as the "tongues" of the "common mouth" (22), and he openly mocks Sicinius as a "wretch" (163), a "Triton of the minnows" (89).

24. Coriolanus blindly adheres to the ancient hero's creed, the concept of *virtus* (D. J. Gordon, "Name and Fame: Shakespeare's *Coriolanus,*" *Papers Mainly Shakespearean,* ed. G. I. Duthie [Edinburgh: Oliver and Boyd, 1964], 40–57); see also J. C. F. Littlewood, "*Coriolanus,*" *Cambridge Quarterly,* II [1966–67], 339–57 and III [1967–68], 28–50; and C. B. Watson, *Shakespeare and the Renaissance Concept of Honor* [Princeton: Princeton Univ. Press, 1960]). F. H. Rouda, on the other hand, would have us see Coriolanus not as a "blustering, bullying mature man, . . . but as a high-minded, emotionally untried youngster" ("*Coriolanus*—A Tragedy of Youth," *SQ,* XII [1961], 103). Shakespeare is reflecting, according to Clifford C. Huffman, the potential tyranny of both royal absolutism and of strictly limited monarchy (*Coriolanus in Context* [Lewisburg, Pa.: Bucknell Univ. Press 1971], pp. 169, 222).

Even his modesty is so intense that in the final analysis it reflects the monstrous ego of the man. It seems genuine enough, for example, when praise is the sole object. In I, ix, the excessive praise of his colleagues is embarrassing; he would not have his little deeds declared in hyperbolical acclamations. His refusal to accept payment of one-tenth of the booty in recognition of his heroic role in the capture of Corioli prompts Cominius to chide him lightly as too modest—"More cruel to your good report than grateful / To us that give you truly" (53–54). Mockingly threatening to put him in manacles if necessary, the general places on him the war's garland and proclaims him henceforth Caius Marcius Coriolanus. On the other hand, when his pride is also at stake, what he advances as modesty is transparently an excuse for condescension. He balks at the thought of standing naked before the people and entreating them for his "wounds' sake to give their suffrage" (II, ii, 136). Since he will "blush in acting," the custom "might well / Be taken from the people" (143–44). In his appearance before the people he mocks the custom rather than fulfilling it; and later, when his mother entreats him to woo them a second time, he bemoans the lie that is given to his "noble heart" (III, ii, 100). When he takes his leave of the city in banishment, he compares himself to a "lonely dragon" whose "fen" will be more "feared and talked of than seen" (IV, i, 30–31).

Such constant emphasis on extreme valor and pride tends to reflect only the outer shell of the man.[25] Moreover, Shakespeare carefully avoids soliloquies, asides, or personal dialogue at those crucial mo-

25. His "one-sidedness and lack of adaptability" has even been labeled "comic" (Norman A. Brittin, "Coriolanus, Alceste, and Dramatic Genres," *PMLA*, LXXI [1956], 801), "near to caricature" (Arthur Sewell, *Character and Society in Shakespeare* [Oxford: Oxford Univ. Press, 1951], p. 126). The play to G. B. Shaw is "the greatest of Shakespeare's comedies" (*Shaw on Shakespeare*, ed. Edwin Wilson [New York: Dutton, 1961], p. 225), and O. J. Campbell (p. 198) calls it a "tragical satire." To Kenneth Burke, Coriolanus resembles the character of a satyr play; not satirical, but scurrilous, he forces our attention to the divisiveness around him (*"Coriolanus*—and the Delights of Faction," *Hudson Review*, XIX [1966], 199). He is a misanthrope (Paul G. Zolbrod, "Coriolanus and Alceste: A study in Misanthropy," *SQ*, XXIII [1972], 56–57) whose "verbal intransigence" evinces his proud integrity (Carol M. Sicherman, "Coriolanus: The Failure of Words," *ELH*, XXXIX [1972], 190).

ments when an inner struggle would presumably be most intense. As Coriolanus considers the position of consul and how he must achieve it, for example, the spectators get no real insight either into any lust for power or into any foreboding discomfort that a position of power unsought and undesired is being thrust upon him. Even more critical, the audience is not permitted to see his private emotional reactions to banishment which lead to his decision to join Aufidius in order to seek personal vengeance against an ungrateful homeland. Similarly, no soliloquy in Act V reiterates the significance of his decision to acquiesce to his mother's pleas and spare his homeland.

Unquestionably, then, the characterization of Coriolanus is far less complex than that of the protagonists of the middle plays. On the other hand—and this is a fact all too easily overlooked by the critic[26] who hastens, sometimes peremptorily, to judge the character by the measure of introspection in the earlier protagonists—he is by no means totally stylized or static. The spectators on several occasions do perceive, beneath this outer shell, the internal struggles where at least a degree of essential dramatic growth occurs.[27] Most obviously, in reaching the crucial decision to spare Rome at the behest of mother, wife, and child, Marcius is aware of the disastrous consequences he must personally face. Volumnia argues at length for an honorable reconciliation between Volscians and Romans. Coriolanus seems to

26. Shakespeare "has become tedious" (Chambers, *Survey*, p. 258); he has "left part of the tragedy half-worked" (Sir Ifor Evans, *The Language of Shakespeare's Plays* [London: Methuen, 1952], p. 174); the play is "a success altogether of a lower order than that of *Macbeth*" (D. J. Enright, "*Coriolanus*: Tragedy or Debate?" *Essays in Criticism*, IV [1954], 19).

27. The text simply will not support the assertion that "Coriolanus at his death has gained neither insight nor wisdom" (Peter F. Neumeyer, "Not Locale Habitation or a Name: Coriolanus," *UR*, XXII [1966], 195; Whitaker, p. 279). As Sailendra Kumar Sen observes, "This simple and haughty soldier" betrays the signs of mental agitation "from the moment he is proposed for consul" ("What Happens in *Coriolanus*," *SQ*, IX [1958], 332; see also Ivor Browning, "Coriolanus: Boy of Tears," *Essays in Criticism*, V [1955], 18–31); it is "a newly-discovered human feeling that [leads] him to make peace" (E. A. M. Colman, "The End of Coriolanus," *ELH*, XXXIV [1967], 18). On the significance of Aufidius' last lines to the theme of reconciliation, see Jay L. Halio, "*Coriolanus*: Shakespeare's Drama of Reconciliation," *Shakespeare Studies*, VI (1970), 302–3.

realize that no such reconciliation is now possible—that he has become involved in a situation from which there is no escape: to destroy Rome will vitiate whatever is human in him as he destroys family and friend to achieve the fruition of his bitter revenge;[28] to exercise mercy will alienate Aufidius and the Volscians in whose hands he has quite literally placed his life. He senses that his decision, in effect, will involve his sacrificing himself in order to save others; foolishly—by the standard of both the world and the ego—he will toss away a victory that is assured:

> Behold, the heavens do ope,
> The gods look down, and this unnatural scene
> They laugh at. O my mother, mother! O!
> You have won a happy victory to Rome;
> But for your son—believe it, O believe it!—
> Most dangerously you have with him prevailed,
> If not most mortal to him.
>
> (V, iii, 183–89)

To assume either that Coriolanus is simply catering once more to his egocentric sense of self-importance or that, like an automaton, he is incapable of disobeying his domineering mother does not do justice to the full context of the scene. To insist that he is not able emotionally to comprehend what he is saying flatly begs the question. Although he does not fully articulate the point and although the experience does not prevent him from losing his temper shortly thereafter in a fit of prideful wrath which precipitates his assassination,[29] Coriolanus has

28. As J. Dover Wilson has noted, Coriolanus, in Plutarch, offers comparatively mild terms to Rome; furthermore he does not intend to burn the city but merely to restore the patricians to ascendency. By making Coriolanus a "complete renegade," Shakespeare emphasizes the significance of the son's capitulation to the mother (ed., *The Tragedy of Coriolanus* [Cambridge: Cambridge Univ. Press, 1960], p. xxxvi).

29. Goddard (II, 240) maintains that Coriolanus' transformation determines the nature of even his final moment: "The old Coriolanus could have held off a dozen assassins, slaughtered them all perhaps, or at the very best sold his life dear. . . . His last act—or failure to act—is that of a new man created by Virgilia's kiss and the love of his child."

at this point subordinated the vengeance demanded by his self-love
to the selfless love of mercy and forgiveness.

Furthermore, considered in its total context, this climactic moment
is not sprung upon the spectators without preparation. The protagonist, for example, does speak four soliloquies, a total of thirty-six
lines. While one of the passages is purely expositional, Coriolanus'
announcement of his arrival at Antium and his intention to disguise
himself (IV, iv, 1–6), and another is merely a reflection concerning
the irony of the treatment that he, in disguise as a beggar, is receiving
from the servants of the household (v, 10–11), the other two reflect,
though only briefly, significant aspects of the inner man. In Act II, the
spectators see Coriolanus' internal agitation concerning the consulship
as he pridefully berates the custom that forces him "to beg of Hob and
Dick" a position he deserves beyond question. The passage concludes
with an abrupt juxtaposition of conflicting sentiments which suggests
that Coriolanus desires the power and authority more than he will
overtly admit even to himself:

> Rather than fool it so,
> Let the high office and the honor go
> To one that would do thus. I am half through;
> The one part suffered, the other will I do.
> (iii, 116–19)

In Act IV Coriolanus muses in soliloquy just prior to entering
Aufidius' home; though he completely ignores the burning issue (the
moral or ethical struggle concerning his decision to attack his homeland), he does reflect upon the play's larger theme of the tainted
mutable world in which man constantly manipulates and uses his
fellow man for self-advantage and in which self-interest dictates
enmity and friendship. Such a sentiment hardly suggests a man totally
devoid of either emotional or logical comprehension of the human
spirit:

> O world, thy slippery turns! Friends now fast sworn,
> . . . .

> shall within this hour,
> On a dissension of a doit, break out
> To bitterest enmity. So, fellest foes,
> Whose passions and whose plots have broke their sleep
>
> . . . .
>
> shall grow dear friends
> And interjoin their issues.
>
> (iv, 12, 16–19, 21–22)

In addition to these two soliloquies, there are numerous passages throughout the play which indicate increasingly meaningful moments of emotional sensitivity. Through the skillful and perceptive actor's delivery of such lines, the capitulation to his mother will occur, not as an unconvincing incident for which the spectators are unprepared, but as the logical and emotional consequence of the cumulative experiences to which Coriolanus has been subjected. An early indication of his humanity involves the "poor man" he wishes to free in Corioli because this citizen has "used [him] kindly" (I, ix, 82) during a previous visit. It is indeed typical of the proud man that he is unable to remember the name of the insignificant commoner, but his intention signals the first charitable thought the spectators have perceived in him. Later when Volumnia insists that her son swallow his pride and if need be practice hypocrisy in order to achieve the consulship, he senses the dear price he may ultimately be forced to pay, avowing that she has forced him to play a role that he shall never perform convincingly. Similarly, in preparing for banishment, he seems to sense the proud man's greatest vulnerability as he ominously assures his mother that he will succeed unless he is "caught / With cautelous baits and practice" (IV, i, 33). Several reflections of increasing humanization heighten the effect of his crucial lines in Act V. Realizing that, by refusing the plea for Rome's pardon, he is breaking the heart of Menenius, who loved him more than a father, he admits that for his old friend's sake he has yielded to the extent of once more offering his first conditions to the city. Moments later as his mother, wife, and child stand before him, his disjointed dialogue signals his emotional turmoil. His determination to stand firm in his will as if

man were his own author and knew no other kin (iii, 33–37), to
expel all "affection," "bond and privilege of nature" (24–25), is
countered briefly by the heart-rending sentiment that the sight of his
family provokes and his begging them to forgive his tyranny. When
his mother kneels before him, he is painfully aware of the unnatural-
ness of the scene; so should the "pebbles on the hungry beach / Fillip
the stars" and "the mutinous winds / Strike the proud cedars 'gainst
the fiery sun" (58–60). He acknowledges himself to be a slave of
passion; his "rages and revenges" are pitched against Volumnia's
"colder reasons" (85–86); and in agony, just prior to agreeing to
his mother's request, he admits that to remain longer in sight of his
family will produce in him "a woman's tenderness" (129).

All things considered, the tragic experience of Coriolanus—the
movement from obdurate self-will to a moment of mercy and selflessness involving an act that costs his life along with the painful achievement of at least a degree of self-knowledge enabling him more truly
to perceive the forces that motivate those around him—is in basic
design similar to those of the earlier protagonists. Yet Shakespeare
has quite clearly structured the play so as to bar the spectators from
sharing fully the intense struggles of the soul that would provoke them
to total emotional identification.[30] In effect, with Coriolanus having
not one line of aside and only limited soliloquies, not for the most
part critically located, Shakespeare draws the spectators back from the
central character even while, more successfully than in *Timon*, sketch-
ing him in sufficient detail to force them to view the tragedy in part
through his eyes.

As a consequence there is—as in *Antony and Cleopatra*—a significant modification of the double vision through which the spectators
are involved emotionally with the protagonist at the same time they
omnisciently view the events that create his dilemma and the judgments he must confront. Whereas the dominant emotional emphasis

30. "The audience is carefully placed," as Michael McCanles has recently
noted, "outside the play as well as outside Coriolanus and is left to contemplate without involvement" ("The Dialectic of Transcendence in *Coriolanus*,"
PMLA, LXXXII [1967], 53). The audience views the first half as a political
tragedy, the last half as an individual tragedy (D. C. Hale, "The Death of a
Political Metaphor," *SQ*, XXII [1971], 202).

for the spectators in the middle tragedies is on the individual and his personal agony, the dominant emphasis in *Coriolanus* is on the larger view, the societal and familial pressure and the ambiguous moral values against which the individual must be measured in a tainted universe.

Indeed, the essential complexity in Coriolanus' character results from the external structural devices—the multiple tragic pointers and the double foils—that control the spectators' response. In Act I Coriolanus is involved in two major actions—the condemnation of the citizens who are struggling for more political power and the awesome feats of courage on the battlefield which deal the Volscians a staggering defeat and earn him the accolade Coriolanus. Before either action Shakespeare carefully draws the spectators' attention to the ambient values of both the class struggle and war.[31] As a consequence the spectators are guided neither to an outright condemnation of Coriolanus' arrogant assumption that the stupid plebeians deserve no greater measure of freedom on the one hand nor to an uncritical admiration for his martial heroics on the other. To be sure, his attitude toward the commoners is cruel and peremptory, but, before his first appearance on stage and his diatribe against them, a group of citizens pointedly blur the spectators' attitude toward them. Against the advice of the second citizen that they consider Coriolanus' services to the city and that they consider cautiously the full effects of any charge brought against him, they—bats and clubs in hand—aver that he is "chief enemy to the people" (I, i, 6–7), "a very dog to the commonalty" (125–26), and would kill him and demand "corn at our own price" (9–10); they would seek revenge for their treatment by the patricians with their pikes before they become rakes; they would prove that they have not only "strong breaths" but "strong arms too" (56–57). Meninius, accepted by the populace as honest and objective, denounces the group as "the great toe of this assembly" (150), the

31. The scenes are "thoroughly ambiguous"; the "audience should not pick sides" (Clifford Davidson, *"Coriolanus:* A Study in Political Dislocation," *Shakespeare Studies,* IV [1968], 263–72). Since every character shares the guilt in the play, the spectator is "prevented from dissociating . . . himself from evil, . . . from locating it exclusively in the other fellow" (Eric Bentley, "Shakespeare's Politics," in *The Dramatic Event* [New York: Beacon, 1954], p. 187).

"lowest, basest, poorest . . . rascals," the "worst in blood," "rats" who turn unjustly on those who nurture them (152, 154, 157). Certainly then, the spectators are consciously guided to an ambivalent response to both the proud Coriolanus and the rebellious plebeians.

By the same token, the spectators see the dehumanizing effects of the conditioning and training that produce the battlefield hero before they are caught up emotionally in his valorous exploits in scenes iv through viii and his idolatrous aggrandizement by his military colleagues Lartius and Cominius in I, ix, and II, ii. Volumnia describes to the sensitive Virgilia (who recoils in alarm) her past rejoicing in the absence of her son "wherein he won honor" (I, iii, 3–4); she has always been "pleased to let him seek danger" (12), to hear his drum as he returns with "bloody brow" (32).[32] When he was but a youth, at an age when another mother would not part with him, she encouraged him to "prove . . . himself a man" (17) in battle. She hears with obvious delight that her young grandson, in one of his father's moods, is beginning to react to the same values. He possesses

> such a confirm'd countenance! I saw him run after a gilded
> butterfly, and when he caught it, he let it go again, and
> after it again, and over and over he comes, and up again;
> catched it again; or whether his fall enraged him, or how
> 'twas, he did so set his teeth and tear it! O, I warrant, how
> he mammock'd it!   (I, iii, 57–62)

Such details obviously temper the spectators' admiration for the military hero who fights without regard to fear like a well-tuned precision machine. Moreover there are several subtle suggestions of fanaticism in Coriolanus' behavior. When he enters the gates of Corioli and shouts for others to follow, the soldiers flatly refuse to be a part of such foolhardiness, and even Lartius observes that Coriolanus "outdares his senseless sword" (I, iv, 53). Marcius later scoffs that he is

---

32. "Obsessed with love of her son's success" (G. W. Knight, *The Imperial Theme* [London: Oxford Univ. Press], p. 170), "an unnatural mother" (M. B. Smith, *Dualities in Shakespeare* [Toronto: Univ. of Toronto Press, 1966], p. 42), Volumnia is concerned only with "the breeding of an over specialized warrior-mechanism" (F. N. Lees, "*Coriolanus*, Aristotle, and Bacon," *RES*, I [1950], 114–15).

not warmed yet when cautioned that his exercise has been too violent for him to fight in a second battle; immediately thereafter, he rushes off to aid Cominius, who could wish the Roman champion were conducted to a gentle bath where balms could be applied. To the impatient Coriolanus, Cominius explains that his soldiers have retreated rather than be "foolish in [their] stands" (vi, 2).

There is, then, in the opening act no simple and single response to what superficially appears to be either the protagonist's vice or his virtue. Similarly while two soldiers contrast further his haughty contempt of the common citizens with his blunt honesty and noble service (II, ii, 1–34), and while Coriolanus proudly offers himself as candidate for consul only to be banished when in a fit of wrath he alienates the people, the factors that motivate first the tribunes and then his mother and the patricians to manipulate him for their own selfish interests become painfully clear. Sicinius and Brutus (whom Menenius describes as "unmeriting, proud, violent, testy" and "ambitious"]II, i, 39–40, 63]) emerge as direct adversaries, fearing not so much that the people will lose liberty as that they themselves will lose power and authority over them. Convinced that their office "may / During his power, go sleep" (211–12), they determine to set the people against him and to prod his arrogance with barbed remarks; they will constantly carry "ears and eyes for the time, / But hearts for the event" (258–59):

> We must suggest the people in what hatred
> He still hath held them; that to's power he would
> Have made them mules, silenced their pleaders, and
> Dispropertied their freedoms, holding them,
> In human action and capacity,
> Of no more soul nor fitness for the world
> Than camels in their war, who have their provand
> Only for bearing burthens, and sore blows
> For sinking under them.   (II, i, 234–42)

Brutus does indeed find the opportune moment to nettle Coriolanus with the observation that a consul must have "a kinder value of the people" (II, ii, 57), followed mockingly with, "Sir, I hope / My words disbenched you not" (68–69). In the face of Coriolanus' difficulty in humbly standing before the citizens and requesting their voices, Brutus sharply observes that the people will bate not one jot of ceremony. Later the tribunes are furious that the plebeians approve Coriolanus as consul, berating them for not treating him as they had been advised. The designing pair persuade the people to revoke their assent, and, by goading his spirit and enraging him, to take advantage of him. The tribunes even slyly suggest that they themselves will take the blame for leading the people to their former vote; in such a guise they obviously can conceal their own devious designs behind the mask of the crowd's mutability. Having, then, incensed the people to a rebellious state, they literally bar Coriolanus' path, confronting him with news of the revocation of his appointment and with fresh charges of his insolence. When Coriolanus in a vitriolic rage calls for the senators to abolish the power of the tribuneship, Brutus and Sicinius have accomplished their aims. They accuse him of manifest treason, of being a "foe to th' public weal" who "deserves death" (175, 207).

Through the mutiny that erupts, the tribunes are able to consolidate their power to the extent that they dictate the terms of reconciliation with the patricians even as they insist that, since Coriolanus has resisted the law, the "law shall scorn him further trial" (268). Again they carefully plan their final round in advance; they will charge him falsely with failure to distribute the "spoil got on the Antiates" (iii, 4) and will plant their supporters throughout the crowd:

> Assemble presently the people hither;
> And when they hear me say, "It shall be so
> I' th' right and strength o' th' commons," be it either
> For death, for fine, or banishment, then let them,
> If I say fine, cry "Fine!"—if death, cry "Death!"
>
> (12–16)

Confronting him again with charges that he is tyrannical, "a traitor to the people" (66), they peremptorily

231

> Even from this instant, banish him our city,
> In peril of precipitation
> From off the Rock Tarpeian never more
> To enter our Rome gates.   (101–4)

In the following scenes, their power virtually complete, they taunt the patricians with the observations that Coriolanus is not much missed and that Rome "sits safe and still without him" (IV, vi, 37), all the while deferentially telling the people that they wished Coriolanus had loved the citizens as they do. Even as Coriolanus and Aufidius move against the empire, the tribunes blindly exercise their new-found tyranny by threatening to whip a messenger who brings word of the attack.

Certainly the spectators' abhorrence of Coriolanus' wrathful pride and arrogance is sharply mitigated by their realization that to a large degree he is victimized by those whose lust for power is far more flagrant and calculated. Neither is he free of manipulation from his mother and the patricians. Volumnia, obsessed with the idea of her son's greatness and determined to drive him to achieve it, thrills that he returns home from Corioli with wounds in the shoulder and in the left arm to add to the twenty–five wounds suffered in previous battles —all of which he can "show the people when he shall stand for his place" (139–40).

Significantly, this first hint of the consulship, the pursuit of which will destroy the son, comes from her lips, and she is quick to greet him with the far bolder implication that only one thing is wanting, which she is certain Rome will cast upon him. Coriolanus himself, in fact, never once mentions the position, even as Cominius and Lartius present his candidacy to the senators and he is proclaimed consul; admittedly he is aware of the political implications and he does not strongly denounce either the honors showered on him or the high office that is suggested, but the impetus for securing him the position comes essentially from external sources. It is also his mother who persuades him, after the mutiny, to return to the people and seek reconciliation in the hope that the citizens will reconsider conferring the consulship upon him. She laments, not that her son is consumed with arrogance, but that he did not put his power well on before wearing it out, that he showed them how he was disposed while they still had "power to cross" him (III, ii, 23). She vigorously counsels him to use his anger to better advantage, to place his own ambition and self-interest above an honesty which is "too absolute" (39); he is told to seem that which he is not for his "best ends" (47); hat in his hand, his knee "bussing the stones" (75), he is told to fawn upon them; honor and policy are in the final analysis synonymous:

> I would dissemble with my nature where
> My fortunes and my friends at stake required
> I should do so in honor.   (III, ii, 62–64)

Once the people are in virtual rebellion the senators too are vitally concerned with the confusion that threatens to "bring the roof to the foundation" (III, i, 205) and destroy the society in which they occupy a favored position. To fight in open defense of Coriolanus would be foolish, like standing "against a falling fabric" (247); the conflict "must be patched / With cloth of any color" (252–53). Hence for reasons quite different from Volumnia's but equally selfish, they agree to acknowledge his faults and to bring him before the people, where he shall answer "to his utmost peril" (325). They assure him that all will proceed legally, that repentance is the only remedy by which to save the city, that he can win the plebeians' hearts and forgiveness. In effect, the self-concerns of Brutus and Sicinius on the one hand, of Volumnia on another, and of the patricians on yet another precipitate a situation for which Coriolanus—despite all his faults—is not directly responsible. And in the banishment that is its final conse-quence, the senators, after having played a large part in persuading Coriolanus to submit himself in reconciliation to the people, suffer his banishment for the sake of peace with woefully little protest. They themselves later admit that his best friends charged him like those who deserved his hate, and therein behaved like enemies:

> We loved him; but, like beasts
> And cowardly nobles, gave way unto your clusters,

Who did hoot him out o' th' city.

(IV, vi, 122–24)

Shakespeare, then, in the middle portion of the play carefully holds in balance the spectators' response to the protagonist through the comments, actions, and intentions of the surrounding characters. In the climactic moments he draws a richly sympathetic focus on Coriolanus' act of selflessness through the further development of Volumnia and Aufidius as character foils. Volumnia, of course, is from the outset a foil to Coriolanus in her obsession with military heroism coupled with her practical devotion to social position. Her entreaties to Coriolanus in Act III to be reconciled with the people grow, as we have seen, out of her private determination to mold him into the political authority she envisions, regardless of the consequences to him. A similar determination and a similar blindness to his personal consequences drive her to play the emissary for peace in the final act. Certainly she is concerned for the welfare of the city and for her own life and safety, but there is virtually no mention of this larger issue. Instead, she stresses the duty he owes to his mother (V, iii, 52–56, 158–60, 164–68, 178) and the miserable life she has led since his exile (94–98), threatening suicide if he perseveres in his attack upon the city (120–25). And, indeed, the old self-interests come indelibly clear in her assertion that her son must reconcile the Romans and the Volscians so that both sides will praise him for bringing peace. Again her obsession with shaping him into a politician who can sacrifice principle to policy and her willingness to resort to any means to achieve it create a dilemma from which he has no escape.

This dilemma the spectators perceive in full as a result of the parallel development of Aufidius, who even more obviously than Volumnia can turn the occasion to personal gain.[33] As early as I, ii,

33. "Designed as an instrument by which certain functions in the total dramatic design might be executed" (Ribner, p. 197), "Tullus Aufidius makes a very effective foil to Coriolanus" (H. N. Hudson, *Shakespeare: His Life, Art, and Characters* [Boston, 1872], II, 487). "Where Coriolanus is proud, Aufidius is ambitious; where Coriolanus is loftily self-conscious, Aufidius is aspiring by self-seeking" (C. C. Clarke, *Shakespeare-Characters* [London, 1863], p. 480).

Aufidius is established as a principal foe of the Roman stalwart and the eventuality of a fateful struggle is implied. When Coriolanus bests him in personal combat (viii) and the Volscians agree to conditions, Shakespeare foreshadows the nature of Coriolanus' destruction through Aufidius' wrathful reaction:

> Where I find him, were it
> At home, upon my brother's guard, even there,
> Against the hospitable canon, would I
> Wash my fierce hand in 's heart.
>
> (I, x, 24–27)

The Volscian leader's opportunity comes with Coriolanus' defection. In light of the venomous hatred that Aufidius has voiced, the spectators can only be sharply suspicious of the excessive flattery he showers on Coriolanus: "all–noble Marcius. Let me twine / Mine arms about thy body. / . . . Thou noble thing. . . . Worthy Marcius. . . . Most absolute sir. / . . . Let me commend thee . . . more a friend than e're an enemy" (IV, v, 107–8, 117, 127, 137, 145, 147). Indeed, two scenes later the suspicion is confirmed; with Coriolanus subjected to a manipulation far more deadly than those in Rome, it is only a matter of time until Aufidius will move against him:

> Be thou sure,
> When he shall come to his account, he knows not
> What I can urge against him.
>
> .   .   .   .
>
> He hath left undone
> That which shall break his neck or hazard mine,
> Whene'er we come to our account.
>
> (IV, vii, 17–19, 24–26)

"So our virtues / Lie in th' interpretation of the time" (49–50): Aufidius in this line speaks indeed aptly for each of those throughout the play who has used Coriolanus to serve his own interest. In the final act, at the moment Coriolanus grants his mother's request to spare

Rome, Aufidius in his lone aside clearly reveals that the Roman's most magnanimous act will be his certain destruction:

> I am glad thou hast set thy mercy and thy honor
> At difference in thee. Out of that I'll work
> Myself a former fortune.   (V, iii, 200–2)

Later in Corioli, like the tribunes earlier, the Volscian leader plants his supporters in the crowd, accuses Marcius of treason, and taunts him as a "boy of tears" (vi, 100) who sentimentally "whined and roared away" the victory (97). At the arranged moment the conspirators assassinate Marcius. Aufidius with a ready explanation gains control of the assembly and emerges with total authority. Thus, for the second time, Coriolanus has been convinced and sentenced without judicious hearing; subject to the destructive frenzies of the mob, he on each occasion finds himself in a predicament inspired both by his own actions and by those of others who have a personal stake in the consequences.

Both Volumnia and Aufidius ironically emerge as heroes in this society, Aufidius as the firmly entrenched martial and political leader of his nation and Volumnia as the "patroness, the life of Rome" (V, v, 1) before whom flowers are strewn. On the other hand, Marcius is clearly the emotional victor. By contrast with the selfish interests that surround him, he in his one act of selflessness—an act which though for far different reasons delights both his mother and the Volscian commander—gains (albeit briefly) the insight that characterizes the Shakespearean tragic hero.

Considering the complexity of the total design, one would do well to pause before condemning the play simply because—in terms of the protagonist's experience and the total dramatic effect—it fails to do what its tragic predecessors do. Whether the result of changing

34. Chapman's heroes—Byron, Bussy, Cleremont, Chabot, Cato—are proud men destroyed both by themselves and by the corruption around them. Indeed the two-part play, *The Conspiracy and Tragedy of Byron*, was apparently written in the same year as *Coriolanus*. Both Edwin Honig ("*Sejanus* and *Coriolanus*: A Study in Alienation," *MLQ*, XII [1957], 407–21) and Stewart P. Sherman (ed., *The Tragedy of Coriolanus* [New York: Macmillan, 1912], p. xvii) suggest that Shakespeare's late style was influenced in part by Jonson.

popular taste,[34] contemporary social conditions,[35] or his own evolving philosophic values, Shakespeare's final tragic perspective is both individual and collective. The tragedy, to be sure, is possible as a consequence of a fundamental flaw in the protagonist; but the dominant thrust of the play is that the tragedy actually occurs as a result of the diverse forces and pressures brought to bear by those around him who manipulate him and others to selfish advantage. The structure of the play guides the spectators, not to a descent into the soul, but to a vision of the protagonist, his decisions, and his actions in the context of those other lives and values that touch and influence him so critically. The protagonist becomes the central agent for reflecting both the personal and the social evil of which mankind is capable. In the fact that those succeed who are willing to practice policy at the expense of integrity and without regard for the consequences to others the tragedy reflects the darkest side of humanity.[36]

Equally important however, both *Antony and Cleopatra* and *Coriolanus* assert, as do the final comedies (the "comedies of transformation"), that it is ultimately the action of the individual, not the action of society, by which life must be measured. The spectators are guided to a positive response to an act of the protagonist which, in relation to the values that have controlled his life to this point, clearly amounts to a moment of selflessness, whether he specifically describes

35. The conjectures range from attacks upon a decadent aristocracy (A. A. Smirnov, *Shakespeare: A Marxist Interpretation,* trans. Sonja Volochova [New York: Critics Group, 1936], p. 78; Wolfgang Wicht, "Mensch und Gesellschaft in *Coriolanus,*" *Shakespeare-Jahrbuch,* CII [1966], 245–97; W. Hazlitt, *Characters of Shakespeare's Plays* [London, 1846], p. 69) to an attack upon the fascist leader (Bertolt Brecht, cited in Jan Kott, *Shakespeare Our Contemporary,* trans. Boleslaw Taborski [Garden City, New York: Anchor, 1966], p. 179) to an attack upon the commons who were attempting to seize power in James' early years (W. Gordon Zeeveld, "*Coriolanus* and Jacobean Politics," *MLR,* LVII [1962], 321–34) to a reflection of the rebellion near Shakespeare's home (E. C. Pettet, "*Coriolanus* and the Midlands Insurrection of 1607," *Shakespeare Survey,* III [1950], 34–42; Sidney Shanker, "Some Clues for *Coriolanus,*" *SAB,* XXIV [1949], 209–13).
36. This tragedy concerns "the decency and integrity of our human responsiveness" (L. C. Knights, "Shakespeare and Political Wisdom: A Note on the Personalism of *Julius Caesar* and *Coriolanus,*" *Sewanee Review,* LXI [1953], 55), and the "failure of Coriolanus . . . represents a failure of a whole

the fact in so many words or not. There is no total redemption for society, no balancing of accounts which, in the earlier plays, stresses the purgation of evil in the kingdom and the cosmos in the face of new moral leadership and revitalized social conscience. On the other hand, as with Alcibiades in *Timon of Athens*, apparently Shakespeare does again intend in Aufidius' final moments to reflect a transfer of the anagnorisis to a character whose critical dilemma closely approximates that of the central figure and whose destiny is inseparably related. At the moment Coriolanus is struck down by the frenzied mob, the Volscian leader avers that his own "rage is gone" (V, vi, 145) and that he is "struck with sorrow" (146). Responding, perhaps, to Coriolanus' finest moment, Aufidius will become a mourner through whom Marcius "shall have a noble memory" (152).

Such a moment is essentially unlike the conventional words of praise spoken over a fallen hero by a secondary figure (as Exton in *Richard II* or Cassio in *Othello* or Fortinbras in *Hamlet*) who has not been significantly engaged in conflict with the protagonist. Nor is the impact precisely similar to the public pronouncements by those adversaries (as Mark Antony in *Julius Caesar* or Octavius Caesar in *Antony and Cleopatra*) whose praise embellishes their own image after their opponent's suicide has prevented the glory of personal combat. Here, since the words come from a principal antagonist who has just slain the protagonist in a bloody and totally unfair coup and who has witnessed the victim's one great act of selfless love, which has rendered him defenseless, the spectators are encouraged to respond more to the sacrifice of the hero than to the fact of his death.

In the final analysis, however, Aufidius' speech is not completely convincing because he has nothing to lose by playing the magnanimous hero—unlike Cleopatra, who has everything to lose as a result of her fidelity to Antony. Consequently, the spectators can only remain suspicious that Aufidius is sorely tainted, self-centered, and materialistic—that practicality and pragmatism, not virtue, endure. In either case, though, the act of human compassion to which the protagonist

society" (D. A. Traversi, "*Coriolanus*," *Scrutiny*, VI [1937], 57). Kott describes the play as "modern" because, in it, history "has ceased to be demonic. It is only ironic and tragic" (p. 186).

(for once not obsessed with the personal consequences) is drawn reflects man's greatest potential. The tragedy is that his own selfishness must destroy him before he can discover that potential.

In essence, this view of tragedy differs only in perspective from that of Shakespeare's earlier work. Philosophically, it is a more profound conception of the diverse factors that coalesce upon and within a particular individual to make his life tragic. Dramatically, however, at least in the sense that we understand Shakespearean tragedy, the impact is less forceful. No longer are the spectators afforded the sharp focus of internalization and the full emotional catharsis that result from close identification. No longer is their attention riveted on the single individual whose life is illumined and enriched through disaster. Now throughout the action and especially in the climactic moments they are never allowed to forget that the characters who compose the surrounding crowd, at best only momentarily touched by the individual's experience, will survive through continued exploitation and compromise. Shakespeare, to achieve this perspective, has guided the spectators' attention beyond man to men; the required angle of vision is oblique. Through the years most playgoers and critics have preferred the direct and intensive vision of the protagonist to whose complete cycle on the tragic wheel of fire all else is subordinated.

Shakespeare's middle plays—in Brutus' agitation over Caesar's growing power, or Hamlet's concern for the heaven-blessed mandate to pursue vengeance, or Othello's perception of Desdemona as the "cunning whore of Venice"—force the spectators to view the protagonist's action in the context of a stage world that affirms the existence of order and of a supra-human control, either an omnipotent God against whom all mortal values must be weighed or a powerful natural force that manipulates the universe to some teleological end. In either case, tragedy centers on the passion arising from some form of blindness, limitation, or error which drives a character to self-destruction. In *Lear* and *Macbeth*, as we have observed, Shakespeare blurs the benevolent nature of that controlling force for protagonist and spectator alike. At the same time, though, he maintains through his characters in these stage worlds a sharp distinction in values, and the anagnorisis in large measure is constructed upon the positive qualities visibly present in the selfless love of Cordelia and Kent, and the political righteousness of Malcolm and Macduff.

The last plays, however, refuse to fit such a convenient mold. To be sure, the protagonist is flawed. But, to repeat, the spectators' concern is also directed specifically to those forces outside the character which produce his tragedy, to the false friends who parasitically prey upon Timon and encourage his prodigality, to the companions who manipulate both Coriolanus' courage and his ego to their own emotional or political profit. Moreover, there is no dominant emphasis on a metaphysical controlling power whose values, upheld by significant characters in these plays, represent the final measure of justice and morality and against whom the central figure struggles in his emerging tragedy. Instead, the dual values are secular; they are set forth through the various characters who people the stage world, and neither is without fault. In the final analysis, for instance, there is little to choose between a mother's pride in Volumnia, who raises a proud military demagogue only to force him into a situation in which his heroics destroy him, and a colleague's treachery in Aufidius, who fawningly courts his favor even while covertly manipulating the conspiracy for his assassination.

In *Antony and Cleopatra*, whether actually his last tragedy or not, Shakespeare achieves his most powerful delineation of these secular values between which man struggles to make the choices for a successful life. Gone is a clear distinction between virtue and vice, between material and spiritual choice.[37] The drama operates within the world

37. Setting forth "two richly endowed but very imperfect people" in a "poetic frame which creates an aura of uniqueness and greatness" (Madeleine Doran, " 'High Events as These': The Language of Hyperbole in *Antony and Cleopatra*," *Queens Quarterly*, LXXII [1965], 33), *Antony and Cleopatra* achieves "swinging ambivalence" (John F. Danby, *Poets on Fortune's Hill* [London: Faber and Faber, 1952], p. 135), a "tangled skein" in which "good grows up together with evil almost inseparably" (William Rosen, *Shakespeare and the Craft of Tragedy* [Cambridge, Mass.: Harvard Univ. Press, 1960], p. 147). Their language sets them apart as "bigger than lifesize" (Rosalie L. Colie, *Shakespeare's Living Art* [Princeton: Princeton Univ. Press, 1974],

of man, within the conflict created out of the struggle for power and influence between a Roman emperor and an Egyptian queen.[38] And the values of these two worlds are equally tainted.

Cleopatra's world, for instance, is decadent and enervating.[39] Nowhere do the spectators have even the slightest sense of the queen's concern for her kingdom and for the welfare of her subjects; nowhere are they convinced that her affairs with heads of the Roman state, past or present, are motivated by any sort of determination to protect her nation at any price. To the contrary, she utilizes her unlimited power and her limited beauty for the gratification of her own vanity. The first visual impression is almost cloying—Cleopatra in lavish array, the elaborate train of attendants, the eunuchs fanning

---

p. 198). See also Robert D. Hume, "Individuation and Development of Character Through Language," *SQ*, XXIV (1973), 300.

38. Depicting dissension on three levels—the individual, the family, and the state (L. E. Bowling, "Antony's Internal Disunity," *SEL*, IV [1964], 239), the play captures "the breadth and life of humanity" (Una Ellis-Fermor, "The Nature of Plot in Drama," *Essays and Studies*, XIII [1960], 67) in its "pageant of human life" reflecting "the order and degrees of society" (Thomas B. Stroup, "The Structure of *Antony and Cleopatra*," *SQ*, XV, No. 2 [1964], 292). With its emphasis on the "external world of Roman business and Egyptian pleasure" (Marilyn Williamson, "Fortune in *Antony and Cleopatra*," *JEGP*, LXVII [1968], 429), the tragedy—according to David Cecil—is concerned, "not so much with man's private inner life, as with his life in the theatre of public affairs" (*Poets and Story-Tellers* [New York: Macmillan, 1949], p. 9). "Aristocratic and heroic appeals" are brought "into tension with a popular and unheroic world" (J. L. Simmons, "*Antony and Cleopatra* and *Coriolanus*, Shakespeare's Heroic Tragedies: A Jacobean Adjustment," *Shakespeare Survey*, XXVI [1973], 97).

39. Critics have long been hard pressed to capture verbally Cleopatra's fascination. She is "mercury, . . . changeable silk, . . . a serpent of the Old Nile" (Van Doren, p. 242), a "brilliant antithesis" of all that we most hate with what we most admire" (Anna Jameson, *Shakespeare's Heroines* [London, n.d.], p. 251), "*la donna è mobile*" (E. E. Stoll, *Poets and Playwrights* [Minneapolis: Univ. of Minn. Press, 1930], p. 13), "half a courtesan and half a *grande amoreuse*" (Chambers, *Survey*, p. 253), a "courtesan of genius" (B. Ten Brink, *Five Lectures on Shakespeare* [New York, 1895], p. 90), a "female Falstaff" (F. S. Boas, *Shakespeare and His Predecessors* [London, 1896], p. 475), "the Hamlet among Shakespeare's women characters" (C. J. Sisson, "The Roman Plays," in *The Living Shakespeare*, ed., Robert Gittings [London: Heinemann, 1960], p. 144).

her, her ladies catering to her smallest whim. Virtually every action through the first half of the play underscores this egocentric posturing. She tauntingly persuades Antony to refuse a message from Rome as a token of his doting affection. Rebuking him moments later, in total disregard for the news of his wife's death and of adverse political developments at home, she is apprehensive not because of his grief but because of the looming possibility that he might escape from her clutches. This same egocentric vanity is evidenced again later when she receives word of Antony's marriage to Octavia. At first striking the messenger and threatening to dispatch him forthwith, she finally resorts to the rather childish ploy of questioning him about Antony's wife feature by feature and then convincing herself that she is superior in every respect. Enobarbus, in mocking hyperbole, brands her passions as "pure love" (I, ii, 144), her sighs and tears as "greater storms and tempests than almanacs can report" (145–46). And she herself admits to the role she plays in maintaining a close rein on Antony by irritating and crossing him at every turn (I, iii).

The Egyptian world is also morally vitiated.[40] For one thing, it reeks of sensuality. The bawdy wit of Iras and Charmian in the opening scene (over where best to have an additional inch of fortune in a husband and over how delightful it would be to see Alexas cuck-

---

40. Those who judge the play on this moral issue alone condemn Antony as a victim of a sinful "passionate lust [which] dominate[s] his life and obliterate[s] his sense of duty" (Louis B. Wright, ed., *Antony and Cleopatra* [New York: Washington Square, 1961], p. xi). Cleopatra's character is best reflected in the numerous references to her as a witch (Daniel Stempel, "The Transmigration of the Crocodile," *SQ*, VII [1956], 66). "Too much subject to the complex of fleshly vices which the Elizabethans often called Pleasure" (J. Leeds Barroll, "Antony and Pleasure," *JEGP*, LVII [1958], 719), their love is "without a soul" (Robert E. Fitch, "No Greater Crack," *SQ*, XIX [1968], 10). Equally extreme are those critics who maintain that the "grandeur of their love . . . [leads us to] forget their crimes" (François Victor-Hugo, ed., *Oeuvres completes de Shakespeare* [Paris, 1895], VII, ix), that Shakespeare is flatly defending an "illicit passion" (Stauffer, p. 234). To the contrary, according to Julian Markels, "Step by step through this play Shakespeare has made us amoral" (*The Pillar of the World* [Columbus: Ohio State Univ. Press, 1968], p. 7). "In the last analysis perhaps we need not say Shakespeare judges; he simply reveals" (L. C. Knights, *Some Shakespearean Themes* [Stanford: Stanford Univ. Press, 1959], p. 134).

olded) is prologue to Cleopatra's own banter with Mardian after Antony has departed for Rome. She takes "no pleasure / In aught an eunuch has" (I, v, 9–10); his affections cannot be shown "in deed" (15); one would do as well to play with a woman as "with an eunuch" (II, v, 5); his "good will" perforce will "come too short" (8). What Octavius terms her "lascivious wassails" (I, iv, 56), Enobarbus describes as occasions for sleeping "day out of countenance" and making "the night light with drinking" (II, ii, 178–79). She recalls with obvious pleasure how often she laughed Antony "into patience" at night:

> and next morn,
> Ere the ninth hour, I drunk him to his bed;
> Then put my tires and mantles on him, whilst
> I wore his sword Philippan.
>
> (II, v, 20–23)

Such a moment, as Maurice Charney observes, visually depicts Cleopatra in "control of her lover's sword, the symbol of his manliness and soldiership."[41] She, in her own words, is one who "trade[s] in love" (II, v, 2), trained by Julius Caesar in her "salad days" (I, v, 73). For another thing, this queen is totally devoid of the fortitude essential to leadership. She finds it easy to articulate her role as commander of her forces, insisting both that Antony fight by sea and that she accompany him as the "president" of her kingdom and fight by his side; with almost equal ease she later assumes she can erase with a word the onus of her retreat which proves so disastrous to Antony: "I little thought / You would have followed" (III, xi, 55–56).

If there is no moral fiber in Cleopatra and her court attendants, so also no such quality is to be found in Octavius and his associates. Robert Ornstein aptly remarks that "the decay of Roman idealism is so advanced that it is difficult to say whether a Roman thought is of duty or disloyalty."[42] In any event, Shakespeare methodically under-

41. *Shakespeare's Roman Plays* (Cambridge, Mass.: Harvard Univ. Press, 1961), p. 130.
42. "The Ethic of the Imagination: Love and Art in *Antony and Cleopatra*," in *Shakespeare: Modern Essays in Criticism*, ed. Leonard F. Dean, rev. ed.

mines the spectators' confidence in the Roman leaders through reflection of Lepidus' dissipation and Octavius' duplicity. Ironically, for
example, despite all the references to the orgies of the East, the only
such scene in the play involves the Western leaders on Pompey's
barge. So drunk are Lepidus and Antony that "the least wind i' th'
world will blow them down" (II, vii, 2–3); their sense "steeped" in
"conquering wine" (106), they dance hand in hand, drowning their
cares in a song to Bacchus. Although the "high-colored" (4) Lepidus
is especially mocked by his servants, both he and Antony have turned
themselves into hollow shells of the power they espouse; with an easy
slit of the throat, as Menas observes, Pompey could be an "earthly
Jove" (66) greater than those "world-sharers" and "competitors"
(69).

Disconcerting also is the Roman marriage by which Octavius intends to insure "perpetual amity" (II, ii, 125) with Antony. Arranged
lock—born not in love but in material convenience—is, of course,
conventional practice both in Shakespeare's day and Caesar's. Even
so, the context of heated words followed by histrionic displays of
affection results in a union which looks cynical indeed to the friends
of the triumvirs, who have no illusions about the game they watch.
Octavius bequeaths a sister to join their kingdoms and their hearts.
Blest by the third triumvir, this business will be the cement with which
to build and hold their love, "the ram to batter / The fortress of it"
(III, ii, 30–31); Octavia will be a "blessed lottery" (II, ii, 244) to
her husband. Again there is little to choose between; in trading in love
Rome can better Egypt at her own game! Most degrading of all,
Octavius forces truth to serve his convenience.[43] While Antony is in
Alexandria with Octavia, Caesar is quick to violate their agreement,
engaging in a new war against Pompey and speaking "scantly" (III,

---

(New York: Oxford Univ. Press, 1967), p. 392. "The politics from which
Antony secedes are . . . the treacheries and back-stabbing of a drunken party
on a pirate's barge" (W. K. Wimsatt, The Verbal Icon [Lexington: Univ. of
Kentucky Press, 1954], p. 96).

43. A "Machiavel" (Thomas McFarland, Tragic Meanings in Shakespeare
[New York: Random House, 1966], p. 98), Octavius "deceives, or tries to
deceive, every other character of political consequence: Pompey, Lepidus,
Antony, Cleopatra" (David Kaula, "The Time Sense of Antony and Cleo-

iv, 6) of his brother-in-law to the public ear. Moreover, on his individual initiative he removes Lepidus from a position of command, denying him "rivality" and seizing him "upon his own appeal" after "having made use of him" in the wars against Pompey (v, 6–10). His claims that he is merely responding to Antony, who has returned to Egypt to dole out kingdoms to Cleopatra's brood, are clearly post facto; Antony's actions subsequent to this power play merely provide Octavius a convenient excuse and a ready response to Octavia's queries. This use of wit to distort the facts he finds useful again in his later pronouncement that only with great hesitation was he "drawn into this war" against Antony, that he ever proceeded with calmness and gentleness in all his writings. Such boasting of leniency and mercy is mocked by the spectators' memory of Antony's earlier plea that he be allowed to "breathe between the heavens and the earth" as a "private man in Athens" (III, xii, 14–15), to which Caesar coldly responded that he would not hear the request. In the same breath he offered audience to Cleopatra only if she drove Antony from Egypt or assassinated him. So, too, Proculeius' claim in Caesar's name that Cleopatra should "fear nothing" from his "princely hand" (V, ii, 22) is belied by the soldiers' stealthy attack upon her immediately thereafter and by Dolabella's later admission that Caesar plans to lead her in triumph.

Between these two worlds Antony is a pawn manipulated to best advantage; each attemps to use him for selfish ends. Cleopatra laments in III, iii, that, were Antony gone, she would not know through whom she would command. Similarly, Enobarbus appropriately observes to Octavius that, if he borrows Antony's love for the instant, he may return it again when Pompey is no longer a threat; and Menas admits that policy was more important in the marriage of Octavia and Antony than the love of the parties. In short, unlike the situation in the middle tragedies in which the protagonist has a particular path of action clearly recognized as desirable, Antony has no "correct" choice through which to calm and control the turbulent

---

patra," *SQ*, XV, No. 3 [1964], 217). As J. Leeds Barroll points out, Dolabella's trick on Caesar in the final act cleverly undercuts his power ("The Characterization of Octavius." *Shakespeare Studies*, VI [1970], 283).

forces of his spirit. Indeed, no such moral structure is assumed. As in Webster's view, a character must transcend the moral ambiguities that surround him. With all values tainted, the protagonist—if he is to achieve tragic proportions—must through his suffering come to envision a potential integrity and selflessness beyond that which can be found in the society of his stage world. This is not to deny the dignity of man, but to emphasize as his highest potential his ability through self-knowledge to achieve a love that meaningfully touches the life of another.

Antony at the outset is no better and no worse than those around him; certainly there is nothing magnanimous about him. In a word, he is an opportunist capable of affection only for himself and ready to compromise truth to protect his reputation and suffer his vanity. Claiming in Act I that kingdoms are "clay" (i, 35) and that the "nobleness of life" (36) is to embrace Cleopatra, he calls for every minute to afford pleasure and sport. In the following scene ego—not principle—prompts a different stance when, confronted by a messenger, he determines to break with the Egyptian because of what the "general tongue" (101) calls him in Rome; the "slippery people" (181) begin to cast their love to Pompey, and his power is threatened. In parting, he easily declares his undying affection for the queen, swearing to make peace or war as she "shall give th' advice" (iii, 68) and sending her an "orient pearl" with the promise to "piece / Her opulent throne with kingdoms" (v, 41, 45–46). With equal ease, though, when opportunity dictates in Rome, he welcomes his new marriage as an "act of grace" (II, ii, 147). One scene later he assures his new wife that, though his past is blemished, henceforth all shall be done "by th' rule" (iii, 7), but, almost immediately he indicates his intention to return to Egypt where his "pleasure lies" (40). Even so, as he and Octavia depart for Alexandria, his face is straight as he comments on the sorrowful parting of brother and sister and as in embrace he wrestles with Caesar in his "strength of love" (III, ii, 62).

Obviously not bound by truth, neither is he bound by responsibility. Through the early acts of the drama he finds in others the cause of his every dilemma. He disclaims responsibility for the wars raised against Octavius by his brother and by his wife; his curt reception of Caesar's missive was the fault of the messenger who stupidly approached him during a hangover; when, according to Caesar, he neglected the plea for arms and aid, the culprit was the "poisonèd hours" which had "bound" him up from his "own knowledge" (II, ii, 90–91). Similarly, the later fiasco at Actium was the consequence of Cleopatra's sudden flight, and the final defeat the result of her treasonous abdication to Rome.

Antony's wheel of fire, then, is built from equal parts of his own blind egocentricity and of the callous avarice of his associates who stand to profit from his alliance or from his destruction. As his tragic experience unfolds, he by degrees is conditioned to hold himself accountable for his actions; at the same time, by becoming progressively more responsive to the suffering of those around him, he develops the ability to extend his feelings beyond himself and thus to experience the disinterested affection that refuses to measure everyone by the standard of selfish gain or self-gratification. As with Coriolanus, Timon, or Lear, only the pain of disaster and destruction seems sharp enough to slice through the egomania nourished by years of autocratic posturing. But their situations are strikingly different. Far more so than Timon, Antony becomes willing to seek out and accept the intimations of love that lie buried beneath the flagrant hypocrisy in man's social relationships. Far more so than Coriolanus, he is provided the opportunity to respond to such affection and thus, through his death, to influence more profoundly the lives of those around him. With *Lear* the dramatic focus is on the inner tragedy of the old king culminating in an anagnorisis to which Cordelia's response is to listen passively and sympathetically; her subsequent death tests these pronouncements, and, while it does not negate them, it does underscore the intensely private nature of his convictions. With Antony, on the other hand, the focus throughout the drama is on the combination of internal and external factors that converge upon a personality to produce his tragedy; appropriately, the anagnorisis is registered, not primarily in the final words and actions of the protagonist, but in the catalytic effects in the final act upon another who has shared in and contributed to the nature of his final moments. Thus, while both plays assert selfless love as man's highest good, the thrust of the one play is inward while the thrust of the other is outward.

The development of Antony's concern for others can be traced in the eighteen scenes from the moment of his first military disaster to his death at the conclusion of Act IV.[44] Although he is by no means ready to accept the blame for the naval defeat in III, xi, his apprehension for the safety of his attendants is significantly new. Admitting that he has lost command, that his "very hairs do mutiny"—with the white reproving the brown for rashness and the brown reproving the white for fear and doting (13–15), he implores his subordinates to divide among themselves his ship laden with gold. Further, he counsels them to flee and to make their peace with Caesar, assuring them of letters from him to "some friends" that will "sweep" their way for them (16–17). From the opposite perspective in IV, viii, he consciously attributes his brief victory over Octavius' forces, not to his own prowess, but to the valor of his soldiers.

> I thank you all
> For doughty-handed are you, and have fought
> Not as you served the cause, but as 't had been
> Each man's like mine: you have shown all Hectors.
>
> (4–7)

He twice uses the pronoun "we" in describing to Cleopatra the heroic actions that have produced the victory, and he voices his regret that the palace lacks the capacity for the entire host to eat together and drink to the next day's fate.

There are further small touches that reflect this growing capacity to appreciate others. In IV, v, for example, Antony makes a point of

44. Possessed of a "Janus-soul" (Dean D. Lyman, "Janus in Alexandria: A Discussion of *Antony and Cleopatra*," *Sewanee Review*, XLVIII [1940], 88), Antony gains "the capacity for devotion and self-forgetfulness which he pitifully lacked before" (M. R. Ridley, ed., *Antony and Cleopatra* [London: Methuen, 1954], p. xxxiv). To the contrary, Whitaker (p. 279) asserts that Antony "is the same man at the end of the play as at the beginning." Rosen would agree, but he notes that "for the first time in the play we are not called upon to judge him" (p. 156).

stopping to converse with a common soldier who earlier had warned him not to fight by sea. His comment, "Would thou and those thy scars had once prevailed / To make me fight at land" (2–3), though brief, acknowledges both the old soldier's bravery and his wisdom. For another example, prior to renewing his struggle against Caesar, Antony calls together his household servants in an unusual display of sentiment. After clasping each of them by the hand and praising their honesty and their devotion to service, he addresses them as his honest and hearty friends and invites them to "burn this night with torches" (41):

> Haply you shall not see me more; or if,
> A mangled shadow. Perchance to-morrow
> You'll serve another master.
> (IV, ii, 26–28)

A similar display of affection occasioned by a sense of foreboding disaster occurs two scenes later as Eros and Cleopatra arm the aging titan for battle. In a touching moment Eros, almost overcome with emotion, fumbles badly in attempting to buckle the armor and Cleopatra can do little better. To Antony's brave front in describing himself as the "spirit of a youth" (IV, iv, 26) who claims "a soldier's kiss" (30) like "a man of steel" (33), Cleopatra's response, as he departs in the company of other soldiers, trails off into virtual incoherence:

> He goes forth gallantly. That he and Caesar might
> Determine this great war in single fight!
> Then, Antony—but now—Well, on.
> (IV, ii, 36–38)

The focal points for the culmination of the development of Antony's character are, of course, Enobarbus and Cleopatra. Clearly the self-centered Antony at the outset of the play was unable to respond without either anger or equivocation to any action that countered his own will. Yet, in IV, v, when he receives news of Enobarbus' defection, he recognizes that his own "fortunes have / Corrupted honest men" (16–17), that his own mismanagement of the military campaign has forced the desertion of one who had no fear of superior odds enjoyed by Octavius, but who could bring himself no longer to follow a leader rendered foolish by romantic passion. Without a touch of rancor he commands that Enobarbus' treasure be sent after him: "Detain no jot, I charge thee. Write to him / (I will subscribe) gentle adieus and greetings" (13–14). Irving Ribner (p. 177) correctly notes that the old soldier's subsequent death both "affirms the greatness of Antony" and also "heightens our sense of the tragic consequences of Antony's fall."

Antony's final confrontation with Cleopatra is even more remarkable. On three previous occasions he has subjected her to vicious and cruel tongue-lashings. Following her desertion in battle, he maintains that she knew he would follow and thus give the victory to Caesar; when he overhears her in conversation with Thyreus, he berates her as a "kite" (III, xiii, 89), a "half-blasted . . . boggler" (105, 110) "found . . . as a morsel cold upon / Dead Caesar's trencher" (116–17); when the Egyptian navy capitulates to Rome, he threatens to kill her, branding her a "foul Egyptian" who has "betrayed" him (IV, xii, 10), a "triple–turned whore" who has "sold me to this novice" (13–14). Now, however, as he faces what in a sense is her cruelest trick—the report of her suicide, which prompts him to fall upon his sword in remorse—his passion is spent. This serenity is the strongest possible affirmation of Antony's growth in self-knowledge.[45] As with Enobarbus, he knows full well that *he* has forced the crisis; whatever the queen's true nature this final ploy is her response to his threats. More-

45. "Inscrutable master of a spontaneous and generous honesty" (Arnold Stein, "The Image of Antony: Lyric and Tragic Imagination," *Kenyon Review*, XXI [1959], 594), Antony asserts "not the integrity of a Roman general," but his "individual integrity" (Eugene M. Waith, *The Herculean Hero in Marlowe, Chapman, Shakespeare, and Dryden* [New York: Columbia Univ. Press, 1962], p. 118). A "sequence of death images" (Katherine M. MacMullen, "Death Imagery in *Antony and Cleopatra*," *SQ*, XIV [1963], 403) culminates in the moment which "embodies the idea of eternity in sexual harmony" (Sheila M. Smith, " 'This Great Solemnity,' A Study of the Presentation of Death in *Antony and Cleopatra*," *English Studies*, XLV [1964], 173) and opens "the way to the poetic assertion of a truly tragic emotion" (Traversi, p. 254). Recently Philip J. Traci, who sees the structure of the play as akin to the sexual act, has described Antony's death as the moment of climax and creation (*The Love Play of Antony and Cleopatra* [The Hague: Mouton,

over, Antony's affection has grown far beyond mere sensual desire. When he receives news that she is still alive, his last request is for reunion with her. Facing her with not a semblance of reproach on his lips, his dying efforts are to give her counsel. He instructs her to seek her honor and her safety of Caesar, to trust none about Caesar but Proculeius.[46] Finally, he implores her not to grieve, but rather to remember him in his "former fortunes" when he lived the greatest and the noblest prince in the world.

Admittedly such a sampling of the middle acts runs the risk of distorting the true nature of an Antony who until his final moments is repeatedly lapsing into momentary emotional tirades against Cleopatra and whose senility appears at its worst in his foolish challenge to Caesar to meet him in personal combat. The far greater risk, however, is that the spectators should not realize how methodically Shakespeare is preparing Antony for his final moments with the Egyptian queen when victory over his own nature is complete. For Shakespeare the question has become, not whether Antony will side with the Roman or with the Egyptian values—ultimately he chooses neither, or rather the whole issue has become so academic that it is not a matter of dramatic concern—but how Antony will come to grips with his own nature and how that resolution will affect those around him. And Shakespeare, as is his wont, has carefully foreshadowed the direction of this resolution through the increasingly significant moments of self-control and compassion that well up from his turbulent and passionate nature even as his physical agony and his despair of materialistic success intensify.

Through six soliloquies totaling sixty-three lines, Shakespeare further underscores this development. While these private moments do not mirror the agonizing moments of actual decision which the spectators share with Hamlet or Othello or Macbeth, they do reflect

---

1970]). Antony symbolizes several significant alternative postures concerning the passing of time (Arthur H. Bell, "Time and Convention in *Antony and Cleopatra*," *SQ*, XXIV [1973], 264); on his posture as a figure of romance, see Donna B. Hamilton, "*Antony and Cleopatra* and the Tradition of the Noble Lovers," *SQ*, XXIV (1973), 251.

46. There is no real evidence to support David S. Berkeley's suggestion that Antony may well have been double-dealing with Cleopatra to gain revenge on

the significant stages of Antony's tragic experience. The first two soliloquies, for instance, establish the depth of his egocentricity. News of his wife's death in Rome triggers a brief moment of introspection that virtually mocks the grief of sincere affection. Using a form of the first-person personal pronoun eight times within nine lines, he admits that he did "desire" (I, ii, 118) her death and held her in contempt. Only now that she is snatched from him does he experience a fleeting trace of sorrow: "she's good, being gone; / The hand could pluck her back that shoved her on" (I, ii, 122–23). But immediately she is out of mind again as he voices apprehension over what effect his "idle-ness" (126) with the "enchanting queen" (124) is having on his political image at home. Similarly, in his second soliloquy, spoken at Rome, he smarts under the soothsayer's assertion that Caesar's fortunes top his. Peevishly admitting that he loses at dice, at drawing lots, at cock fighting, and at quail fighting, he determines that he will return to Egypt where, if not his marriage, at least his pleasure lies.

This same self-concern impels Antony in his third and fourth solilo-quies to disavow any responsibility for the desertion of the Egyptian fleet which his own mismanagement has prompted. His scapegoat is Cleopatra; he maintains that he has been betrayed by "this false soul of Egypt," this "grave charm" (IV, xii, 25). Bemoaning that he and Fortune "part here" (19), he brands her a "right gypsy" who has beguiled him "to the very heart of loss" (28, 29). A few lines later he determines that the "witch shall die" for "this plot" of selling him to "the young Roman boy" (47–49), and in his blindest moment he likens himself to Hercules, who with the shirt of Nessus suffers blame-lessly from the deceit of another.

The final soliloquies provide the spectators an insight into an Antony purged of this self-centeredness. Now his every thought bends toward Cleopatra, for whose presumed death he now assumes com-plete responsibility. Since she is dead, he will "lie down, and stray no farther" (IV, xiv, 47):

---

her by suggesting that she trust Proculeius ("On Oversimplifying Antony," CE, XVII [1955], 96–99).

ANTONY AND CLEOPATRA

I will o'ertake thee, Cleopatra, and
Weep for my pardon. . . .
                                    Stay for me.
Where souls do couch on flowers, we'll hand in hand,
And with our sprightly port make the ghosts gaze.
                              (IV, xiv, 44–45, 50–52)

After informing Eros that, since Cleopatra died he has "lived in such dishonor that the gods / Detest [his] baseness" (56–57), he faces death—as he will shortly face the living Cleopatra—without the saber-rattling bravado that has characterized him to this point. Interestingly, in his final private lines he establishes the same metaphor of marriage that Cleopatra will use in her dying moments an act later: "I will be / A bridegroom in my death, and run into 't / As to a lover's bed" (99–101). Through this image and the selfless concern that it signals in soliloquy, Antony has indeed transcended the tainted societal values which are an integral part of his tragedy and against which his experience must be measured. In the final analysis the drama asserts the value of neither illicit passion nor heroic action; Antony's full tragic stature, like Lear's or like Macbeth's, arises from the fact that he comes to know himself and the true meaning of human relationships through the disasters that produce his suffering and his death.

The most striking accomplishment of the play is the manner in which Shakespeare is able to balance the spectators' emotional interest in the man Antony with their objective concern for the social forces that prompt his tragedy. Antony's soliloquies, for example, strengthen the emotional bond between the character and the audience. Yet, as we have noted, since they are not located strategically in the play, they do not force the spectators into the soul of the protagonist where they must share the intense introspection that would reveal the moral bases of his decisions; instead they are but cursory glimpses into the inner man, reflecting either a fixed state of mind or a fleeting emotional response to the event of the moment. In other words, while using the soliloquy to provide Antony a semblance of philosophic complexity, Shakespeare sharply limits the extent to which the spectators are sub-

253

stantially able to know the man and, thus, to commit themselves emotionally to him. For another thing, as we have also noted, Shakespeare carefully despiritualizes the universe of this stage world.[47] There is no prevailing religion that presumes a general code of behavior based on accepted concepts of good and evil; neither is there a religion of honor or duty which tacitly constrains a man to treat his fellow humans with integrity and respect. To the contrary, the characters act with no moral qualms whatever, and the only prevailing social code of conduct is policy. The spectators, without either a total emotional commitment to Antony or a moral guideline to judge his behavior, are forced to evaluate his character—not vertically against some higher code—but laterally against the conduct of those around him and against the interpretation of his actions through the eyes of his associates.

Shakespeare controls this perspective through various structural devices. Through the soothsayer, for example, he establishes a pattern of anticipation. In I, ii, this divine foretells the future of Charmian and Iras; and, while humor is the immediate effect, the scene also points to a future fraught with impending disaster. He enigmatically foresees that Charmian, though she has had a "fairer former fortune / Than that which is to approach" (32–33), will yet be "far fairer" (16) than she now is. "More beloving than beloved" (22), she will "outlive the lady" whom she serves (30). Similarly, in II, iii, the soothsayer renders Antony's decision to forsake Octavia and Rome inevitable with the assertion that, in a contest with Caesar, Antony is sure to lose:

> Hie you to Egypt again.
>
> · · · · · · ·
>
> stay not by his side.
>
> · · · · · · ·
>
> near him, thy angel

47. This is "a world of the senses; it is physical" (Spencer, *Nature,* p. 169). "The only deity [Shakespeare] mentions is Isis" J. D. Wilson, ed., *Antony and Cleopatra* [Cambridge: Cambridge Univ. Press, 1954], p. xiv); "the conventional moral terms necessary for the definition of sin and corruption, the standard abysses of tragedy, do not apply here with their usual

Becomes a fear, as being o'erpow'red.

. . . .

           I say again, thy spirit
Is all afraid to govern thee near him;
But he away, 'tis noble.

             (15, 18, 21–22, 28–30)

Another device for tragic foreshadowing is the departure from Antony in IV, iii, of the god Hercules to the strange sound of music in the air and under the earth. This brief scene, set in Alexandria on the eve of Antony's fateful battle, is not found in Plutarch, who reports instead that a statue of Bacchus was thrown down by the wind in Athens. The substitution of Hercules for Bacchus obviously enhances Antony's heroic stature.[48] Moreover, although the god is never actually seen on the stage (indeed their association is sketched in only the most superficial terms), the moment does effectively heighten the spectators' anticipation of the impending disaster. A similar touch occurs in Act III prior to the initial battle at Actium in the old soldier's warning not to fight by sea, not to trust "rotten planks" (vii, 62). Dismissed peremptorily the soldier pointedly observes that "by Hercules," he thinks he is "i' th' right" (67). A final example is noted in Scarus' lines immediately before Antony realizes he is defeated. The augurers refuse to predict victory; instead they say they "know not," "look grimly," and "dare not speak their knowledge" (IV, xii, 5–6). All of these devices, then, the soothsayer, Hercules, the old soldier, the augurers—much like the curses of Queen Margaret in *Richard III* or the witches' prophecy in *Macbeth* or Iago's methodic delineation in advance of his every move in *Othello*—function to control the spec-

---

rigor" (Anthony Caputi, "Shakespeare's *Antony and Cleopatra:* Tragedy Without Terror," *SQ*, XVI [1965], 191).

48. Antony "has the physique and temperament to profit by his claim to descent from the legendary hero" (William Blissett, "Dramatic Irony in *Antony and Cleopatra*," *SQ*, XVIII [1967], 157). Raymond B. Waddington has suggested that the allusions to Hercules are "subsumed typologically by Mars and Venus" whose "mythical and cosmological affair" the play "is designed to evoke" ("*Antony and Cleopatra*: 'What Venus Did with Mars,'" *Shakespeare Studies*, II [1966], 210).

tators' interest by establishing a pattern of anticipated tragic action that intensifies their concern for character rather than for plot.

More particularly, Shakespeare utilizes minor characters as external pointers to establish the societal dimensions of Antony's predicament.[49] Through critical comments aimed in turn against both the Egyptian and Roman worlds, specific comparisons of Octavia and Cleopatra, and observations about Antony himself, these characters constantly remind the spectators of the characters around the protagonist who contribute to his tragedy. Demetrius and Philo, for instance, note at the outset the lethal qualities of Cleopatra's "tawny front" (I, i, 6) and "lust" (10) which have transformed the "triple pillar of the world" (12) into "a strumpet's fool" (13). So also, Enobarbus in Act III scoffingly deplores the Egyptian queen's stupidity and vanity in insisting that she accompany Antony to battle and in encouraging him to fight by sea at the cost of every military advantage. Canidius, in the same vein, observes that their leader is led, that they are "women's men" (vii, 70). Three scenes later the comments are even more pointed. Scarus, following the first battle at Actium, claims that they have "kissed away" kingdoms and provinces (x, 7–8). Cleopatra is a "ribaudred nag of Egypt" (10) whose only fitting reward is leprosy for her cowardly flight "like a cow in June" (14). Antony is now but the "noble ruin of her magic" (19). In deciding to defect to Caesar, Canidius observes that, had their general been himself, all would have gone well. When Enobarbus observes what he assumes to be flagrant duplicity in Cleopatra's responses to Caesar through Thyreus and even more flagrant stupidity in Antony for not denouncing her forthwith, he reasons through a series of asides that he too must find some way to leave him. Convinced that Antony's judgments are failing with his fortunes, he believes his leader, because of Cleopatra, to be "so

49. Creating a "kaleidoscopic" effect (Robert Speaight, *Nature in Shakespearean Tragedy* [London: Hollis and Carter, 1955], p. 135), "Shakespeare was inviting us to bring our intelligence to bear" on the action (H. A. Mason, "*Antony and Cleopatra*: Angelic Strength—Organic Weakness," *Cambridge Quarterly*, I [1966], 220). Harley Granville-Barker (III, 74 n.) speaks of the advancement in "Shakespeare's stagecraft" from the "older, conventional, plot-forwarding use of the soliloquies."

leaky" that sinking is inevitable: "I see still / A diminution in our captain's brain / Restores his heart" (197–99).

Such comments direct the spectators' attention no less forcefully to Antony's victimization by the corruption of Rome. Pompey notes that Caesar—without Antony's support—"gets money where / He loses hearts" (II, i, 13–14) and that Lepidus neither loves nor is loved by the other triumvirs. Servants in II, vii, observe the drunken state of the Roman leaders; and Enobarbus and Agrippa two scenes later imply that Lepidus, because of both his hangover and his fawning flattery of his cohorts, makes a mockery of his position. In III, v, Enobarbus and Eros note that Caesar, through the several ways in which he has violated the pact with Antony, is precipitating some form of a military confrontation. Probably nowhere is Antony's dilemma so sharply reflected as in his relationships with Cleopatra and Octavia, both of whom represent the weight and authority of a kingdom. Following the betrothal of Antony and Octavia in II, ii, Enobarbus describes the lavish sensuality of Cleopatra's barge; to Maecenas' comment that Octavia possesses "beauty, wisdom. modesty" (242), he retorts that Antony will never leave Cleopatra: "Age cannot wither her, nor custom stale / Her infiinite variety" (236–37). He reiterates this point to Menas four scenes later: Antony "will to his Egyptian dish again: then shall the sighs of Octavia blow the fire up in Caesar"; that which is the strength of their friendship shall prove the immediate cause of their enmity (III, vi, 123–26).

Two character foils are developed briefly in the middle of the play to emphasize further the duplicity of this stage world. First, Pompey in his refusal to seize dishonorable advantage of the drunken trio on his barge and by slashing their throats become ruler of the Western world stands in ironic distinction to the triumvirs themselves (especially Caesar), to whom opportunity and self–advantage are the highest values. Certainly Pompey has the power base and the popularity with the people (II, ii, 9–11) as well as the motive (II, vi, 10–23) to make such a move. Admittedly, in the final analysis he is a "moralistic trimmer" who—like Henry IV with Sir Pierce of Exton —would have his power by murder and retain the "ethic of his father" too.[50] Nevertheless, as he indicates in response to Menas' offer to "cut the cable" (II, vii, 70) and "fall to their throats" (71), he will have none of the method:

> Ah, this thou shouldst have done,
> And not have spoke on't! In me 'tis villany,
> In thee 't had been good service. Thou must know,
> 'Tis not my profit that does lead mine honor;
> Mine honor, it.   (II, vii, 72–76)

This singular statement comes only brief scenes after Antony has contracted a marriage without honor and only brief scenes before Caesar is flatly to violate the very terms agreed to on the barge by raising a new war in which Pompey's political murder will be the Roman reward for his present honor.

Second, Ventidius' actions in Parthia underscore Antony's selfishness in the early acts. Further, the scene provides a satiric commentary on the hollowness of the world, both the pettiness of the leaders and of the soldier who caters to the general's vanity at the expense of the empire's cause. Having put the Parthians to rout, Ventidius might well have taken full advantage of the moment to sweep through Media and Mesopotamia. This, however, he dare not do in Antony's absence for fear of offending his leader; in another of Shakespeare's additions to Plutarch, Ventidius explains that Sossius, Antony's lieutenant in Syria, lost his favor for doing more than his captain could.

In the final scenes, as Antony's actions reflect his growing capacity for compassion, Shakespeare also uses the comments of external pointers to help develop the spectators' sympathetic perspective for the central character. When the guards find Antony moments after his self-inflicted wound, for example, their remarks metaphorically stress his noble and heroic nature: "The star is fall'n" (IV, xiv, 106). "And time is at his period" (107). Eros a few lines earlier had killed himself rather than act as Antony's executioner; so again neither of the

50. Ornstein, p. 393. "Taken straight from the experience of the Renaissance" (Kott, p. 174), the scene "parallels and foreshadows Antony's own fall" (H. S. Wilson, p. 164). Moreover, the "Menas-Pompey relationship parallels the relation of Enobarbus to Antony" (Brents Stirling, *Unity in Shakespearian Tragedy* [New York: Columbia Univ. Press, 1956], p. 170).

guards can bring himself to honor the request to kill him. Dercetas, likewise, stressing Antony's "honor," "courage," and "most noble blood" (V, i, 22, 23, 26), reports to Caesar the death of a master "who best was worthy" and "best to be served" (6, 7). Nor are those in Caesar's camp unaffected. To Maecenas' observation that Antony's "taints and honors" waged equal with him, Agrippa responds that a "rarer spirit" never steered humanity (31). And Caesar himself is touched with tidings to "wash the eyes of kings" (28) as he laments the fate of his "brother," "competitor," and "mate in empire," the "friend and companion," and "arm of his own body" (42–45):

> The breaking of so great a thing should make
> A greater crack. . . .
> > The death of Antony
> Is not a single doom, in the name lay
> A moiety of the world.
> > (V, i, 14–15, 17–19)

The major impact of the play occurs in the final act with the transferral of the anagnorisis which focuses the spectators' attention upon the societal responses to—as earlier upon the causes of—the individual tragedy. Admittedly, a tainted society prevails beyond the tragedy it has occasioned. Octavius, standing over the dead Cleopatra, pompously asserts that the death of this famous pair of lovers will redound to his glory:

> > High events as these
> Strike those that make them; and their story is
> No less in pity than his glory which
> Brought them to be lamented.
> > (V, ii, 358–61)

Obviously this is the same world leader who, rankling under the weight of a triumvirate, in turn cast off Lepidus and defied Antony's authority; "the lies of Egypt are amateurish compared with those of Octavius."[51] Nor, presumably, has society improved—whether it be

---

51. Ornstein, p. 394. "The victory of Octavius brings glory to no one and promises nothing" (Georg Brandes, *William Shakespeare: A Critical Study*

the turncoat Egyptian naval force or the fickle Roman populace. If human nature is still tainted, however, individual lives have not remained untouched by Antony's experience. Through Cleopatra and her attendants—far more effectively than in Alcibiades in *Timon of Athens* or Aufidius in *Coriolanus*—Shakespeare forces the spectators to realize this fact. Indeed, Antony like the Duchess of Malfi is dead at the end of Act IV, and the final thrust of the drama—for Cleopatra as for Bosola—is on the catalytic effect of his death upon even the most tainted of those who have helped to produce it.

Shakespeare effectively foreshadows Cleopatra's action in Act V through Enobarbus' response to Antony's love in Act IV. Delivering more private lines than Antony himself (a total of seventy-two lines in six soliloquies and six asides), Enobarbus informs the spectators of the difficulty of his decision to desert his leader and in turn his anguish and remorse when Antony returns compassion for treason. That is, when he is told that Antony sends after him, not words of invective and denunciation, but his treasure and gentle greetings, Enobarbus is forced to recognize the potential for love and magnanimity that has been buried under his captain's ego and passion. In soliloquy he relates that his heart is swollen to bursting and that he seeks only to die (IV, vi, 30–39). In confessing to the moon (ix, 7–10), his final words reflect his response to Antony's selfless act:

<blockquote>
On Antony,
Nobler than my revolt is infamous,
Forgive me in thine own particular,
But let the world rank me in register
</blockquote>

[London, 1898], p. 476); see also, John W. Draper, "Political Themes in Shakespeare's Later Plays," *JEGP*, XXXV (1936), 88. As R. A. Foakes has observed, the late plays "show us men and women as they are rather than as they might be" ("Shakespeare's Later Tragedies," in *Shakespeare: 1564–1964*, ed. E. A. Bloom [Providence: Brown Univ. Press, 1964], p. 109). To the contrary, both C. E. Nelson ("*Antony and Cleopatra:* The Triumph of Rome," *UR*, XXXII [1966], 199–203) and Marilyn Williamson ("The Political Context in *Antony and Cleopatra*," *SQ*, XXI [1970], 241–51) argue Shakespeare's emphasis on Caesar's achievement of peace and unity in a divided kingdom. Shakespeare forces us to judge at the same time he reveals to us the folly of judging (Janet Adelman, *The Common Liar* [New Haven, Conn.: Yale Univ. Press, 1973], p. 39).

A master leaver and a fugitive.
O Antony! O Antony!   (18–23)

Cleopatra's response is no less transforming, but she is a far more complex and ultimately more powerful character. One consequence of this complexity is that critics describing her character have disagreed with a vengeance. Those, for example, intent on seeing her from first to last as a flirt, a whore, and an opportunist charge duplicity in her response to Caesar through the messenger Thyreus (III, xiii), in her role in the Egyptian navy's defection (IV, xii), in her false report of her suicide to Antony (xiii), and in the insincerity of her scheme for suicide (V, ii) as noted in her reception of both Proculeius and Dolabella and of her withholding from Caesar half of the funds from her treasury. She speaks not one line of actual soliloquy to provide an explanation for her actions; moreover, her lustfulness and vanity in the early acts condition the spectators to be ready to assume the worst about her.

To be sure, a part of the power in her characterization lies in the ambivalence common to humanity which Shakespeare so carefully preserves in Act V. Indeed, Willard Farnham (p. 148) has pointed out that the playwright methodically makes her more paradoxical than does his source: "He makes her paradoxical both before and after Actium. He is more kind than Plutarch to the earlier Cleopatra and less kind to the later. But he makes her rise to grandeur in death even more surely than Plutarch does." In attempting to slice through the enigmatic moments in order to grasp the general direction of her development, one must remember in the first place that Cleopatra never once blames Antony for the ruin he has brought upon them. "When all is finally lost," as H. S. Wilson (p. 174) writes, "she protects herself against Antony's violence by deceit—it is part of her charm, in happier times, and now her only weapon; and even thus she helps Antony to achieve his final grandeur."

In the second place, none of her enigmatic moments is without explanation. Berated by a furious Antony for her conversation with Thyreus, the Cleopatra who interrupts his tirade with only a few calm comments such as "Not know me yet?" (III, xiii, 157) is far different indeed from the histrionic queen who used such a volume of words to her advantage in parting with Antony in Act I or in receiving the messenger with news of Antony's marriage in Act III. If one assumes her complicity in the naval defection, her ready return to Antony instead of to the safety of Caesar's camp makes no sense.[52] Nor, if one assumes ulterior intentions in reporting her suicide to Antony (rather than a desperate, albeit unwise, attempt to allay his threats to kill her) does her rushing Diomedes to him with the truth for fear of the consequences. As for her actions in the fifth act with Proculeius, Dolabella, and Seleucus,[53] if Shakespeare intended them as scattered ploys in every direction to save herself, her private moments perforce would be checkered with the same frantic desperation; in actuality, just the opposite is true.

In the third place—and by far the most significant—the structure of the play fully supports only one interpretation. In Acts III and IV she has already begun to respond haltingly to Antony's increasing moments of selflessness—in her self-defense concerning Caesar's messenger, in her refusal to save her life by attempting either to assassinate Antony or to drive him out, and in the touching scene in which she helps to arm him for battle.[54] His death, in turn, spurs her finest

52. Moreover, as J. Leeds Barroll has pointed out, the fact that "Antony's troops are more hilarious about this rapprochement than are their prototypes in the source" suggests that "they have deserted on their own rather than at the queen's instigation" ("Shakespeare and the Art of Character: A Study of Antony," *Shakespeare Studies*, V [1969], 202).

53. While Roy W. Battenhouse (p. 166) argues that the tantrum provides her an opportunity to flirt with Caesar, both Ridley (pp. xv–xvi) and J. Shaw ("Cleopatra and Seleucus," *RES*, VII, No. 4 [1966], 79–86) explain the scene as Cleopatra's ruse to trick Octavius, to which the audience should be privy. Brents Stirling, steering the middle path, says that in the scene Cleopatra's "ambiguity is complete" ("Cleopatra's Scene with Seleucus: Plutarch, Daniel, and Shakespeare," *SQ*, XV, No. 2 [1964], 310).

54. Critics have labored in various ways to articulate this growth. L. L. Schucking (*Character Problems in Shakespeare's Plays* [London: Harrap, 1922], p. 134) and E. M. W. Tillyard (*Shakespeare's Last Plays* [London: Chatto and Windus, 1958], p. 22) would see two entirely different Cleopatras at the beginning and at the end. Cleopatra in her actions is like "the penitent Christian" (Dolora G. Cunningham, "The Characterization of Shakespeare's Cleopatra," *SQ*, VI [1955], 14)—a view sharply refuted by Elizabeth Story

hour in her determination to answer in the only way possible—by a commitment in love to another which will force her to face death with both courage and dignity. Such a commitment is obviously not a simple matter for one who previously has devoted her every moment to the pursuit of life sated with physical pleasure; nor, despite Caesar's comment in V, ii, 353–54, has anyone seriously suggested that a poisonous asp provides an easy way to die.

Nevertheless, she makes this engagement in the closing lines of Act IV, achieving the conventional effects of soliloquy in her conversation with Charmian and Iras. These characters, who live and die with Cleopatra, exist only in dramatic combination with her; like the Fool in *Lear*, they function as internal pointers or objects of dialogue through whom the spectators are able to see beneath the deceptive layers of the Egyptian queen. Since with Antony dead all is "but nought," it is no sin to "rush into the secret house of death" (xv, 81, 84). With "that huge spirit . . . cold" her only friend is "resolution, and the briefest end" (92–94). They will "do't after the high Roman fashion" and "make death proud" to take them (90–91). In similar dialogue later she asserts that her "desolation does begin to make / A better life" (V, ii, 1–2). Steadfast in the face of Caesar's lengthy personal protestations that he will use her with pomp and majesty, she informs her attendants, "he words me, girls, he words me, that I should not / Be noble to myself" (V, ii, 191–92). At this moment—*prior* to Dolabella's warning of Caesar's plans to apprehend her within three days—she sends Charmian with a message

---

Donno ("Cleopatra Again," *SQ*, VII [1956], 233). "She will prove herself worthy to be a Roman's wife" (G. L. Kittredge, ed., *The Tragedy of Antony and Cleopatra* [Boston: Ginn, 1941], p. xi) as she "moves toward the fulfillment of her resolve" (Ruth Nevo, "The Masque of Greatness," *Shakespeare Studies*, III [1967], 111). She accomplishes "the triumph of spirit over flesh" (Geoffrey Bullough, *Narrative and Dramatic Sources of Shakespeare* [New York: Columbia Univ. Press, 1964], V, 252). To Adrian Bonjour it is the "depth of Cleopatra's real despair" which "makes the play a tragedy" ("Shakespeare and the Toil of Grace" in *Shakespeare: 1564–1964*, p. 94). Keith Rinehart has recently argued that Elizabeth I was a partial source for the characterization ("Shakespeare's Cleopatra and England's Elizabeth," *SQ*, XXIII [1972], 81).

for the asps secretly to be brought. Further, she instructs her attendants
to dress her in full royal array, crown and all.

> Show me, my women, like a queen. . . .
>   I am again for Cydnus,
>   To meet Mark Antony.   (227, 228–29)

When she receives news of the arrival of a rural fellow who brings
the asps, she speaks again of the "noble deed" that will bring her
"liberty" (237); and there is not the slightest hint of hesitation: "My
resolution's placed. . . . I am marble–constant" (238, 240). Moments
later, applying an asp to her arm, she has "immortal longings" (280)
and hears Antony praise her noble act:

> Husband, I come:
> Now to that name my courage prove my title!
> I am fire, and air; my other elements
> I give to baser life.   (286–89)

The spectators, then, can trace a steady resolve through her private
moments in the final act. Any surface deviation, whether with
Proculeius, Dolabella, Seleucus, or Caesar himself, is but the counter-
action to her capture by the Roman soldiers and her audience with the
Roman emperor. In order to gain sufficient freedom for her secret
resolve, she obviously must convince them of her continued determination to live and of her willing resignation to yet another army of
occupation.

The spirit of Antony, in brief, pervades Act V, and Cleopatra best
reflects a primary characteristic of Shakespeare's final vision that
tragedy is a social rather than an individual phenomenon. Since the
flawed central figure is manipulated by the selfish interests of those
around him, they inevitably must share the guilt of his destruction.
But they are also capable of responding to the tragic insights he
achieves. The final significance of life, Shakespeare again seems to be
saying, lies in the manner in which one is touched by and in turn
touches the lives of those around him.[55] To be sure, *Antony and Cleo-*

55. Both Battenhouse (p. 173) and Blissett (p. 165) argue that Shakespeare denigrates the passion of the lovers through various allusions which

patra lacks the intense inner focus, the powerful emotional involvement, of Shakespeare's middle tragedies. As in *Timon* and *Coriolanus* the spectators, blocked from total commitment to the protagonist, are forced to view the emerging tragedy in the full context of the pervasive evil that produces it. Of these final plays, however, *Antony and Cleopatra* is clearly the most powerful. Through the structural devices that force the spectators to consider the causes and the effects of Antony's destruction from a wide variety of angles and that project his tragic insights beyond his limited individual experience, Shakespeare has largely overcome the problems of the two preceding plays in achieving a perspective that involves the social dynamics of tragedy even while it effectively centers on the tragedy of the individual.

---

create a parody of the Christian birth; contrarily, Ethel Seaton (*"Antony and Cleopatra* and the *Book of Revelation*," *RES*, XXII [1946], 223) maintains that such allusions help the spectators to feel that "the lovers themselves undergo a purification of passion." More to the point is Speaight's comment that the play ultimately exalts a love which is "beyond good and evil, . . . [which] purifies its own degradations, . . . [and which] necessarily at odds with actuality . . . can only be perfected in death" (p. 156).

VI

CONCLUSION

Shakespeare's final tragedies have always been considered something of an anticlimax. Each of the plays—especially *Antony and Cleopatra* —has had its admirers who argue all the more passionately and, not infrequently, persuasively in order to compensate for this assumption. For that matter, even the majority of the negative critics still admit these tragedies to be among the best of English Renaissance drama— anticlimactic though they may be in Shakespeare's canon. But the fact remains, whatever position the scholar may take from the armchair of his study, as stage plays these works over the years have been less in demand than most of Shakespeare's earlier tragedies.

The greatest irony is that, while the final works may not be as effective as stage pieces, they are in some respects the most complex both structurally and philosophically. Certainly one need not quibble with Bradley's assertion (in defense of the unparalleled greatness of *Hamlet, Othello, Lear,* and *Macbeth*) that "the tragic emotions are stirred in the fullest possible measure only when such beauty or nobility of character is displayed as commands unreserved admiration or love; or when, in default of this, the forces which move the agents, and the conflict which results from these forces, attain a terrifying and overwhelming power."[1] The vital question is whether Shakespeare's final plays should be evaluated only in terms of the degree of the spectators' emotional involvement or the forces of overwhelming power, whether Shakespeare was not purposefully moving toward a tragic vision that sacrifices such total emotional rapprochement in order to achieve a more profound delineation of the societal nature of evil. From his earliest efforts in tragedy, Shakespeare moves relatively consistently (the notable exception is *Romeo and Juliet*) toward a dramatic focus that concentrates on the flaw, the passion, the lack of wisdom within the protagonist. While the spectators' double vision permits them to see in those around this central character the evil of which he at least for a time is oblivious and to which he falls prey, the structural devices

1. *Oxford Lectures on Poetry* (London: Macmillan, 1909), p. 305.

primarily emphasize the individual's culpability; and with increasing effectiveness the asides and soliloquies prompt the spectators to share emotionally the ultimate consequences of that flaw and the human wisdom that can emerge from such suffering. In *Lear* and *Macbeth* the focus is broadened to include an emphasis on both the protagonist's error and the hostile or indifferent universe in which man struggles; still, however, the necessity of individual self-control is paramount, and the devices of internalization force the spectators to share the experience of one whose own actions render him susceptible to the forces around him.

In the final plays, while Shakespeare does not minimize the protagonist's culpability in inducing a tragic dilemma, he does stress sharply the pervasive evil that surrounds the central figure. No single character (like Iago) or select group (like Edmund, Goneril, and Regan) functions as the villain of the piece; instead the protagonist is surrounded by numerous characters who, in their avarice or lust or pride, manipulate him to their own material or emotional ends. The causes of tragedy, in other words, exist not in isolation but as a combination of destructive human forces from within and without, and Shakespeare is concerned in his last years with directing the spectators' critical attention to those external forces that contribute to the tragedy of the individual.

Throughout his life, then, Shakespeare probed and experimented in a determined effort to expand the limits of the form. And central to this exploration was the development of an effective perspective through which to provoke the spectators to share the genuine ambivalence of the tragic experience. As his vision of this experience deepened, so obviously did the significance of his dramaturgical skills in utilizing various structural devices to create in the spectators the ambiguities and the contrarieties integral to it. Based on the assumption that reality is more complex when viewed from two or more points of view, this tragic perspective holds the emotions of the spectators in tension, simultaneously arousing sympathy for and censure upon the protagonist. The spectators observe his predicament, his choice of action, and his destruction from his limited point of view and also from a more omniscient view that reveals the attitudes of those around him who in large measure have provoked the tragedy and of those who must innocently suffer as a consequence of it.

A sense of the significance of plot and structure he inherited, to be sure, from his immediate predecessors. Kyd's Hieronimo and Marlowe's Edward II, for example, are characters who provoke both pity and disdain from the spectators, even though the tension is not sustained. A sorrowing father caught in the tragic dilemma of choosing between private and public vengeance in the early acts, Hieronimo degenerates into a calculating and ruthless avenger in the closing scenes; moreover, the framing action depicting Revenge and Don Andrea, peripheral at best to the major plot, emphasizes the inexorability of vengeance, not the agony of human involvement in such action, and parallel incidents such as Villupo's villainy and Isabella's madness are so sensational and grotesque that they fail to underscore similar qualities in the principals Lorenzo and Hieronimo. King Edward is disgustingly effeminate and injudicious in the opening scenes, but Marlowe is able to maintain a degree of ambivalence through extensive use of secondary characters who comment on the divine sanctions of kingship as well as on his personal abuses. And, if Edward is never an individual truly perceptive of his flaws, he is made sympathetic in the final acts through the soliloquies voicing his suffering and torment and through the development of Mortimer, who in his tyrannous ambition becomes an effective foil to the king. In Tamburlaine, also, the commentary of the surrounding characters is a principal structural device for establishing and controlling the spectators' attitude toward a character who possesses in combination the cruelty and the rapaciousness of a barbarian and the regality and magnetism of a prince. Even though judgments about *Dr. Faustus* are extremely dangerous, because of the garbled condition of the text, two structural devices are clearly significant—the soliloquies, which provide a powerful expression of the protagonist's inner tension, and the use of Wagner, albeit never fully developed, as a parody of the central figure.

The distinctive quality of Shakespeare's drama arises from his ability to utilize such structural devices in combination to achieve a complex vision of tragedy that effectively mirrors not only the weltanschauung of an age caught in the cross-currents of ideological change but also the passions and tensions to which man is universally subject. And, as this investigation reveals by tracing his efforts as a craftsman for almost two decades, Shakespeare is able to do so with increasing confidence, sophistication, and effectiveness. Such critics as A. P. Rossiter and Norman Rabkin, among others, have pointed the way to this study, and I would offer no apology for the absence of novel interpretations of the tragic canon. Indeed the greater significance lies in the fact that this analysis of certain of the devices by which Shakespeare constructed his tragedy tends in the main to support what might be called the current consensus. In other words, such an analysis helps to explain the existence of a consensus among those who have examined Shakespeare's work more specifically in terms of character, theme, or language.

Shakespeare, by Virgil Whitaker's account, wrote several kinds of tragedy—tragic romances, unified *de casibus* tragedies, revenge tragedies, and quasi-Aristotelian tragedies. More important to this present study is the consistency of Shakespeare's concern for artistic control and his determination to develop the form into a subtle and responsive instrument for exploration of different aspects of the tragic personality. Certainly this approach can claim to provide no single key to Shakespeare's artistry. No doubt the morally neutral and the morally committed—the Christian, the skeptic, the humanist, and the agnostic —will continue to claim him as their own; of a single work we shall continue to read that it makes a "tragic mockery of all eschatologies, . . . of both Christian and secular theodocies, of cosmogony and of the rational view of history, of the gods and the good nature"; that "its effect is ultimately one of despair"; that it reflects the redemptive process of Christian salvation; that its doctrine is humanisic, demanding a vital distinction between "theology" and "religion."[2] One can

2. Views cited are from Jan Kott, *Shakespeare Our Contemporary*, trans. Boleslaw Taborski (Garden City, N. Y.: Doubleday, 1964), p. 147; Herbert Weisinger, "The Study of Shakespearean Tragedy since Bradley," *SQ*, VI (1955), 392; Roy Battenhouse, *Shakespearean Tragedy* (Bloomington: Indiana Univ. Press, 1969); Irving Ribner, *Patterns in Shakespearean Tragedy* (London: Methuen, 1960); and Helen Gardner, *Religion and Literature* (New York: Oxford Univ. Press, 1971), pp. 13–37.

reasonably assume that any great work of art can provoke a multiplicity of responses. At the same time this examination of various aspects of structure that in large measure reflect how Shakespeare intends the spectators to respond to the primary characters and the dominant issues of the tragedy does help to establish the fundamental constraints within which these interpretations must take shape.

INDEX

INDEX

Richardson, W., 29
Richardus Tertius (Legge), 41
Richmond, H. M., 51, 105
Ridley, M. R., 136, 248, 262
Rieman, D. H., 60
Righter, Ann, 20, 198
Rinehart, Keith, 263
Ringler, William, 171
Rogers, Robert, 148
Romeo and Juliet, 47, 59, 69–91, 92, 93, 108, 112, 156, 266; free will vs. fate, 69–70, 72–75; as adaptation of Brooke, 70–71; Friar Lawrence's role, 72–73, 83; Romeo's and Juliet's soliloquies, 76–79; Mercutio and Tybalt, 80–82; Chorus, 82–84; societal perspective, 84–88, 91; and other *novelle* plays, 87–88; and *The Rape of Lucrece*, 88–90
Rose, Mark, 6, 74
Rosen, William, 240, 248
Rosenberg, John D., 177
Rosenberg, Marvin, 141
Rosinger, Lawrence, 157
Rossiter, A. P., 2, 26, 27, 35, 49, 60, 139, 269
Rötscher, H. T., 84
Rouda, F. H., 221
Rowley, William, 20
Rusche, Harry, 172
Rymer, Thomas, 136

Sampley, Arthur M., 9, 25
Sanders, Wilbur, 199
Santayana, George, 195
Schanzer, Ernest, 93, 101
Schlegal, W., 117
Schuking, L. L., 98, 262
Seaton, Ethel, 265
Seibel, George, 133
Sejanus (Jonson), 202, 236
Semper, L. J., 123
Sen, Sailendra Kumar, 223
Sen Gupta, S.C., 56
Senecan tragedy, 5, 29

Sewell, Arthur, 222
Shanker, Sidney, 237
Shaw, G. B., 39, 98, 142, 222
Shaw, John, 166, 262
Shepherd, Geoffrey, 3
Sherman, Stewart P., 236
Sicherman, Carol M., 222
Siddons, Sarah, 183, 184
Sidney, Philip, 3; *Arcadia*, 158
Siegel, Paul N., 78, 115, 176, 206
Simmons, J. L., 6, 93, 219, 241
Simpson, R., 28
Singer, Irving, 195
Sisson, C. J., 241
Skulsky, Harold, 114, 164
Smidt, Kristian, 37, 189
Smirnov, A. A., 237
Smith, Gordon Ross, 101
Smith, M. B., 70, 229
Smith, Sheila, 250
Smith, W. B., 109
Smith, Warren D., 78
Snider, D. J., 180
Solyman and Perseda (Kyd), 87
Somerville, H., 109
Sommers, Alan, 10
Spanish Tragedy, The (Kyd), 8, 14, 17, 24, 25, 115, 268
Speaight, Robert, 161, 178, 256, 265
Spencer, Hazelton, 201
Spencer, T. J. B., 94
Spencer, Theodore, 72, 117, 154, 172, 197, 203, 220, 254
Spenser, Edmund, 55
Spevack, Marvin, 85
Spivack, Bernard, 20, 142
Sprague, A. C., 61
Spurgeon, C. F. E., 58, 137, 198
Stampfer, Judah, 176, 177, 217
Starr, G. A., 98
Stauffer, D. A., 10, 77, 93, 201, 242
Stein, Arnold, 194, 250
Stempel, Daniel, 137, 242
Stephens, Martin, 83
Stevenson, Robert, 133
Stevenson, Warren, 166
Stewart, J. I. M., 145, 156, 187

INDEX